URBAN FORESTRY

URBAN FORESTRY

C.1

GENE W. GREY
Kansas State University

FREDERICK J. DENEKE
(United States Department of Agriculture)
Forest Service

JOHN WILEY AND SONS
New York • Santa Barbara • Chichester • Brisbane • Toronto

Text and cover designed by Mark E. Safran
Production was supervised by Linda Indig
Copy editing was supervised by Eugene Patti

Library of Congress Cataloging in Publication Data

Grey, Gene W., 1931–
Urban forestry.

Bibliography: p.
Includes index.
1.   Trees in cities.   2.   Forests and forestry.
3.   Forest management.   I.   Deneke, Frederick J.,
1942–   joint author.   II.   Title.
SB436.G73   635.9'77   78-5275
ISBN 0-471-01515-6

Printed in the United States of America

10 9 8 7 6 5 4 3 2 1

TO SANDRA AND JODY

FOREWORD

Efficient, effective management of urban vegetation, especially trees and forests, is essential to the environmental and social well-being of all our citizens. By the year 2000 between 80 and 95 percent of all North Americans will probably be living in or adjacent to metropolitan centers. Although culture and language may vary and climatic–vegetation zones differ, urbanites of every region will face similar problems and have comparable requirements for goods and services. High density populations living and working on land that is steadily being compacted, yielding a declining and degrading environment will undoubtedly demand compensating, high quality outdoor experiences on residual greenspace. Unfortunately municipal budgets will be hard-pressed to respond. This will be the urban forester's challenge: to solve the dilemma of meeting urban man's demands and needs for enduring trees and forests in the midst of severe economic and environmental constraints.

Today's North American is highly mobile and usually migrates to a new neighborhood or city every five years. Be it a new job opportunity, retraining or advanced education, or retirement, our citizens have created and are part of a migrant society. When roving individuals or a family arrive at a new locale, they expect to be greeted by well-treed streets and landscapes. The average urbanite demands green boulevards and parks while his suburban neighbor anticipates a tree or two at the street side or in the front yard. But as people move communities change. Old neighborhoods disappear, are abandoned, or redeveloped. New residential or retirement tracts sprout like the ubiquitous tree-of-heaven. Examples of urbanization are evident on the prairies of Alberta, the Sonoran desert of Arizona, and the palmetto flats of Florida. In each situation woody vegetation is subjected to stress and strain as urban change alters the environment.

In response to people's needs, the urban forester has the obligation to preserve the mature trees of established neighborhoods, conserve the fringe forests being invaded by development, and establish and maintain sturdy saplings in treeless city landscapes. Today's plantings and protection programs, however, present challenges to the urban forester that were not evident just a few years ago. In the later 1960s urban renewal and environmental issues created newspaper headlines prompted by public awareness and action followed by political response. The relative affluence of municipal governments, reinforced by federal grants, encouraged the widespread planting of trees and shrubs in urban renewal projects, in expanding suburbs, and along city streets. Since then, however, budgets for municipal tree planting and maintenance have been drastically reduced throughout North America. Energy shortages, rising unemployment, creeping inflation, and the spectre of recession haunt the urban mind. City planners have lost some of their clout and creditability as urban problems continue to fester. All of these shifts away from pressing environmental issues have made the thrust of high priority tree management to beautify and ameliorate our human settlements a subordinate concern. The urban forester must overcome these new constraints!

In spite of altering municipal management priorities, fluctuations in the soft money of grant and support programs, and political apathy, the need for well-managed urban trees and community forests is stronger than ever. Noise and other outdoor environmental discomforts have continued to mount in most urban centers. "Acid rain" keeps falling on trees and other city vegetation already under severe stress. Soil pollution from deicing salts, automotive fumes, and dogs continue to weaken tree root systems. And mechanical abuse from many sources scars the bark of trees and scalds their leaves.

Field and laboratory data from ten years of significant research conducted by governmental agencies and universities have "reinforced" the importance of trees within and near urban centers. But many "critics" of urban-oriented endeavors have emphasized that there is an unnecessary lag of five years or more between publication of research results and their implementation at the municipal level. In the present book Professors Grey and Deneke have responded to the critics and closed the gap.

In several surveys recently conducted in Canada and the United States, urban foresters and public works officials were asked to identify what assistance was needed to develop viable urban forestry management programs. Among the responses, four were repeated again and again:

1. The need for advice on how to establish an urban forestry administrative and action program.

2. A call for a series of modern, model tree ordinances (bylaws in Canada) to support urban forestry activities.

3. Requests for guidance on the marshaling of public interest and participation.

4. Inquiries about ready reference materials that list sources of financial aid and assistance plus bibliographical citations of current literature and programs applicable to arboriculture and urban forestry. The text *Urban Forestry* responds to all four needs, and more!

As we confront the last twenty years of our century—a period that will determine the future of people on earth—there is no viable alternative but to face and solve history's accumulated problems. Solutions must come from urban people and their institutions because the survival stakes of the metropolitan masses are paramount. Urban foresters must be a part of the problem solving team since they have much to contribute to the future of urban life.

J. W. Andresen
Director
Urban Forestry Studies Programme
University of Toronto

PREFACE

The benefits of trees and other vegetation in and near cities and towns have long been recognized. A large number of property owners has been generally responsible for the care of individual trees. Only recently, however, has the concept of urban trees as a forest generally been recognized and the proper management systems applied.

Most cities are indeed forests—communities of trees and other woody plants both on and in the soil. One has only to stand on a high vantage point or fly over a city to perceive that below is a true forest. It is composed of trees along streets, in parks, around public buildings, and on all kinds of other public and private property. It is located on all land use zones—residential, recreational, business, and industrial. This forest is in a near-constant state of adjustment to use of the land on and in which it grows. Construction, repair, and demolition of streets, sidewalks, waterlines, sewers, power and communication lines, buildings, parking lots, and other structures occur continually somewhere in the forest.

Management of the urban forest is the responsibility of public and private owners. It involves any combination of property owners, city park or forestry departments, city tree boards or commissions, private tree care firms, nursery people and others. Optimum management, however, requires a system that considers both the needs of individual trees and the forest as a whole. Ideally, it must be a system that provides for the social values of the forest while protecting the rights of all property owners as much as possible.

We chose "Urban Forestry" as the title for this book, recognizing that considerable confusion and perhaps even less agreement exists over what the total involvement with this special forest should be called. The terms "urban forestry, municipal forestry, city forestry and community forestry" are often used. Some people believe, also, that involvement with trees in urban areas should not be called forestry at all but more properly arboriculture. We believe, however, that "urban forestry" is properly the umbrella under which all matters concerning the urban forest environment should fall. It is also the term with which most foresters are now familiar and has the widest application. We recognize, though, the obvious problem with the term when it is applied to small towns in rural areas. Other terms, however, present other problems. "Municipal forestry" implies a forestry program directed only to city-owned or city-controlled trees. "Community forestry" seems too restrictive because it seems to refer to either a small town or a particular part of a larger city or urban area, or a segment of society. "City forestry" has the same shortcomings as "municipal forestry" and lacks the wide applicability of the more popular term, "urban forestry."

Let us grapple no further with such definitions and turn to the task at hand. Please read on and understand that what we call urban forestry refers to all of the terms we have just discussed.

Gene W. Grey
Frederick J. Deneke

Acknowledgments

We are particularly grateful to Professor John W. Andresen of the University of Toronto for unselfishly referring us to the publisher and his review of the manuscript; to Dr. Robin Higham, Professor of History at Kansas State University, for his counsel and encouragement during the formative stages of this work; to Dr. Robert S. Dewers of Texas A&M University for his positive review; and to the students in the course "Urban Forestry" at Kansas State University from 1974 to 1976 for their critique of many of the topics in the book that were presented to them.

G.W.G.
F.J.D.

CONTENTS

URBAN FORESTRY

1
HISTORY
OF URBAN
FORESTRY

Although the term "urban forestry" is relatively new (Jorgensen, 1970), certain practices and disciplines that make up the field of urban forestry have been long established. The use of trees to enhance the environment and many of the principles relating to their care are extremely old. Indeed, one can find biblical reference to the planting of trees in the Garden of Eden.

Early History

Trees have been esthetically important to people since earliest civilization. The Egyptians, Phoenicians, Persians, Greeks, Chinese and Romans held trees in high esteem and in certain situations worshipped them. They used trees for their esthetic benefits, developing formal gardens and sacred groves to enhance temple settings. Even in these early cultures trees were also used to complement statues and provide a landscape for buildings. Along with these uses developed a rudimentary knowledge of tree care. Transplanting of trees was common as early as 1500 B.C. in Egypt (Winters, 1974). Theophrastus and Pliny both contributed much knowledge in these early times toward the maintenance and care of trees (Chadwick, 1970).

This knowledge continued to develop as civilization advanced. Botanical gardens began to evolve during the Middle Ages with particular emphasis on plants with medicinal properties. Since this was a time of separatism and survival, such gardens were necessary features. As the Renaissance period evolved, man embarked upon new adventures in scientific achievement and trade. As part of this increased trade and travel plants from other countries were introduced. These plant species were exhibited in private gardens and collections and led to the establishment of large botanic gardens in many countries. This increase in plant species resulted in greater knowledge of plants and their care.

Early England contributed much to our knowledge concerning trees. The first recording of the term "arborist" can be found in James Lyte's book *Dodens* in 1578 (Chadwick, 1970). *A New Orchard and Garden,* a book written by William Lawson in 1618, is quite detailed in its references to tree maintenance as we know it today (Chadwick, 1970). John Evelyn in 1662 wrote a monumental work on trees called *Sylva* (Evelyn, 1776). In it he discussed all known aspects of forestry and fruit trees and included references to past works on trees. In Evelyn's book there are passages concerned with arbor walks and the ornamental use of trees along with his recommendations on which species to plant. There are many other early books on trees, but suffice it to say that by the 1700s the use of trees in urban settings, a respect for their importance in natural areas, and the knowledge of their growth and maintenance were well developed. Botanic gardens had ceased to be as important for medicinal purposes and became places to study horticultural and arboricultural practices. Interest in landscape design was developing, and visitors to garden areas came away with new ideas for their own homes. Thus the use of plants in ornamental settings became more widespread. As time passed, plant materials became more available and designs became less formal as the emphasis shifted from decoration to relaxation and enjoyment.

In the early 1800s the open spaces in various London squares were laid out with freely planted trees and lawns. In fact the image of London at that time was one of trees and grass. Many of these were residential green spaces surrounded by housing, resulting in quiet, comfortable residential neighborhoods (Zube, 1973). Tree-lined boulevards were introduced to Paris in the mid-1800s. The main reason for boulevards, however, was to control movement of troops, and the trees provided them with some measure of defense (Zube, 1973). Such plantings also provided beauty and unified architectural elements.

North America

In the early settlement years, trees were often considered a detriment. Though providing fuel, shade, and food, they harbored real and imagined dangers ("horror sylvanum") and occupied soils desirable for food crop production. The popular image of a New England town square with trees and grass did not evolve until the late 1700s and early 1800s (Zube, 1973). Philadelphia did not have street trees until the late 1700s because prior to that time insurance companies would not insure houses that had trees in front of them (Zube, 1973). Eventually cities developed and expanded into forested areas, particularly in eastern North America. The forested areas were modified considerably. Demands would often dictate their total removal; in other areas some native trees remained in the home setting; and on occasion certain forested areas that posed site difficulties in construction would be left intact and development would evolve around them. Many of the these forested areas eventually would become parks. In still other areas, such as the Great Plains, urban forests were to be created from areas naturally devoid of woody vegetation.

Settlers and immigrants often brought seed or propagation materials of their favorite tree species from their homelands. These found their way into the "landscape" around homes in both urban and rural settings. In areas cleared or devoid of forests, they were our first street trees. Botanic gardens were occasionally developed by private individuals. Often the decision to incorporate a given plant species was because of its rarity or botanic inter-

3

est. These gardens were the proving grounds for exotic plant species that would eventually find their way into the general urban landscape. Examples of some of the early botanic gardens were: Henry Shaw's collection (now the Missouri Botanical Garden in St. Louis), the James Arnold Arboretum in Jamaica Plains, Massachusetts, and Longwood Arboretum in Kennett Square, Pennsylvania. During the late 1700s and 1800s several tree species were introduced that became popular lawn and street trees; these were the Lombardy poplar, Norway maple, English elm, and ailanthus (tree-of-heaven). The planting of introduced tree species in lawns and gardens was quite popular until the mid-1800s. This happened primarily for two reasons: (1) most of the early trained horticulturists and foresters were of European origin and training and favored trees with which they were familiar; and (2) most of the early nurseries obtained their ornamental stock from Europe. It should be noted that planting European stock persisted even until the 1900s, and often the planting stock of native North American tree species originated from Europe. This presented other problems, however, such as the introduction of exotic insect and disease pests. White pine blister rust on eastern white pine originated in such a manner.

As the use of plants in lawn and street settings became more widespread, so did the science of caring for them. Horticultural societies were organized and numerous books and magazines about gardening were published. In the mid-1800s, there developed more of an impetus to use native instead of exotic species. One of the leaders in this movement was Andrew Jackson Downing. He worked with Calvert Vaux and Frederick Olmstead in designing parks and wrote several books on landscaping. His principle was to select the best indigenous trees, believing that the soil and climate of the area would most favor these. He was especially fond of the native maples, oaks, and elms for city tree plantings. His influence can still be found in many cities established after 1850. Of course one cannot leave this era without noting the influence of Frederick Olmstead on city park development. The classic example of his work is Central Park in New York City. Anyone who has lived in or visited New York can appreciate his brilliance and foresight. His work is evidenced in Chicago and other cities and has been emulated in countless others.

The landscape concept in the United States grew as a result of increasing industrialization and was used in the development of suburbs during the mid-1800s. Suburbs were designed to allow an escape to areas of natural beauty; streets curved through wooded and rolling hills. Llewellyn Park in Orange, New Jersey, was one of the earliest of these towns. If trees were not already present, they were added to give a natural woodland effect (Zube, 1973).

4

In 1872, J. Sterling Morton, a farmer–legislator, then living in a relatively treeless Nebraska, proposed that an annual Arbor Day be observed especially for the purpose of planting trees—a practice that is now observed in most of North America.

It should be noted that one of the early texts of the twentieth century dealing with street tree maintenance and arboriculture practice was issued by a forester of great renown. B. E. Fernow published a book in 1911 titled *The Care of Trees in Lawn, Street and Park*. At the time he was on the faculty of the department of forestry at the University of Toronto, Canada. Jorgensen comments that this was the birthplace of both forestry education and arboriculture in Canada (Jorgensen, 1970). This is probably also true for urban forestry in North America; in fact he devoted one chapter in his book to "esthetic forestry." However, Fernow disagreed that the term "forestry" or "forester" should be applied to street and lawn trees. He preferred the term "tree warden." The term proposed by Fernow was not new. Towns in Massachusetts and other northeastern states had tree wardens as early as the 1700s.

The practice of arboriculture also took some giant steps forward in the early twentieth century. At the turn of the century, John Davey, often called the father of modern arboriculture, founded a company that specialized in tree maintenance (Wysong, 1972). In 1924, the International Shade Tree Conference (now the International Society of Arboriculture) had its beginning. Here people interested in the care and management of shade trees could meet, share ideas, and further advance the field of arboriculture. The Society marks the first organizational effort by both lay and professional people to respond to public concern for the planting and care of lawn and street trees.

In the 1930s the National Park Service approved the special care of trees in areas of concentrated use or of historical significance within their jurisdiction. A. Robert Thompson, a forester in the Park Service, was commissioned to write a series of bulletins on tree maintenance. The Civilian Conservation Corps (CCC) also made a significant contribution by its involvement not only in afforestation, reforestation, and windbreak plantings, but also in the planting of street trees in many cities.

Recent Developments

Past developments focused on tree planting, tree maintenance, and landscape architecture. The concept of urban forestry or total management of the urban forest system did not mature until the mid-1960s. However, pressures

5

toward building such a management concept came as early as the 1930s. Ironically, the major impetus for such a concept was the result of factors outside the developing system. Dutch elm disease, phloem necrosis, and oak wilt were among them. With the advance of such diseases came a recognition for the need of knowledge and management systems to cope with them. Research was directed to appropriate areas and specific courses in arboriculture were introduced at many universities. The need for individuals competent in shade tree management was recognized in many cities. Individuals, and in many cases entire staffs, were added to cope with the growing problems of managing the tree resources in urban areas. Individually these became, for example, the city forester, the tree warden, and the municipal arborist. Collectively, they became the park and tree departments or the park and landscape divisions.

Yet such programs were still limited in scope and focused on the concept of the individual tree and its needs. Cities had not yet dealt with the concept of integrated urban forest ecosystem management. The concept of urban forestry was introduced first at the University of Toronto in 1965 (Jorgensen, 1970). Jorgensen states that urban forestry as developed in Canada

> does not deal entirely with city trees or with single tree management, but rather with tree management in the entire area influenced by and utilized by the urban population. This area naturally includes the watershed areas and the recreational areas serving the urban population, as well as the areas lying between these service areas and politically designated urban areas and its trees. The politically established boundaries for municipalities rarely include the entire geographical area influenced by urbanization.

An early spokesman for urban forestry in the United States was Professor John W. Andresen, formerly Forestry Chairman at Southern Illinois University, Carbondale. Professor Andresen is now Director, Urban Forestry Studies Programme at the University of Toronto.

In 1967 a report was published by the Commission on Education in Agriculture and Natural Resources that referred to the need for foresters to be responsive and sympathetic to an increasingly urban America (Commission on Education in Agriculture and Natural Resources, 1967). The rationale was that the urban trend would continue and that foresters would be forced to respond to the demands of growing urban constituencies. In fact a recent Louis Harris poll, a section of which involved desired American life-styles and environmental values, reported that 95 percent of those polled listed "green grass and trees around me" as an important environmental value (Zube, 1973).

In 1968, the Citizens Advisory Committee on Recreation and Natural Beauty, chaired by Laurance S. Rockefeller, submitted their Second Annual Report to the President of the United States. Part of the report focused on the theme that city trees constituted a resource that was not being adequately cared for. They recommended that

> an urban and community forestry program be created in the United States Forest Service. The program should encourage research into the problems of city trees, provide financial and technical assistance for the establishment and management of city trees and develop Federal training programs for the care of city trees.

It was also suggested that

> The U.S. Forest Service should create an urban and community forestry program in cooperation with the states to protect, improve, and establish trees in community, suburban and urban areas. A Federal–State program would provide technical and financial assistance to local governments, organizations and individuals to establish and manage trees and related plants in community parks, open spaces, streets, greenbelts, and on private properties.

With the acceptance of this report by the President came the official recognition of urban forestry in the United States.

In response to this challenge, the Pinchot Institute of Environmental Forestry Studies was created in 1970. This is an interdisciplinary division of the USDA, Forest Service, Northeastern Forest Experiment Station in cooperation with several universities. Its express purpose is to improve, through environmental forestry research, human environments in the densely populated areas of the Northeast. In October 1971, U.S. Congressman Robert L. F. Sikes (Florida) introduced a bill, H.R. 8817, that included authorization for the expenditure of $5 million for a new program of urban environmental forestry. Although this bill was passed by both houses of Congress, the President vetoed it in deference to other national priorities.

In 1972, the Cooperative Forest Management Act of 1950 was ammended by Public Law 92-288. This gave the U.S. Forest Service responsibility for developing an active program in urban forestry. This program was funded for fiscal year 1978 at $2.5 million. As of this writing a formula for state allocations is being developed.

7

Recent efforts to develop urban forestry programs have not been limited to governmental agencies. In 1972, the Society of American Foresters initiated an Urban Forestry Working Group. The Working Group put forth this policy statement:

> *Urban forestry is a specialized branch of forestry that has as its objective the cultivation and management of trees for their present and potential contribution to the physiological, sociological and economic well-being of urban society. Inherent in this function is a comprehensive program designed to educate the urban populace on the role of trees and related plants in the urban environment. In its broadest sense, urban forestry embraces a multi-managerial system that includes municipal watersheds, wildlife habitats, outdoor recreation opportunities, landscape design, recycling of municipal wastes, tree care in general, and the future production of wood fiber as raw material.*

In addition, the International Society of Arboriculture (formerly the International Shade Tree Conference) convened an Urban Forestry Committee in 1973. Since 1968, 33 forestry colleges have initiated new courses and curricula in urban forestry (Andresen and Williams, 1975) (Appendix I).

Although urban forestry is still in its infancy, it has developed rapidly in response to the expressed needs of the urban populace. It is now emerging as a full-fledged profession and will continue to grow as urban needs become more acute.

BIBLIOGRAPHY

Andresen, J. W., *Community and Urban Forestry: A Selected and Annotated Bibliography,* USDA, Southeastern Area State and Private Forestry, 195 p., 1974.

Andresen, J. W., and B. M. Williams, "Urban Forestry Education in North America," *Journal of Forestry,* 73(12):786–790, 1975.

Chadwick, L. C., "3000 Years of Arboriculture—Past, Present and Future," in *Proceedings of the 46th International Shade Tree Conference,* 73a–78a, 1970.

Citizens Advisory Committee on Recreation and Natural Beauty, *Second Annual Report to the President,* 1968.

Commission on Education in Agriculture and Natural Resources, *Undergraduate Education in the Biological Sciences for Students in Agricul-*

ture and Natural Resources, Publ. 1495, National Academy of Sciences, Washington, D.C., 1967.

Fernow, B. E., *The Care of Trees in Lawn, Street and Park,* H. Holt and Co., New York, 392 p., 1911.

Jorgensen, Erik, "Urban Forestry in Canada," in *Proceedings of the 46th International Shade Tree Conference,* 43a–51a, 1970.

Society of American Foresters, *Directory of Urban Foresters,* SAF Urban Forestry Working Group Publ., 7 p., 1974.

Winters, Robert K., *The Forest and Man,* Vantage Press, New York, 393 p., 1974.

Wysong, Noel B., "Urban Forestry," *Arborist's News,* 37(7):76–80, 1972.

Zube, Ervin H., "The Natural History of Urban Trees," in *The Metro Forest, A Natural History Special Supplement,* 82(9), 1973.

2
DISTRIBUTION AND OWNERSHIP OF THE URBAN FOREST

The urban forest includes all woody vegetation within the environs of all populated places, from the tiniest villages to the largest cities. In this sense it includes not only trees within city limits but trees on associated lands that contribute to the environment of populated places—for example, greenbelts, municipal watersheds, recreation sites, and roadsides. Andresen has described the urban forests of megapolitan New York as "forests that invade the abandoned fields of the countryside and recolonize deserted lots and back alleys; forests that yield but do not surrender to the building contractor and the tract developer and the forests that, despite constant abuse, provide continual bounty." Thus, in New York State, the urban forest enlarges from rows of street trees and clusters of park trees in New York City to ever-broadening greenbelts in contiguous suburbs, to coalesce in the forests of the Catskills, Adironacks, and Allegheny Highlands (Andresen, 1975).

Nationwide, the urban forest covers an estimated 69 million acres (28 million ha).* As with New York, any heavily populated area in the nation has elements of the urban forest. However, a small town on the Great Plains—an oasis of trees surrounded by open prairie—is also an urban forest (Figure 2.1).

The distribution of urban forests in a particular geographic area is not difficult to determine. One has only to look at a map showing population centers to correctly determine that the larger part of the urban forest is in and near the larger cities. The distribution of the forest of individual cities, however, is much more complex and deserves a closer look.

Within city environs, it is necessary to look at the various land-use areas on which trees are likely to occur. The land-use data for metropolitan Dade County, Florida, shown in Table 2.1, are an example (Goodman, 1968). Nearly 35 percent of the total land area is in residential use, with most of this used for single family residences. Since residential areas are located either in natural forests or are generously planted to trees, it is reasonable to conclude that they constitute a major portion of the urban forest. Other land-use areas on which the urban forest most logically occurs are park and recreation areas (3.8%), transportation areas—particularly streets (24.6%), agricultural areas (2.2%), institutional lands (3.1%), and undeveloped areas (23.5%). Definition is made difficult by commercial and industrial areas, for instance, where trees are often less abundant. There are occasional trees in these areas, however, that make a contribution to the urban environment.

*Precise figures for the urban forest area are not available. The estimated 69 million acres (28 million ha) is based on our judgment that approximately 3 percent of the nation's land area could be considered as urban forest. For a summary of special land use areas from which this figure was derived see: Economic Research Service, USDA, *Major Uses of Land in the United States* (Agricultural Economic Report No. 247) 1969, p. 26.

Figure 2.1 The urban forest encompasses all of the woody vegetation within the environs of all populated places. A small town on the Great Plains is also an urban forest.

Any definition of the urban forest should be abstract as well as physical and should deal with all woody vegetation within cities and their environs. Thus, the data discussed above show only where one is most likely to find the urban forest. However, it can be everywhere within and around the cities.

For those who cannot perceive the urban forest as a partial abstraction (and must have acreages), a solid case can be made for including the total acreage of city environs. The rationale here is that roads, streams, lakes, meadows, and other open areas are not subtracted from acreages in National Forests or other large forested areas. By this reasoning we arrive at an estimated 69 million acres (28 million ha) as the total area of the urban forests in the nation.

Perhaps the most straightforward way of looking at the distribution of the urban forest is according to public and private ownership and public or private responsibility. We estimate that 30 percent of the trees in urban areas are publicly owned. The remainder is in private ownership.

TABLE 2.1

Existing Land Use,
Metropolitan Dade County

Category	Acreage	Percent of Urban Area
Residential	(0.405 ha)	
Single family	39,526	31.0
Two family	1,800	1.4
Multifamily	1,783	1.4
Rooms	78	0.1
Camps	24	0.0
Trailers	328	0.3
Mixed[a]	708	0.6
Total	44,248	34.8
Commercial		
Retail	3,940	3.1
Mixed[a]	458	0.4
Total	4,398	3.5
Tourist		
Hotels	549	0.4
Motels	264	0.2
Mixed[a]	54	0.0
Total	870	0.6
Industry		
Extraction	339	0.3
Light manufacturing	639	0.5
Heavy manufacturing	434	0.3
Light storage	569	0.4
Heavy storage	250	0.2
Mixed[a]	343	0.3
Total	2,575	2.0
Institutional		
Education	1,909	1.5
Cultural	199	0.2
Medical	232	0.2
Religious	498	0.4
Public administration	641	0.5
Penal	6	0.0
Mixed[a]	351	0.3
Total	3,835	3.1
Parks and Recreation		
Parks	2,629	2.0
Play grounds	218	0.2
Golf courses	1,604	1.3
Cemeteries	344	0.3
Total	4,796	3.8

14

TABLE 2.1 *(continued)*

Category	Acreage	Percent of Urban Area
Transportation		
Terminals	6,784	5.3
Railroads	830	0.6
Utility	529	0.4
Streets	22,966	18.0
Parking	249	0.2
Mixed[a]	158	0.1
Total	31,516	24.6
Agriculture		
Groves	687	0.5
Crops	2,102	1.7
Mixed[a]	48	0.0
Total	2,834	2.2
Undeveloped		
Vacant	29,815	23.4
Glades	20	0.0
Marshes	78	0.1
Total	29,913	23.5
Water		
Lakes	1,104	0.9
Courses	1,290	1.0
Bays		0.0
Total	2,394	1.9
Total, all categories	127,381	100.0

[a]Indicates two or more categories of use on the same parcel of land.

Source: Metropolitan Dade County Planning Advisory Board and the Metropolitan Dade County Planning Department, *Preliminary Land Use Plan and Policies for Development,* The Department, Miami, p. 18, 1961.

Public Lands

Parks

In the urban setting parks are probably the most relatable areas as forests (Figure 2.2). Many are magnificent examples of manmade forests while other examples have been developed in residual natural wooded areas. Parks vary from tiny green spots in central business districts to large acreages, which are often beyond the city limits. There are few parks without trees, and passive recreational areas are usually heavily forested. Most parks are publicly owned, but there are also recreation areas on private lands owned by churches, industries, labor unions, and other organizations.

Figure 2.2 Parks with trees and open spaces are probably the areas in the urban setting most easily identifiable as forests.

Most public parks are municipally owned and managed. However, there are occasional examples of county, state, and federally owned parks in or adjacent to cities.

Street rights-of-way

Street rights-of-way constitute a substantial part of public urban forest lands (Figure 2.3). These are strips adjacent to streets or medians between divided boulevards. They are often called treelawns, parkways, or parking strips. Streetside rights-of-way vary in width and often provide space for sidewalks. There is usually space for a single row of trees except that median areas are often wide enough for trees, shrubs, and other landscape design features. Streetside tree spacing varies according to lot width, driveways, utilities, and other spatial factors; but 50 ft (15¼m) apart or 200 trees per street mile (1.61 km) is generally the recommended standard in residential areas. It must be stressed that the streetside tree situation varies greatly within most cities. The factors responsible for these variations are discussed in Chapter 6.

Highway and railroad rights-of-way

There are virtually no cities or towns in modern America that are not served by public highways or railroads. Most cities have one or more railroads and perhaps several county, state, and federal highways. The land adjacent to

16

Figure 2.3 Street rights-of-way constitute a substantial part of public urban forest lands.

these arteries, at intersections, and in medians often supports a significant part of the urban forest (Figure 2.4). Along some highways, particularly those maintained by counties or states, tree situations are similar to those along streets. However, federal highways (often called interstates, freeways, or trafficways) generally involve large land areas where trees, shrubs, and other landscape plants have been planted.

Railroad rights-of-way make only a minor contribution to the urban forest environment as they were rarely landscaped in the past. In recent years, however, abandoned roadbeds and yard areas have been converted to bicycle trails, parks, and other recreation areas with appropriate landscape plantings.

Public buildings and grounds

Grounds adjacent to public buildings (e.g., schools and colleges, hospitals, auditoriums, museums, penal institutions, courthouses, and utility plants), are important parts of the urban forest (Figure 2.5). Quite often these grounds are well landscaped with generous plantings of trees and shrubs. Other public grounds may be used as military installations, cemeteries, airports, golf courses, and nurseries (Figure 2.6). These segments of the urban forest may be owned and managed by all levels of government and represented by a myriad of departments and agencies.

17

Figure 2.4 Lands adjacent to highways support a significant part of the urban forest.

Figure 2.5 Grounds next to public buildings are important parts of the urban forest.

18

Figure 2.6 Cemeteries are often forests.

Extraterritorial lands

The urban forest often goes beyond the populated limits of the city. Green-belts, groves, forest preserves, and even vegetated landfills, although often removed from the city proper, must be considered as part of the urban forest. These areas are usually publicly owned and often dedicated to a primary use with secondary multiple uses. These forests are extremely valuable to the urban environment as they may provide watershed protection, recreation, scenery, solace, or a place for disposal of waste products.

Although only partially extraterritorial, the Chicago area forest preserves are an excellent example of such lands. The Cook County Forest Preserves were authorized by the Illinois State Legislature in 1913 and organized as a Forest Preserve District in 1915. The Preserves total more than 47,000 acres (19,000 ha) in many tracts of various sizes located north, west, and south of Chicago. They comprise a network of forested lands dedicated as naturalistic sanctuaries for the education, pleasure, and recreation of the public (Otte and Vlasin, 1963).

Most tracts are maintained in a primitive state. Their interiors are accessible only by trails established for walking, bicycling, or horseback riding. Although they are not intended as parks in the traditional sense, there has been intensive development of recreation facilities on exterior areas.

19

Many of the preserves are within the corporate limits of Chicago and its suburban towns. The many tracts are connected by public roads or trails on strips of public land.

The Forest Preserve District is governed by a board of 15 Forest Preserve Commissioners. Over many years the Board of Commissioners has withstood near-relentless pressure by individuals, groups, and public agencies seeking forest preserve lands for conventional parks, schools, cemeteries, housing developments, and commercial purposes.

An occasional village forest still remains, particularly in the eastern United States. Originally set aside as commons to provide fuel and other wood products for village residents, these forests are now most often parks or other recreation areas.

Recently solid waste disposal areas, when filled, have been planted to trees and converted to a variety of recreational uses. Such reclaimed landfills are reasonably certain to add substantially to the urban forest in the future.

Riparian areas

Riverfronts, canals, levees, channel diversions, lakeshores, and even seashores are parts of the urban forest (Figure 2.7). Quite often these lands are developed as parks or recreation areas. They serve also as greenbelts and open spaces within cities. Such water-related areas are extremely varied, and trees are important elements when their presence is not inconsistent with the primary use of the land.

Private Lands

The urban forest occurs on all kinds of residential, commercial, and industrial lands. The largest area is in residential districts either in naturally forested areas or where property owners have often created magnificent forests (Figure 2.8). Residential areas vary from highrise apartment complexes to single family dwellings, and trees are associated with both settings except in infrequent situations where site factors are too limiting. Trees are a part of the appeal of home ownership, and a sturdy shade tree is one of the first introductions to a new house. As suggested by the Dade County, Florida data, residential areas constitute a substantial part of urban land use. Although precise figures on the total urban forest area do not exist, it appears reasonable that 20 to 30 percent of the nation's urban forests are in residential areas.

Commercial areas make up a less significant part of the urban forest. This is because of the relatively small land area devoted to commercial

Figure 2.7 Riparian areas such as this riverfront recreation site contribute to the urban forest.

purposes and the relative lack of trees there. Tree plantings and other landscaping vary greatly but appear to have increased in recent years, perhaps reflecting the growing environmental concerns of business.

Industrial districts are often more utilitarian than beautiful. However, many industries contribute substantially to the total urban forest with landscaped grounds, screen plantings, and outdoor park and recreation areas for employees. Many cities, seeking to attract industry, have developed industrial parks. Tree plantings are sometimes made as an esthetic inducement to industry and are often required of industry after construction.

Public or Private Management Responsibility

Ownership of land on which the urban forest grows is never total and absolute. Some rights must be given for the benefit of society. Private property

21

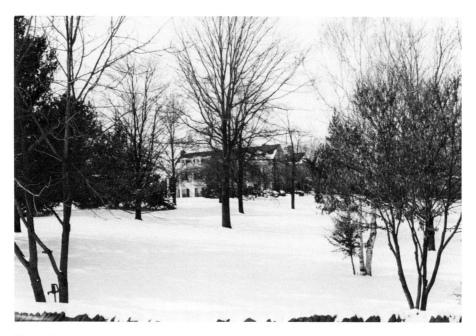

Figure 2.8 The largest area of private ownership in the urban forest is in residential districts.

rights are commonly given (taken) in the form of easements for streets, power lines, sewers, and other utilities. Such easements often restrict the planting of trees to certain areas and numbers and require pruning and other management practices to limit interference. Conversely the public may give rights and/or responsibilities to private property owners. Title to trees growing on street rights-of-way sufficient to claim injury damage is commonly given to adjacent private property owners. The responsibility for pruning and care of streetside trees is also often transferred to property owners. The transfer of rights and responsibilities is generally prescribed by ordinance or code. In many cities and towns, however, streetside tree responsibility is based on policy or tradition rather than ordinance.

These factors are illustrated by a four-block section of Manhattan, Kansas (Figure 2.9). This area was platted prior to 1900 and is typical of older residential neighborhoods in many cities. The blocks are divided into eight 50 × 150-ft (15.25 × 47.75 m) lots on either side of a 15-ft (4.57-m) alley. The streets are 30 ft (9.14 m) wide with 15-ft (4.57-m) parkways on both sides. Sidewalks, 4 ft (1.22 m) in width, are located near the private property side of the parkways, leaving 9-ft treelawns.

Treelawns are part of street rights-of-way and are owned by the city. Title to trees on them is held by adjacent property owners. City ordinances

Figure 2.9 Urban forest distribution on public and private property in a selected area of Manhattan, Kansas.

give the city the right to plant, prune, spray, and otherwise manage parkway trees, but also allows property owners to do so by permit. Dead trees are removed by the city and new trees are planted where appropriate. However, watering and other postplanting care are by policy the responsibility of property owners.

Overhead power lines run along the alleys on city property. Pruning of interfering trees on adjacent private property is the right of the city. Responsibility for pruning, however, is transferred to the utility company. The right of owners to manage trees on their property is further influenced by city ordinances that require removal at the owner's expense of dead or diseased trees.

Ownership and distribution are of particular significance to the management of the urban forest. Even in a small city or town the urban forest might be owned by several thousand private property owners plus numerous departments of the city, county, state, and federal governments. In addition, there are transferred responsibilities by easements, ordinances, and policies. Such a diversity of ownership and responsibility both facilitates and complicates management of the urban forest. It offers opportunities for intensive care by individuals of small segments of the forest but poses definite problems when management systems that apply to the total forest are considered. Management of the urban forest is discussed in detail in Chapter 6.

BIBLIOGRAPHY

Andresen, John W., "New York's Urban Forests," *NAHO,* The University of the State of New York, The State Education Department, Vol. 8, No. 1, p. 6, Spring 1975.

Goodman, William I., *Principles and Practice of Urban Planning,* International City Managers' Association, Washington, D.C., p. 122, 1968.

Otte, Robert C. and Raymond D. Vlasin, "Districts That Manage Resources," *A Place to live,* The Yearbook of Agriculture 1963, U.S. Government Printing Office, Washington, D.C., p. 434, 1963.

3
COMPOSITION OF THE URBAN FOREST

The urban forest can be both natural and manmade. In total area, it is perhaps the largest of all planted forests in the nation. Precise figures are not available, but we estimate that approximately 45 million acres (18.225 million ha) have been planted in urban and recreation areas, at public installations and facilities, and along roads and other transportation areas. The urban forest includes also a large area of native woodlands both within and adjacent to cities and towns. In many cases, native forests have been urbanized as cities have grown into them (Figure 3.1). Often in these situations, the original forests have been so altered by the supplemental planting of introduced species that they have taken on the characteristics of manmade forests. In areas such as the Great Plains or desert Southwest, the urban forest may be entirely manmade.

It is virtually impossible to discuss the total composition of the urban forest. It is more meaningful to discuss specific areas of the nation. The urban forests of New England, for example, are composed of generally similar species that are quite different from those in the urban forests of the Gulf States, Lake States, Great Plains, Rocky Mountains, or West Coast. However, even within these areas considerable climatic differences occur that influence the composition of the forests.

A common approach to urban forest composition is the use of plant hardiness zones. These zones were delineated by the Arnold Arboretum and are based on annual average minimum temperature. Species of trees and other plants generally adaptable to the climatic conditions of each zone have been identified. A map showing hardiness zones is shown in Figure 3.2*. Hardiness zones have the obvious limitation, however, of not taking into account more localized site factors such as soils and exposure. These factors are discussed in Chapter 5.

In forested regions of the United States, urban forests are composed largely of indigenous species. This is because cities have been built inside forests, and native species are often those generally most available for planting. Exceptions are in regions of sparse natural forests where introduced trees must be used, or in subtropical areas where exotic species are so easily adaptable. In forested regions, however, there are more exotic species within cities, which give way to indigenous species in suburban and exurban areas.

The composition of urban forests is influenced primarily by physical elements. The limiting factor is which species will grow in an area and ranges from hundreds of species in the south to a handful in the high elevations of the Rocky Mountains. Moreover, within the limits imposed by na-

*For a detailed listing of tree species by zones, see Donald Wyman, *Trees for American Gardens*, MacMillan, New York, 1965.

Figure 3.1 Native forests have become urbanized as cities have grown into them.

APPROXIMATE RANGE OF
AVERAGE ANNUAL MINIMUM
TEMPERATURES FOR EACH ZONE

ZONE		
ZONE 1	BELOW -50°F	
ZONE 2	-50 TO -40°	
ZONE 3	-40 TO -30°	
ZONE 4	-30 TO -20°	
ZONE 5	-20 TO -10°	
ZONE 6	-10 TO 0°	
ZONE 7	0 TO 10°	
ZONE 8	10 TO 20°	
ZONE 9	20 TO 30°	
ZONE 10	30 TO 40°	

Figure 3.2 Plant hardiness zones as delineated by the Arnold Aboretum.

27

ture are the personal, social and economic factors that influence human choice. While often interrelated, these factors may be summarized as purpose or function, popular species, public control, socioeconomic factors, mobility, and nostalgia.

Purpose or Function

The composition of the urban forest is influenced largely by the purposes its various segments are intended to serve—such as for shade, screening and esthetics. For example, a picnic area in a public park would probably have large deciduous shade trees. Screen planting for a salvage yard would be composed mainly of evergreens. Streetside plantings for shade and esthetics are usually colorful deciduous trees. A single tree might be chosen for size, form, color, or other characteristics to fill a particular need in the landscape.

Popular Species

The composition of urban forests often reflects the popularity of certain species. In the Midwest and the East, remaining American elms attest to the species' popularity prior to the spread of Dutch elm disease. Sugar maples, honeylocusts, sweetgums, and pin oaks appear to be in vogue now. A species' popularity is often based on practical reasons such as its form and strength, as in the case of American elms. More often, however, it is based on brilliant leaf or blossom color or other desired characteristics. Maples, oaks, gums, and crabapples are often planted for these reasons. Popularity is often created by advertising and promotion by nurseries and landscape firms. There are currently, for example, full-page ads for red maple, royal paulownia, and zelkova in popular magazines. Popularity is also influenced by the recommendations of public forestry and horticulture specialists, lawn and garden editors, and others. Unfortunately, a species' popularity often leads to planting mistakes, because a tree chosen only for leaf color or one other characteristic may be unsuitable for its planting site.

Public Control

Planting programs instituted by city forestry departments have the most controlling influence on the composition of urban forests. Directed principally to street rights-of-way, parks, and other public grounds, these programs range from recommendations or regulations intended for adjacent property owners to total implementation by city crews. Many cities have "official" street lists of trees from which adjacent property owners may choose. Other cities prohibit by ordinance the planting of certain "undesirable" species. Streetside planting may also be controlled or influenced by subdivision regulations that require developers or property owners to plant trees. The most positive control, however, is in cities where all streetside tree planting is done by municipal forestry departments.

Less formal and most applicable in small cities that do not have forestry departments are planting projects sponsored by civic and service clubs, garden clubs, youth groups, and other organizations. Such projects are usually intended for parks, school grounds, highway entrances, or other public areas. The Bicentennial of 1976 has shown a dramatic increase in such projects with the idea of establishing memorials to last another 100 years.

Socioeconomic Factors

The composition of urban forests varies greatly according to economic areas. In areas of low resident income, the urban forest is often composed of declining older trees remaining from times of greater economic prosperity. When new trees are planted, there is a tendency to select fast-growing species such as silver maple, willows, poplars, and tree-of-heaven. Volunteer, or naturally seeded trees, are common, having established themselves on vacant lots and other untended areas.

The urban forests of middle and upper income areas are generally well planted and well tended, reflecting the options of affluence. It is also in areas of higher income where most native woodlands on private property are found. This is not only because large lots are common but wooded areas are often premium sites for home construction. Schmid (1975) observed that in such areas of Chicago homeowners must be interested in or tolerant of native vegetation; "at the very least, a resident must feel no obligation to convert the whole of his property into lawns and flower beds in order to acquire neighborhood respectability."

Mobility

Although difficult to separate from socioeconomic factors, the mobility of Americans also has an influence on composition of urban forests. People in low and middle income areas tend generally to own homes for only a few years. Tenure is longer in districts of higher income. People who view their residence in a particular location as temporary tend not to plant trees.

29

However, the frequent resale of property increases the chances of ownership by individuals who will plant trees, often in the hope that such plantings will increase property values. When trees are planted, fast-growing species are most often used because there isn't time to wait for oaks, hickories, and other slower growers.

Nostalgia

Nostalgia for the familiar has had a profound influence on the composition of urban forests. Trees from the "old country" or "back East" were often brought by settlers. Although many species could not tolerate the new sites to which they were introduced, many of them flourished. Often such introductions were for utilitarian as well as esthetic purposes as attested by the early introductions of apple, pear, peach, and nut trees.

Occasionally a love of trees once known became a crusade, as in the case of J. Sterling Morton, founder of Arbor Day. Remembering fondly the large trees of his native New York State, Morton set about to have the planting of trees on the Nebraska plains made an official act. His zeal not only changed the Nebraska landscape but has influenced the urban forests of virtually every city in North America.

Manhattan, Kansas

All of the factors just discussed have influenced the composition of the urban forest of the authors' hometown of Manhattan, Kansas. Manhattan is located within hardiness zone 4. It has a typical continental climate with warm summers and moderately cold winters. Normal low temperatures are 30°F (−1°C) in January and normal highs are 82°F (27°C) in July. Extremes have ranged from −30°F (−34°C) to +112°F(44°C). Average rainfall is 32 in. (81.28 cm) with approximately 70 percent of it falling during the growing season. In summer, the rate of evapo-transpiration is moderately high. Prevailing summer winds are from the south. Periods of high winds can be expected particularly in March, April, and May.

Manhattan is located in the Flint Hills region of Kansas. The original city was built in the bottomlands of the Kansas River. Subsequent development of the city took place on adjacent uplands. Lower slope and bottomland soils are moderately deep silty clays on undistrubed sites. Upland soils are shallow, stony, and gravelly. All soils tend to be alkaline.

Manhattan has a population of 29,500. It was settled in 1855 by farmers and traders of varying ethnic backgrounds. The city developed primarily around Bluemont College, which later became Kansas State College (now Kansas State University).

The urban forest of Manhattan is mostly manmade, although some development of the city has extended into naturally wooded ravines and hillsides. The urban forest extends beyond the city limits to include public recreation areas adjacent to a large lake owned by the federal government. The forest within the city limits can be divided into three general areas: (1) older; (2) intermediate; and (3) new (Figure 3.3). The "older" area includes the originally platted city plus its expansion on the high river bottoms east and south of the university. The "intermediate" area is west and north of the campus and was developed generally from 1940 to 1960. The "new" area is located on the uplands to the west. In July 1975, a complete inventory was made of streetside trees in each area.

Figure 3.3 The urban forest of Manhattan, Kansas can be divided into three areas: (1) older; (2) intermediate; and (3) new.

TABLE 3.1

City Street Trees
City of Manhattan, Kansas
Older Area
July 1, 1975

Species	Number of Trees	Average Age	Average Diameter (in.) (2.54 cm)	Percent of Species Total				Percent of Total Trees
				Good(1)	Fair(2)	Poor(3)	D & D(4)	
American elm	2158	60	19	31	25	24	20	33
Hackberry	1090	60	16	59	31	10	0	18
Siberian elm	376	40	14	4	33	59	4	6
Hard maple (sp.)	328	10	4	74	5	18	3	5
Green ash	320	15	6	48	31	21	0	5
Pin oak	320	40	15	69	10	20	1	5
Sycamore–planetree	302	20	8	76	9	15	0	5
Honeylocust	288	20	9	71	8	20	2	4
Silver maple	280	15	10	39	13	48	0	4
Red oak	218	10	5	56	23	13	8	3
Redbud	138	10	4	78	2	20	0	2
Black walnut	130	55	15	34	54	12	0	2
Hybrid elm	82	15	6	7	56	37	0	1
aMiscellaneous	466							7
Totals	6496							

(1) *Good:* Healthy, vigorous tree. No apparent signs of insect, disease, or mechanical injury. Little or no corrective work required. Form representative of species.

(2) *Fair:* Average condition and vigor for area. May be in need of some corrective pruning or repair. May lack desirable form characteristic of species. May show minor insect injury, disease, or physiological problem.

(3) *Poor:* General state of decline. May show severe mechanical, insect, or disease damage, but death not imminent. May require repair or renovation.

(4) *Dead or Dying:* Dead or death imminent from Dutch elm disease or other causes.

a Less than one percent each: bur oak, tree of heaven, flowering crab, sweetgum, basswood, black locust, Kentucky coffeetree, eastern redcedar, chinquapin oak, hawthorn, mimosa, catalpa, pine (sp.), cottonwood, willow, Osage-orange, purpleleaf plum, white birch, mulberry, fruit (sp.), Japanese pagodatree, shingle oak, English oak, Russian olive, ginkgo, boxelder.

Older area

The "older" area of Manhattan supports 6496 street trees composed of more than 40 species (Table 3.1). In spite of sustained losses from Dutch elm disease, American elm is still the most abundant species, comprising 33 percent of the total population. (A 1948 inventory showed that 66 percent of them were American elm.) Hackberry is the second most common species with 18 percent. The remaining tree population is well distributed, with no single species making up more than six percent of the total. The American elms and hackberrys have an estimated average age of 60 years. All of the "original" street trees were planted by adjacent property owners as there were no city-sponsored planting efforts until the late 1940s. The choice of species was based largely on the local availability of elms and hackberrys. Both species are native to the area, and wild seedlings and saplings were frequently transplanted. A local commercial nursery also promoted these species. Because there was no forewarning of epidemic disease, the selection of elms and hackberrys could hardly be faulted. Because of their hardiness and vase-shaped ascending form, both species were admirably suited for streetside planting.

There is little clear evidence that nostalgia was an important factor in street planting except for a few large black walnuts that were planted along a farm lane that later became a city street. These were planted by an individual who remembered fondly the large walnut trees in the eastern states and who also relished black walnut nutmeats. Ethnic factors seem not to have been important since significant numbers of a particular species that could be associated with "mother" countries do not exist.

The "older" area of Manhattan includes sections of both high and low resident income, and the streetside tree data are not separate. Thus, conclusions can be based on observations only. The lower income areas appear to have fewer trees. Elm losses have been high but significant replacements have not been made. Streetside planting is done by city crews while post-planting care is the responsibility of adjacent property owners. Because of generally poor care exercised by residents, the city forestry division has discontinued planting unless it has a prior agreement with the property owners for maintenance. Tree planting request and care agreement forms are published in the local newspaper prior to the planting season. Few forms are submitted by residents of low income sections of the city.

Forty species of streetside trees is a relatively high number for Kansas towns. (The Department of Forestry at KSU has inventoried 110 towns.) Observations suggest that there is also a generally greater number of additional species on private property than in other towns. This can be reasonably attributed to the proximity to the Departments of Horticulture and Forestry at Kansas State University. The experimental and extension work

TABLE 3.2

Recent Street Tree Planting in the
Older Area of Manhattan
(Trees Less Than 3 In. Diameter)

Species	Number of Trees	Percent of Total
Hard maple (sp.)	105	24
Green ash	50	12
Red oak	52	12
Sycamore–planetree	52	12
Silver maple	43	10
Redbud	19	4
Sweetgum	18	4
Pin oak	14	3
Hackberry	8	2
Honeylocust	7	2
Basswood	7	2
Flowering crab	8	2
Fruit (sp.)	8	2
Siberian elm	4	1
Black walnut	5	1
Hybrid elm	5	1
Cottonwood	4	1
American elm	8	>1
Eastern redcedar	1	1
Catalpa	1	1
Bur oak	3	1
Willow	1	1
Mulberry	1	1
Russian-olive	2	1
Ginkgo	1	1
Black locust	1	1
Mimosa	3	1
Purpleleaf plum	1	1
White birch	1	1
Japanese pagodatree	1	1
	429	

of staff horticulturists and foresters has had both a direct and indirect influence on the composition of Manhattan's urban forest. The department operated an experimental nursery for several years from which excess trees were made available to the public. Department personnel have served as consultants to the city forestry division on numerous occasions. Information on tree selection, planting, and care has long been readily available to Manhattan residents.

TABLE 3.3

City Street Trees
City of Manhattan, Kansas
Intermediate Area
July 1, 1975

Species	Number of Trees	Average Age	Average Diameter (in.) (2.54 cm)	Percent of Species Total				Percent of Total Trees
				Good(1)	Fair(2)	Poor(3)	D & D(4)	
Honeylocust	648	20	10	80	18	2	0	20
Sycamore–planetree	504	20	11	90	6	4	0	16
Green ash	322	20	10	61	30	8	0	10
Hackberry	250	25	12	69	22	8	1	8
American elm	164	30	16	45	47	5	4	5
Red oak	158	20	9	90	6	4	0	5
Siberian elm	158	20	11	28	34	38	0	5
Flowering crab	128	15	6	91	9	0	0	4
Silver maple	110	15	8	58	35	7	0	3
Hard maple (sp.)	106	10	4	77	17	6	0	3
Hybrid elm	90	20	10	36	49	15	0	3
Redbud	66	10	4	73	24	3	0	2
Pine (sp.)	62	20	9	81	16	3	0	2
Goldenraintree	50	20	8	88	12	0	0	2
Pin oak	50	20	10	88	0	12	0	2
Sweetgum	50	10	4	56	36	8	0	2
Japanese pagodatree	46	20	10	48	43	9	0	2
Eastern redcedar	40	20	10	15	55	30	0	1
aMiscellaneous	166							5
Totals	3194							

(1) *Good:* Healthy, vigorous tree. No apparent signs of insect, disease, or mechanical injury. Little or no corrective work required. Form representative of species.

(2) *Fair:* Average condition and vigor for area. May be in need of some corrective pruning or repair. May lack desirable form characteristic of species. May show minor insect injury, disease, or physiological problem.

(3) *Poor:* General state of decline. May show severe mechanical, insect, or disease damage, but death not imminent. May require repair or renovation.

(4) *Dead or dying:* Dead, or death imminent from Dutch elm disease or other cases.

a Less than one percent each: white birch, bur oak, cottonwood, willow, basswood, baldcypress, black walnut, Kentucky coffeetree, mimosa, mulberry, black locust, fruit (sp.), paw paw, hawthorn, catalpa, Russian-olive, chinquapin oak, boxelder, Osage-orange, and white poplar.

TABLE 3.4

City Street Trees
City of Manhattan, Kansas
New Area
July 1, 1975

Species	Number of Trees	Average Age	Average Diameter (in.) (2.54 cm)	Percent of Species Total				Percent of Total Trees
				Good(1)	Fair(2)	Poor(3)	D & D(4)	
Sycamore–planetree	380	10	6	42	40	18	0	15
Hard maple (sp.)	222	10	4	59	32	5	4	9
Honeylocust	220	15	7	36	47	17	0	9
Green ash	152	10	5	38	47	12	3	7
Fruit (sp.)	148	10	4	76	24	0	0	6
Hybrid elm	138	15	7	45	43	12	0	6
Silver maple	108	10	4	50	43	7	0	5
Pin oak	104	15	7	46	52	2	0	4
Red oak	104	10	6	75	23	2	0	4
Hackberry	92	10	5	24	44	30	2	4
Sweetgum	92	10	3	65	26	9	0	4
American elm	80	35	15	5	27	50	18	3
Pine (sp.)	70	10	4	97	0	3	0	3
Basswood	66	10	3	33	67	0	0	3
Bur oak	62	10	4	52	29	16	3	3
Mulberry	48	10	3	54	42	4	0	2
Eastern redcedar	32	20	9	38	31	31	0	1
Siberian elm	32	30	14	6	50	44	0	1
Redbud	30	10	3	73	7	13	7	1
White birch	24	10	3	100	0	0	0	1
aMiscellaneous	130							6
Totals	2334							

(1) *Good:* Healthy, vigorous tree. No apparent signs of insect, disease, or mechanical injury. Little or no corrective work required. Form representative of species.

(2) *Fair:* Average condition and vigor for area. May be in need of some corrective pruning or repair. May lack desirable form characteristic of species. May show minor insect injury, disease, or physiological problem.

(3) *Poor:* General state of decline. May show severe mechanical, insect, or disease damage, but death not imminent. May require repair or renovation.

(4) *Dead or dying:* Dead, or death imminent from Dutch elm disease or other cases.

a Less than one percent each: white birch, bur oak, cottonwood, willow, basswood, baldcypress, black walnut, Kentucky coffeetree, mimosa, mulberry, black locust, fruit (sp.), paw paw, hawthorn, catalpa, Russian-olive, chinquapin oak, boxelder, Osage-orange, and white poplar.

The planting program of the city forestry division does not preclude property owners from also planting streetside trees. A planting permit is required, but the system is poorly enforced, and much streetside planting is done in ignorance of, or deference to, the permit "requirement." Of 30 species (429 trees) planted in recent years, 24 percent are hard maples (Table 3.2). This is an apparent reflection of the popularity of hard maples, primarily because of their brilliant fall leaf color. Several magnificent specimens of these species on a prominent estate within the city have contributed greatly to this popularity.

Intermediate area

There are 3194 streetside trees in the "intermediate" area of Manhattan (Table 3.3). There are 38 species present, most of which were planted during the past 30 years. The thornless honeylocust is the most common (20 percent), followed by the planetree (16 percent), green ash (10 percent), and hackberry (8 percent). No other single species makes up more than 5 percent of the total population. Most streetside trees were planted by the city as the area was developed. This program was undertaken by the city forestry division shortly after World War II. With counsel from the university, planting standards and policies were developed and species were selected according to general site conditions. It can be argued that there is a slight overabundance of honeylocusts and planetrees here, but thus far neither species appears to have serious problems.

Three percent of the streetside trees in this area are hybrid elms. These are Christine Buisman elms, *Ulmus carpinafolia* H.V., which were highly touted replacements for the American elms lost to the Dutch elm disease. They were planted by the city forestry division in response to the sentiment of the mid-1960s that elms should not disappear from the landscape. Although apparently highly resistant to Dutch elm disease, these particular trees appear to lack the qualities that made American elms such popular shade trees. They lack the ascending form of American elms and are subject to severe annual attacks by elm leaf beetles.

New area

Essentially the same factors that influenced the composition of streetside plantings in the intermediate area are present in the new area (Table 3.4). Most trees have been planted by city crews. Species composition is similar with minor differences in percentages. The increased number of hard maples is perhaps noteworthy. Their presence appears to reflect the same popularity that is responsible for their recent planting in the older area of Manhattan. There are relatively few of them in the intermediate area only because there has not been the need for recent planting. Most of the hard maples here were planted by adjacent property owners. The city forestry division plants few maples in new areas because these species have difficulty withstanding the harsh elements of exposed sites.

BIBLIOGRAPHY

Schmid, James A., *Urban Vegetation*, Research Paper No. 161, University of Chicago, Department of Geography, Chicago, p. 63, 1975.

4
BENEFITS OF
THE URBAN FOREST

The urban forest is important to the city dweller in many ways. Its trees provide shade, beauty, and a long list of other benefits. In most instances these benefits are taken for granted. Indeed, the urban dweller may not even be aware of many or even relate to them. The various benefits can be grouped under the following four broad categories:

1. Climate amelioration
2. Engineering uses
3. Architectural uses
4. Esthetic uses

Climate Amelioration

The major elements of climate that affect us are solar radiation, air temperature, air movement, and humidity; and we have comfort zones associated with the interactions of these four elements. We can be too hot, too cold, or just right. This comfort zone of "just right" varies according to individual, sex, age, and the particular climate to which one is adjusted. From an engineering aspect, we control this comfort zone very precisely in buildings. With a twist of a knob or push of a button, we can regulate indoor temperature, light, humidity, and air movement. If only similar controls could be applied to the out-of-doors environment! To a degree they can be; by the proper use of trees and shrubs, a microclimate can be created that may ameliorate the climate sufficiently for us to be comfortable.

Temperature modification

Human comfort essentially depends on the factors that affect skin temperature and the perception of heat and cold. The optimum core temperature for a human body is 98.6°F (37°C). Discomfort occurs when thermal energy is either lost or gained in relation to this optimum. This energy transfer, when carried to extremes, can result in either sunstroke or hypothermia. We generate heat through our metabolic processes. Inactive persons generate about 50 kcal of heat per hour. With physical exertion the amount of heat generated increases; to maintain comfort in either case, this heat must be dissipated.

Heat is dissipated from the body in three ways: radiation, convection, and evaporative cooling. Heat energy is radiated by people and their surroundings. This occurs through infrared thermal radiation from the skin or other surfaces. A two-way flux of radiation is involved. First, if the surroundings are cooler than the human body, the flux will be away from the body and cooling will result. Second, if the surrounding surfaces are warmer, the net flux of energy will be toward the human body. Heat is also transferred by convection. If the air is cooler than the skin or clothing, convective transport of heat will be toward the air. If the air is warmer, the transport will be from the air to the body. Wind also plays a very important role in convective heat transfer. It will speed up the transfer and can be especially critical where air temperatures are lower; these are the chill factors. Evaporative cooling is the loss of heat through perspiration and contact with the air. Evaporative cooling also occurs in the lungs in the breathing process. Decreasing humidity and higher wind speeds will increase evaporative cooling (Herrington, 1973).

Cities tend to be warmer than the surrounding countryside on an average of 0.5 to 1.5°C (Federer, 1970). This difference may be desirable in the winter, but in the summer it can cause discomfort. The summer difference is mainly because of the lack of vegetation in the city and its role in the absorption of solar radiation and in evaporative cooling.

As solar radiation enters the earth's atmosphere, part of it is lost through cloud-cover reflection; some of it is scattered and diffused by particles in the atmosphere; some is absorbed by gaseous pollutants (e.g., carbon dioxide, water vapor, and ozone); the remainder (approximately one-half) penetrates to the earth's surface.

During the daylight hours, solar radiation is absorbed by city surfaces—asphalt, concrete, steel, glass, tar roofs, and others. All of these are poor insulators—gaining, but also losing heat more readily than vegetation or soil. Thus, there is usually a considerable temperature differential between these surfaces and the surrounding air. Heat is then either convectively transferred to the air, causing an increase in surrounding air temperatures or is conducted to subsurface materials. Usually, the resulting increase in air temperature will also bring about a decrease in relative humidity.

Trees, shrubs, and grass ameliorate air temperatures in urban environments by controlling solar radiation. Tree leaves intercept, reflect, absorb, and transmit solar radiation (Figure 4.1). Their effectiveness depends on, for example, the density of species foliage, leaf shape, and branching patterns. Deciduous trees are very instrumental in heat control in urban settings in temperate regions. During the summer they intercept solar radiation and lower temperatures. In the winter the loss of their leaves results in the pleasant warming effects of increased solar radiation (Figure 4.2).

Trees and other vegetation also aid in ameliorating summer air temperatures through evapotranspiration. Trees have been called nature's air conditioners. A single isolated tree may transpire approximately 88 gallons (400 liters) of water per day (provided that sufficient soil moisture is available) (Kramer and Kozlowski, 1970). This has been compared to five average

45

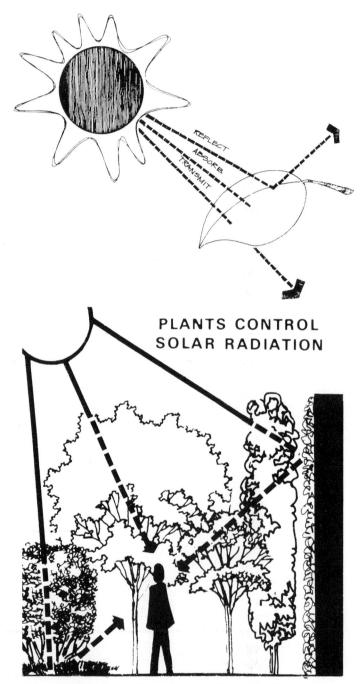

Figure 4.1 Plants benefit man by controlling solar radiation.

SUMMER

WINTER

Figure 4.2 Deciduous trees intercept the sun's rays during the summer months and allow them to pass through during the winter.

room air conditioners, each with a capacity of 2500 kcal/hr, running 20 hours a day (Federer, 1970). In a forest situation on a calm day, temperature decreases and relative humidity increases downward through the canopy profile (Figure 4.3).

At night heat is lost primarily through the exchange of infrared radiation between city surfaces and the atmosphere. On cool, clear nights, city surfaces cool more rapidly, on cloudy nights, there is less cooling. In addition, the rate of infrared heat loss varies with the type of material originally receiving heat from solar radiation during the day. Heavy, high density materials cool slowly; thus, releasing heat that may be desirable. At night, tree canopies slow the loss of heat from city surfaces, providing a screen between the cooler night air and the warm surface materials (Figure 4.4). Thus, the night temperatures are higher under trees than in the open (Federer, 1976). In urban areas, this differential may often be as great as 10 to 15°F (5 to 8°C) (Federer, 1970).

Another major influence on heat loss is the actual physical makeup of the city. A city is not a uniform object; it has many different parts and many different structures, all of which work together in varying ways: for example, narrow streets, tall buildings, factories, low buildings, wide streets, parking lots, parks, courtyards, lakes, hills, and rivers among others. Each location within a city has its own microclimate and is unique in its effect on the inhabitants and their sense of comfort. These microclimatic effects will be further discussed in Chapter 5.

47

	TEMP.	HUMIDITY
	96°F	33%
	95°	35%
	93°	32%
	92.5°	35%
	92°	33%
	71°	87%

Figure 4.3 Temperature decreases and humidity increases downward through a forest canopy.

CANOPY EFFECT—NIGHT

Figure 4.4 A tree canopy will slow the loss of heat at night.

Wind protection and air movement

Air movement, or wind, also affects human comfort. The effect may be either positive or negative depending largely on the presence or absence of urban vegetation. Wind can increase evaporative cooling during the day (Figure 4.5). The cooling will vary with the surrounding terrain and the wind speed (Federer, 1970).

48

	TEMP.	HUMIDITY
	67°F	94%
	67°	96%
	67°	96%
	67°	96%
	67°	97%
	65°	100%

Figure 4.5   Wind can negate cooling effects normally found within a forest canopy.

During summer, air movement has relatively little effect on air temperature unless the wind is part of a cool front. Instead, it simply causes a cooling sensation because of convective heat loss and evaporative cooling. In Figure 4.3, it is shown that because trees screen sunlight and transpire moisture, the area below the forest canpoy can be as much as 25°F (14°C) cooler on a still summer day than in an open area. Wind can reduce this temperature differential by replacing moist, cool air with dry, warm air. Hot, dry foehn or chinook winds can actually cause heating. Winds themselves can also be caused by temperature differences. Warm air rising over cities adjacent to oceans or lakes may pull in low, cool breezes; warm air rising from hot, dry open areas may pull in cool air; or cool air may flow downhill into low areas.

Trees reduce wind velocity and create sheltered zones both leeward and windward. Thus, trees can interfere with the evaporative cooling process, allowing higher temperatures to prevail in protected zones. This effect is greater from dense coniferous plantings than deciduous tree and shrub plantings and may be positive or negative depending on the time of the year. In the winter, a dense row of coniferous trees planted next to the north and west walls of a home in an area where prevailing winds come from these directions may create a "dead-air space" or insulation zone that prevents heat loss from a building (Figure 4.6). With a constant 70°F (22°C) house

DEAD
AIR
SPACE

Figure 4.6 The placement of coniferous trees next to a house can reduce heat loss during winter.

temperature, this could result in a fuel savings of nearly 23 percent (Robinette, 1972).

Conifers planted on slopes can impede the movement of cold air that would normally flow to low points, thus preventing the formation of localized frost pockets.

In many parts of the world, trees are used as effective wind controllers. This is particularly true in the Great Plains and other relatively treeless areas where severe winds cause discomfort, irritability, and occasional loss of life and property. In these regions, a belt of trees to slow the wind is a welcome relief (Figure 4.7).

Before discussing how trees are used in controlling wind, it is necessary to understand wind movement. Two types of wind or airflow are generally recognized:

1. Laminar airflow: layers or streams of air that flow one on top of another.

Figure 4.7 One of many shelterbelts in the Great Plains that are effective in reducing wind movement.

  2. Turbulent airflow: air masses moving in the same direction but in a
     random pattern.

     Turbulence in airflow is governed by disturbances in the airstream and
roughness of the surfaces over which it flows. The more streamlined the
surface obstruction, the less the turbulence. Layer separation can occur
when air moves around sharp corners. Usually wind without obstruction
flows in parallel layers (laminar flow). When wind flows over an obstructive
surface, the layer of air adjacent to the surface—the boundary layer—
usually speeds up, creating a low pressure area between this boundary and
the surface obstruction. Such low pressure will either result in the movement of the obstruction or will tend to pull the boundary layer back into its
original position. This process is affected by the intensity of the wind speed
and shape of the obstruction. Usually the leeside of the surface barrier is
protected (air movement is slowed). This leeward area of protection de-

51

creases as wind speed increases. The protected area on the leeward side increases as steepness of the slope on the windward side of the barrier increases. In addition, pierced and incomplete barriers may actually increase comfort in the leeward zone as they prevent rapid return of the original wind speed for a greater distance on the leeside.

Trees and shrubs control wind by obstruction, guidance, deflection, and filtration. Effect and degree of control vary with species size, shape, foliage density and retention, and the actual placement of the plants. Obstruction involves the placement of trees to reduce wind speed by increasing resistance to wind flow (Figure 4.8). An example is the prevention of heat loss by dense rows of conifers adjacent to a building, as mentioned earlier. Trees, by themselves or in combination with other barriers, may alter airflow over landscapes and around buildings. Plants can be situated to eliminate wind currents around corners or at entrances to buildings. Careful placement is necessary, however, as plants can also obstruct desired air movement through buildings.

Deflection of wind by trees and shrubs has been a topic of study since the 1930s in the Great Plains. Windbreaks perpendicular to prevailing winds may reduce wind two to five times the height of the tallest trees in front of the barrier and for distances of 30 to 40 times on the leeward side (Figure 4.9). Maximum wind reduction occurs in leeward distances of 10 to 20 times the height of the tallest trees. Here, downwind velocities may be reduced as much as 50 percent. The actual degree of protection depends on the height, width, penetrability, row arrangement, and species in the windbreak.

The wake zone depends largely on tree height; the taller the trees, the greater the protected distance. As trees increase in height, they generally become more open and allow increased airflow in the lower portions. Here more rows of trees in combination with low shrubs are usually required to

WIND

DENSE PLANTINGS CAN REDUCE WIND SPEED 75% TO 85%

Figure 4.8   Trees aid human comfort by reducing windspeeds.

Figure 4.9 Windbreaks provide protection for considerable distances.

provide adequate protection. Thus, the effectiveness of a windbreak depends on both height and penetrability. Usually the width of a windbreak has a negligible effect in reducing wind velocity on the leeward side; it can. however, create a noticeable microclimate within the sheltered area. Windbreaks with a cross-section design of a pitched roof are less effective in blocking winds than those with vertical edges.

While very dense windbreaks provide a greater wind reduction on the leeward side, the total zone of effective shelter is less. A penetrable wind barrier may not provide as much wind reduction on the leeward side, but the wake zone extends for a greater distance (Figure 4.10). Movement of air through the windbreak gives some lift to the boundary layer and acceleration to normal wind speed is more gradual. The optimum density for a shelterbelt is estimated at 50 to 60 percent (Robinette, 1972).

Species selection is important in windbreak efficiency. Conifers with dense foliage, are best on the north and west sides where protection from winter winds is desired. Deciduous species are preferred on the south and east as they protect against hot, dry winds in the summer and allow incoming solar radiation in winter.

Trees can provide effective wind protection for roads and highways. Highways perpendicular to prevailing winds are often subjected to strong crosswinds and gusts. Wind movement is also affected by highway cuts, breaks in terrain, and nearby buildings. Wind movement can often be controlled in such problem areas by the proper placement of trees and shrubs (Figure 4.11).

Trees can also be used to control snow drifting. As wind velocity is slowed to the leeward, snow particles are deposited. Windbreaks containing low shrub rows are most effective in the control of drifting. Drift patterns vary with windbreak density (Figure 4.12). Dense windbreaks yield drifts that are narrow and quite deep. As penetrability increases, drifts become wider and shallower. Higher velocity winds cause drifts to be narrow and

53

A 30ft. high shelterbelt affects wind
speed for 100yds. in front of the trees
and 300yds. down wind.

Effect of moderately penetrable windbreaks on wind.

Effect of dense windbreak on wind
flow.   H=30ft.

Figure 4.10   Density affects the downwind
protection zone of any given windbreak.

54

PLANTINGS CHECK CROSS-WIND GUSTS ADJACENT TO HIGHWAY CUTS

Figure 4.11 Tree plantings can be used to increase highway safety in areas subjected to high winds.

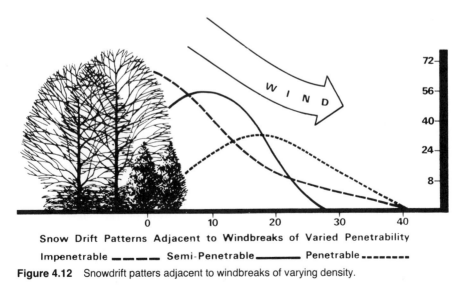

Snow Drift Patterns Adjacent to Windbreaks of Varied Penetrability

Impenetrable ▬ ▬ ▬ ▬ Semi-Penetrable ▬▬▬▬ Penetrable ▬ ▬ ▬ ▬ ▬

Figure 4.12 Snowdrift patters adjacent to windbreaks of varying density.

55

deeper. The following formula has been derived for computing windbreak drift patterns (Jensen, 1954):

$$L = \frac{36 + 5h}{K}$$

where: L = the length of the drift in feet
h = the height of the screen in feet
K = the function of the screen density, 1.0 for 50 percent density and 1.28 for 70 percent density

Windbreaks may be more desirable than snowfences since maintenance costs of snowfencing can be high, and certainly trees are more esthetically pleasing. Trees and shrubs can be used to provide drift-free parking lots, roads, and sidewalks (Figure 4.13). In addition, they may be used to cause snow deposition where desired, such as ski areas, toboggan runs, and where soil moisture from melted snow is desired.

Precipitation and humidity

Trees intercept and filter solar radiation, inhibit wind flow, transpire water, and reduce evaporation of soil moisture. Thus, beneath a forest canopy, humidity is usually higher and evaporation rates are lower. Temperature beneath the canopy is also lower than the surrounding air during the day and warmer during the evening.

In addition to their effects on temperature, trees and shrubs are important in the hydrologic cycle. They intercept precipitation and slow its descent to the soil surface. This can increase infiltration and decrease runoff and soil erosion. Trees may also reduce soil moisture evaporation. However, their high transpiration rates and interception process may actually reduce the amount of water available for aquifer recharge or reduce stream flow when compared to other types of vegetative cover. All of these factors are important in urban areas where natural underground aquifers are the main source of water.

Effectiveness in controlling runoff and increasing infiltration varies with soil type, organic content of the soil, topography, type and intensity of precipitation, and composition of vegetative cover. Interception of precipitation by coniferous trees is usually greater than that of hardwoods (Figure 4.14). An estimated 60 percent of the rainfall will reach the ground through a pine canopy as compared to 80 percent through a hardwood canopy. This is because the leaf structure of conifers enables better entrapment of water droplets (Figure 4.15). Pubescence is another leaf characteristic important in water entrapment. Branching patterns also affect interception rates, horizontal branching patterns being the most effective (Figure 4.15). In

WINDBREAKS FOR COLLECTING SNOW

ROAD

WINDBREAK DESIGNED TO TRAP SNOW
ADJACENT TO A ROAD

Figure 4.13 Windbreaks can be used to assist in keeping sidewalks and roads free of snow drifts.

addition, rough bark slows the movement of water down tree trunks (Figure 4.15). The more intense the rainfall, however, the less effective a tree will be in interception. The same is true of duration of rainfall. Resultant runoff will also be affected by the nature of the shrub canopy, ground cover, litter, and topography.

Engineering Uses

In recent years, highly specialized uses for plants in solving environmental engineering problems have been developed. Involved are not only landscape

57

RAIN 100%

60%
REACHES
GROUND

Pine forest.

RAIN
100%

80%
REACHES
GROUND

Hardwood forest.

Figure 4.14 Coniferous forest trees intercept more rainfall than do hardwood forest trees.

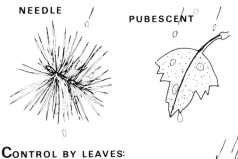

NEEDLE   PUBESCENT

CONTROL BY LEAVES:
LEAVES VARY IN THEIR
ABILITY TO HOLD WATER AND
BREAK RAINDROP IMPACT.

SMOOTH   BLADE

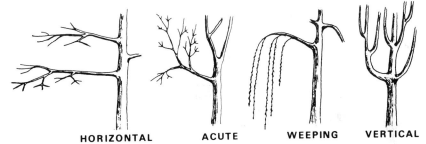

HORIZONTAL   ACUTE   WEEPING   VERTICAL

CONTROL BY BRANCHING:
    HORIZONTAL BRANCHING IS MOST EFFECTIVE IN PREVENTING WATER
    RUNOFF DOWN TREE TRUNK AND EROSION AT BASE OF TREE.

DIAMOND   ROUGH   SMOOTH   PEBBLED

CONTROL BY BARK:
    ROUGH BARK HOLDS AND SLOWS WATER RUNNING DOWN
    TRUNK AND PREVENTS EROSION AT BASE OF TREE.

Figure 4.15 Differences in plant species morphology will affect how much
rainfall is intercepted.

esthetics but soil erosion control, air pollution, noise abatement, wastewater management, traffic control, and glare and reflection reduction. Robinette (1972) has listed the following plant characteristics and their effects that help to solve environmental engineering problems:

1. Fleshy leaves that deaden sound.
2. Branches that move and vibrate to absorb and mask sounds.
3. Pubescence on the leaves to entrap and hold dust particles.
4. Stomata in the leaves to exchange gases.
5. Blossoms and foliage that provide pleasant smells to mask odor.
6. Leaves and branches to slow wind.
7. Leaves and branches to slow rainfall.
8. Spreading roots to hold soil against erosion.
9. Dense foliage to block light.
10. Light foliage to filter light.
11. Spiny branches to deter human movement.

Erosion control and watershed protection

Because of environmental impacts associated with most construction activities, erosion control is perhaps the most important engineering use of plants. Soil erosion is the loss of topsoil by wind or water movement, usually resulting from improper soil protection. Soil erosion is influenced by exposure of the site to wind and water, the physical characteristics of the soil, and topography.

Wind erosion in the urban forest is not as well recognized as water erosion. Wind erosion is mostly associated with rural agricultural lands where large land surfaces may lie unprotected, where winds are frequent and strong, and where precipitation is minimal and unpredictable. Visibility is often reduced, presenting a safety hazard. Wind erosion is affected by speed, duration, and direction of the wind along with such soil factors as moisture, physical structure, and cover. Normally, as the wind moves over exposed dry soil, the smaller soil particles are moved. This results in saltation, a condition where larger particles moving along the soil surface act as abrasives, causing smaller particles to dislodge and become windborne. Trees and shrubs have long been used to reduce wind erosion. During the 1930s, thousands of windbreaks were established in the Great Plains for this purpose, and new ones are still being planted.

Soil erosion in urban areas is usually associated with construction activities where soil surfaces have been exposed. Splash erosion from the impact of falling raindrops causes soil particles to be dislodged and to move into runoff suspension where they act as scouring agents removing even more soil.

There are four types of runoff erosion: (1) sheet, (2) rill, (3) gulley, and (4) slip. Sheet erosion is the removal of the entire top soil layer from an exposed site. As this continues, soft areas in the soil surface may be removed faster, resulting in rills or troughs. Channeling of runoff water in rills results in gulley erosion. Slip erosion is the mass movement of water-saturated soils downslope. The latter is associated with steep slopes in regions of high rainfall following vegetation removal by fire or other causes.

Drastic changes occur in watershed hydrology when agricultural or forested areas are converted to urban land use. The most important thing city planners can do to minimize adverse hydrologic effects of urbanization is to retain partial watersheds. This entails reserving areas along streams, around lakes, or other areas as greenbelts to be maintained in their natural state (Figure 4.16). Other measures that can improve the hydrology of urban areas include:

1. Perforation of compacted lawns to improve water absorption and infiltration.
2. Planting of trees and shrubbery.
3. Use of conservation practices such as terracing, contour planting, mulching, and sod waterways in yards and gardens.
4. Construction of gravel drainage areas for roof runoff.
5. Use of flat roofs to reduce runoff and aid building cooling.
6. Temporary mulching of construction sites.

Plants reduce water-caused soil erosion by intercepting rainfall, by holding soil with their roots, and by increasing water absorption through the incorporation of organic matter (Figure 4.17). In addition, plants are more attractive than mechanical water erosion control devices.

Wastewater management

Rapid population growth accompanied by an expanding industrial base has greatly increased the demands on our nation's water resources. This growth is also creating ever-increasing waste disposal problems. In 1970 approximately 25 billion gallons (113 billion liters) of municipal sewage effluent were discharged daily into surface streams in the United States. It is estimated that the population of the United States will reach 300 million by the year 2000 A.D. and the municipal waste load of the nation would increase correspondingly (Nutter, 1971).

Wastewater disposal begins with "primary treatment." Large objects are removed and the remaining material is ground in a grit chamber and piped to sedimentation tanks where sand, silt, and suspended organic material are allowed to settle. After the water is skimmed, it is discharged into

61

Figure 4.16 Retaining of forested areas adjacent to streams not only reduces erosion but is also more esthetic.

lakes or streams. At this stage about one-third of the biochemical oxygen demand (B.O.D.)* still remains. Only a very small portion of the nutrients, however, have been removed. In about 30 percent of the United States' treatment plants, this is all that is done.

*B.O.D. is a measure of the oxygen consumed during decomposition of organic compounds.

62

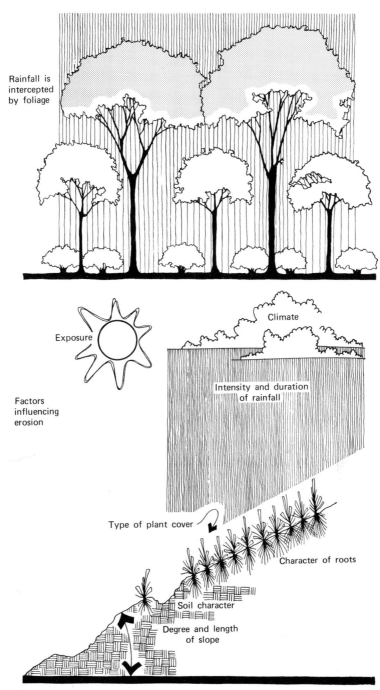

Figure 4.17 The various factors that influence water-related soil erosion.

63

Secondary treatment is primarily biological in nature and involves the use of microorganisms (bacteria) to decompose organic compounds. Approximately 60 percent of the treatment plants in the United States incorporate this step (Owen, 1975). In this process, about 90 percent of the B.O.D. and 90 percent of the suspended solids are removed. However, 58 percent of the nitrogen compounds and 30 percent of the phosphorus compounds (elements responsible for stream eutrophication), still remain. Discharge of this nutrient-rich secondary effluent into lakes or streams causes abundant aquatic growth. These plants grow profusely, die, decompose, and increase the B.O.D. of the water. This accelerated process utilizes available dissolved oxygen that is necessary for other aquatic life. Nutrients are re-released to be recycled in the same manner. As a result, streams may become even more polluted after receiving secondary treatment water than they were when receiving raw sewage.

Recently a third process, called a tertiary treatment, has been developed to aid in nutrient removal. In this process secondary effluent is mixed with lime to remove phosphorous by precipitation. Nitrogen, present primarily as ammonia, is removed by blowing large amounts of air through the effluent. Though highly effective, these treatments are expensive—30¢ per 1000 gallons (4545 liters) of effluent as compared to 12¢ per 1000 gallons (4545 liters) for secondary treatment. Thus, tertiary treatment may not be feasible in many urban and industrial areas.

Because of the high cost of current methods, other solutions for effluent disposal should be considered. A promising alternative is land sewage disposal. Land disposal systems reduce stream water pollution, conserve and recycle water, and allow nutrients to be recycled for further use. The suitability of effluent for land disposal depends on its chemical composition. Wastewater from residential areas can generally be used for this purpose whereas industrial wastewater may require some treatment to remove toxic substances that could affect biological systems. Industrial waste from food processing plants and pulp mills are usually well-suited for land disposal. Land disposal is not a recent innovation. Most of the early systems, however, were concerned only with waste disposal and did not consider water conservation or the recycling of nutrients.

The following case is made for productive land disposal systems by Sopper (1971):

A more feasible method might be to apply the wastewater to the land so as to utilize the entire biosystem—soil and vegetation—as a "living filter" to renovate the effluent for groundwater recharge. Under controlled application rates to maintain aerobic conditions within the soil, the mineral nutrients and detergent residual might be removed and degraded by micro-organisms in the surface soil horizons, chemical precipitation, ion exchange, biological transformation, and biological absorption through the root systems of the vegetative cover. The utilization of higher plants as an integral part of the system to complement the microbiological and physiochemical systems in the soil is an essential component of the living-filter concept and provides maximum renovation capacity and durability to the system.

Land sewage disposal has been used for centuries in the Orient, and many European cities have had operational systems for years. Systems in Berlin and Paris date back to 1850. Israel has adopted this type of sewage disposal system because of water shortages. The sewage of Tel Aviv has been used to grow fruits and vegetables in the Negev Desert instead of polluting the beaches of the Mediterranean.

In the United States, sewage was used for crop irrigation only on a small scale in the nineteenth and early twentieth centuries, and until recently the process was relatively unknown. The primary reasons for this were:

1. Low population densities and greater abundance of land and water resources.
2. Availability of inexpensive chemical fertilizers.
3. Generally negative public attitude about eating food that was produced from human effluent.

However, these factors have changed in recent years, and agronomists, horticulturists, ecologists, and others are now investigating the use of renovated wastewater for fertilization and groundwater recharge. Industrial wastes have been used for irrigation purposes. For example, at Seabrook Farms in Bridgeton, New Jersey the 10 million gallons (45 million liters) of water used daily to wash vegetables are afterwards disposed of on forest land. Other companies have initiated similar systems, and many paper and pull mills have incorporated land disposal systems into their operations.

The Pennsylvania State University Waste Water Renovation and Conservation Project is another example (Sopper, 1971). Water pollution and supply were problems in State College. Sewage water was discharged into the area's main watercourse, depleting the stream of necessary oxygen for aquatic life and reducing its recreational value. The main water supply came from groundwater reservoirs that were being depleted by a drought of nine years duration. Millions of gallons of water were released into the stream, thus removing it from the water supply.

65

The need to solve both the water quality and the water supply problems prompted studies involving the land disposal of wastewater and the living filter concept. The removal of the effluent from local streams to overland disposal sites would reduce stream pollution and enhance renovation and recharge of the groundwater reservoir. A team of scientists studied changes in plant community structure, monitored foliar and soil nutrient changes and absorptive capacities of soils at various levels of effluent application. Their work indicates that the living filter concept is feasible given the following site conditions (Sopper, 1971):

1. *The soil must have an infiltration and percolation capacity high enough to accommodate applications of wastewater at the recommended rates. Soil permeability must be high enough to permit drainage of the renovated effluent and to maintain aerobic soil conditions. Forest soils are well-suited because they are usually very porous, and have high infiltration and percolation rates, and remain so during the winter season.*
2. *The soil must have sufficient chemical absorptive capacity, water retentive capacity and depth to the groundwater table to hold dissolved minerals for use by plants and micro-organisms, thereby preventing groundwater contamination.*
3. *Land must have low relief and good vegetative cover along with accumulated surface organic matter to minimize surface runoff. This is particularly true in the winter months.*
4. *There must be a groundwater aquifer with a fairly deep water table to accommodate subsequent changes in groundwater storage, and with sufficient horizontal permeability to allow for adequate lateral displacement of the renovated wastewater.*

Renovation and reuse of wastewater is more widespread in the United States than one might imagine. At Whittier Narrows in Los Angeles County, California, 10 to 15 million gallons (45 to 68 million liters) of sewage waste per day are recovered, purified, and diluted to recharge groundwater supplies for municipal reuse. At Santee, California municipal wastewater is reclaimed and used in a series of recreational lakes. Chanute, Kansas during a severe drought in 1957 impounded its own wastewater, treated it, and reused it for several months. The Desert Inn Hotel and Country Club in Las Vegas, Nevada uses purified sewage effluent to irrigate its 130-acre (52-ha) golf course.

According to the Pennsylvania State University study, the living filter system is best adapted to small cities and suburbs because of the availability of open land close to a treatment facility. In their studies, they found that an application rate of 2 in. (5.08 cm) per week required only 129 acres (52 ha) of land to dispose of one million gallons (4.5 million liters) of wastewater per day. It is estimated that a city with a population of 100,000, discharging 10 million gallons (4.5 million liters) of wastewater daily, would require only 1290 acres (522 ha) for a living filter system.

Although large blocks of agricultural and forest land may be used for disposal, cities might also use golf courses, recreation fields, forest preserves, parks, greenbelts, scenic parkways, and perhaps even highway medians.

Noise abatement

Noise is commonly thought of as excessive or unwanted sound. Experts in the field often refer to noise as "invisible pollution." Noise involves both physical and psychological effects. The physical effects deal with transmission of sound waves through the air, while the psychological effects involve the human response to sound. Sound is defined as a pressure variation in an elastic medium that affects the hearing mechanism. Sound moves in waves; the high pitches or frequencies have shorter wavelengths and the low frequencies longer wavelengths. Sound frequency is measured in cycles per second (CPS). The human ear can detect sound in the range of 20 to 20,000 CPS. The sound pressure level (SPL) or intensity of sound is measured in decibels (dB). The decibel scale, when adjusted by weighting the sound level meter to the dBA scale is approximately related to loudness, but that relationship is not intended (Figure 4.18). The lowest sound that can be detected by a keen human ear under very quiet conditions corresponds to zero decibels, and the highest sound corresponds to about 120 decibels (Table 4.1). The decibel scale is logarithmic, and is defined by an equation.* Because of the logarithmic nature of the decibel and the response characteristics of the ear, an increase of 10 dB corresponds to the approximate doubling of the loudness of a sound.

Propagation of outdoor noise is caused by: (1) the nature of the source (e.g., its frequency, composition, location, and whether or not the source is of a linear or point nature); (2) the nature of the terrain and vegetation over which the sound is passing; and (3) the state of the atmosphere (e.g., speed and direction of the wind and temperature conditions).

Outdoor sounds are normally attenuated (reduced in intensity) before reaching the receiver. Attenuation usually assumes a dual nature; it is called *normal* attenuation when it is related to distance and *excess* attenuation when it results from the introduction of elements or barriers between the sound source and the receiver.

---

*SPL (decibels $= 20 \log p/P^0$, where p is measured pressure and P^0 is a reference pressure of 0.0002 microbars or 0.00002 Newtons per square meter.

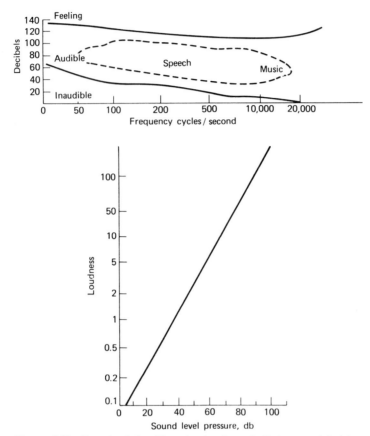

Figure 4.18 Sound relationships showing how decibels are related to sound frequency and loudness.

TABLE 4.1

Sound Levels in dBA (from Herrington, 1973)

Source	SPL, dBA
Threshold of pain	130
Jet takeoff (200 ft away)	120
Large truck, noisy motorcycle or pneumatic drill (50 ft away)	80
Vacuum cleaner (10 ft away)	70
Average residence	50
Residential area, night	40
Soft whisper (5 ft away)	30
Threshold of hearing	0

Noise originating from a point source (as from a mountain top) radiates spherically away from the source. Acoustic energy decreases in proportion to the reciprocal of the square of the distance. Studies have shown that each time the distance from a point noise source is doubled, there is a reduction of 6 dBA. Thus, if a truck produced an SPL of 80 dBA at roadside [10 ft (3.1 m) from the truck], the SPL at 20 ft (6.3 m) would be 74 dBA; at 40 ft (12.5 m), 68 dBA; at 80 ft (25 m), 62 dBA; etc. However, with a noise coming from a line source (a busy freeway), the reduction is only 3 dBA for each doubling of the distance.

Excess attenuation of sound propagated along the ground is greatly affected by the presence of temperature and wind gradients. Attenuation measured upwind may exceed those measured downwind by as much as 25 to 30 decibels. In general, sounds passing downwind from a source are directed downward toward the surface, while sounds traveling upwind from a source are directed upward from the surface. At night, when the atmosphere is coldest near the ground, sound waves will be directed toward the surface, while during the day when the atmosphere is warmer near the ground, sound will be directed away from the surface.

Elements introduced between the source and the receiver reduce sound by absorption, deflection, reflection, and defraction. Another phenomenon, masking, may also aid in reducing noise.

Absorption occurs when an object receives sound waves and entraps them, converting the sound into other energy forms and, eventually, heat. If the material is sufficiently porous, up to 95 percent of the energy may be absorbed. *Deflection* occurs by introducing an element that will cause the noise to bounce from a recipient into an area of direction less offensive to the hearer. *Reflection* causes the sound to be directed back to the source, thus protecting the hearer. *Refraction* is the dissipation, diffusion, or dispersion of acoustical energy when it strikes a rough surface. This may also be caused by wind turbulence. Masking, though not a form of attenuation, is the introduction of a pleasing sound that tends to override undesirable noises (e.g., piped-in music in an office).

Research documentation of plants as attenuators is limited. Robinette (1972) lists three early works in his discussion of plants and acoustical control: Eyring (1946); Weiner and Keast (1959); and Embelton (1963). The most recent studies have been by Cook and Van Haverbeke in Nebraska (1971, 1974, 1977).

How effectively plants control sound levels is determined by the sound itself, the planting involved, and the climatic conditions. The properties of sound include type, origin, decibel level, and intensity. Planting factors include the species, arrangement in relation to the sound source and the receiver, and planting height and density (Figures 4.19 and 4.20). Climatic

NOISE SOURCE CITY TRASH CREW AT A DISTANCE OF 90'
PLANTING   CONIFEROUS EVERGREEN HEDGE
NOISE REDUCTION 50%

NOISE SOURCE LAWNMOWER EXHAUST AND BLADE WHINE
PLANTING   6' HIGH 10' THICK MIXED CONIFEROUS AND DECIDUOUS
NOISE REDUCTION 40%

NOISE SOURCE CHILDREN PLAYING AT A DISTANCE OF 50'
PLANTING   DECIDUOUS PLANTING
NOISE REDUCTION 50%

Figure 4.19 The function of plants in reducing noise pollution in different urban settings.

NOISE SOURCE : SHOPPING CENTER PEDESTRIAN SOUNDS
PLANTING : DECIDUOUS PLANTING
NOISE REDUCTION : 25%

Figure 4.20 Plants can reduce sound in downtown urban areas.

factors include wind direction and velocity, temperature, and humidity. In addition to deflection, absorption, refraction, reflection, and masking, plants may also attenuate sound by their influence on local climate; that is, their stabilization of temperature, their modification of wind speed, and other factors. Weiner and Keast (1959) pointed out that sound propagation patterns over woodland areas differ from those over open level terrain. They attributed this difference not only to absorption and scattering, but also to wind velocities and vertical wind gradients, which are reduced over woodland areas. Also air temperatures are fairly uniform because such areas are not subject to the large diurnal lapse rates and nocturnal inversions common to open terrain.

Plant attenuation of sound is shown in Figure 4.21; sound waves are absorbed by the leaves, branches, and twigs of trees and shrubs. These plant parts are light and flexible. It has been postulated that the most effective plants for absorbing sound are those having many thick, fleshy leaves with petioles. This combination allows for the highest degree of flexibility and vibration (Robinette, 1972). Sound is also deflected and refracted by the heavier branches and the trunks of trees. It has been estimated that, on the average, forests can attenuate sound at the rate of 7 dB per 100 ft (30 m) of distance at frequencies of 1000 CPS or less (Embleton, 1963).

A recent study involving trees and shrubs as sound attenuators was conducted by the School of Engineering at the University of Nebraska and the Rocky Mountain Forest and Range Experiment Station, U.S. Forest

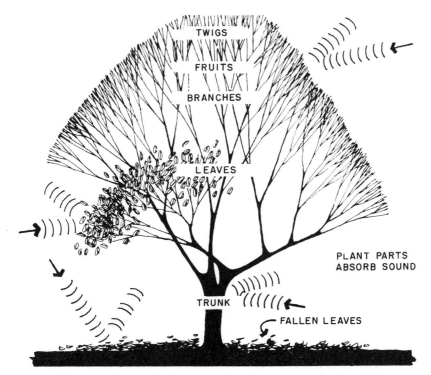

Figure 4.21 A graphic illustration of how plants attenuate sound.

Service. These studies showed that the potential of trees and shrubs for sound reduction is quite promising. Attenuations of 5 to 8 dB and even as much as 10 dB for wide belts of tall, dense trees were recorded. These levels were even greater when harder surfaces were compared with tree-shrub-grass combinations; then attenuations of 8 to 12 dB were common (Cook and Van Haverbeke, 1971). Generally, wide belts of tall trees were found to be most effective, and species did not differ greatly in their ability to reduce noise levels, provided that deciduous trees were in full leaf. Evergreens are desirable for year-round screening (Figure 4.22).

The relative position of the screen between the sound source and the hearer (receiver) is very important. A screen close to the sound source is more effective than one close to the area to be protected.

Urban residential property can be effectively screened from passenger car noise with a single row of dense shrubs backed by a row of taller trees, totaling a depth of 20 feet (6.3 m). Screening for rural areas or freeways requires wider belts consisting of several rows of tall trees in dense plantings. In general, 100 ft (30 m) or more of such a planting between the noise source and the area to be protected are desirable.

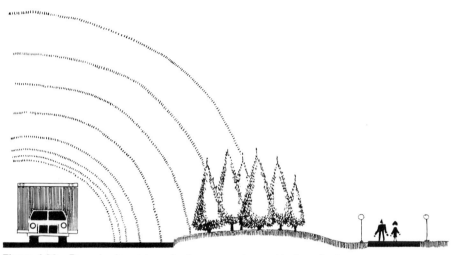

Figure 4.22 Properly placed, tree plantings can reduce vehicular noise in residential areas.

Specific recommendations based on these studies are as follows (Cook and Van Haverbeke, 1971):

1. *Reduction of noise from high-speed car and truck traffic in rural areas is best achieved by tree and shrub belts 65 to 100 feet (20 to 30 m) wide with the edge of the belt within 50 to 80 feet (16 to 20 m) of the center of the nearest traffic lane. Center tree rows should be at least 45 feet (14 m) tall.*
2. *To reduce noise from moderate-speed car traffic in urban areas, tree and shrub belts 20 to 50 feet (6 to 16 m) wide may be used effectively with the edge of the belt from 20 to 50 feet (5 to 16 m) from the center of the nearest traffic lane. Shrubs six to eight feet (2 to 2.5 m) tall should be used next to the traffic lane followed by backup rows of trees 15 to 30 feet (4.5 to 10 m) tall.*
3. *For optimum results, trees and shrubs should be planted close to the noise source as opposed to close to the protected area.*
4. *Where possible, use taller varieties of trees which have dense foliage and relatively uniform vertical foliage distribution (or use combinations of shrubs and trees). Where the use of tall trees is restricted, use combinations of shorter shrubs and tall grass or similar soft ground cover, as opposed to paving, crushed rock, or gravel surfaces.*
5. *Trees and shrubs should be planted as close together as practical to form a continuous, dense barrier. The spacing should conform to established local practices for each species.*

73

6. *Evergreens (conifers) or deciduous species which retain their leaves should be used where year-round noise screening is desired.*

7. *Belts should be approximately twice as long as the distance from the noise source to the receiver, and when used as a noise screen parallel to a roadway, should extend equal distances along the roadway on both sides of the protected area.*

Traffic noise can also be alleviated by proper highway design. Studies have been conducted on sound propagation from highways that are depressed, raised, or on a grade. Proper planting in such situations can aid tremendously in sound control. A publication dealing with optimum planting for sound control along highways was published in the early 1950s (Simonson; 1957). This report also discussed planting design for retaining walls and buffer plantings on roadsides to control noise. Figure 4.23 illustrates some of the design combinations for various highway situations.

Where rights-of-way are limited, a combination of wall (masonry, barrier, or embankment) and planting can be used effectively. The effectiveness of the barrier can be increased by the use of vines that cover the wall.

Depressed highways reflect traffic noise upward. Planting on the lower parts of the slope, however, will cause secondary reflection and may reduce effectiveness. Planting along highways is very effective in suppressing noise transmission to adjacent areas.

Preliminary studies indicate that if grass, vines, or other plants are on barrier slopes facing the noise, the noise may be reduced by as much as 8 to 10 dB. Hedges and trees with dense foliage act as sound absorbers and deadeners. The effectiveness of the barrier increases with the increasing thickness, height, and density of the planting.

In work related to the previous discussion Cook and Van Haverbeke (1974) compared bare and tree-covered landforms as attenuators of highway noise. They found that for highway noise abatement, a combination of the two is more effective than either one used separately. The choice is governed by several factors, including cost and availability of material, the time frame involved, and esthetics. The specific recommendations Cook and Van Haverbeke put forth in their study are as follows:

1. *To reduce noise from high-speed traffic, land-forms should be sufficient in height to screen the traffic from view. Several rows of trees and shrubs should be planted adjacent to and on the land-form for progressive improvement with conifers used in preference to deciduous species for year-round noise control.*

2. *The reduction of noise from suburban traffic can be ac-*

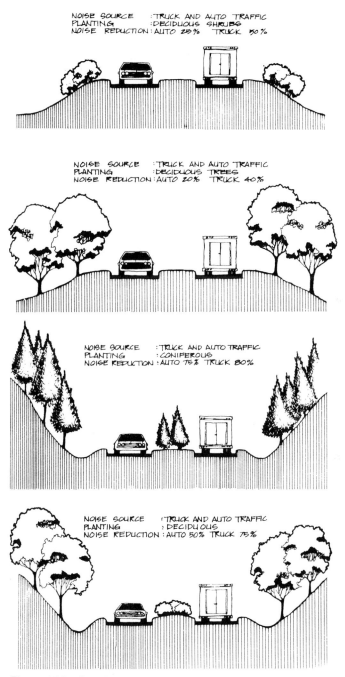

NOISE SOURCE   : TRUCK AND AUTO TRAFFIC
PLANTING   : DECIDUOUS SHRUBS
NOISE REDUCTION : AUTO 25% TRUCK 50%

NOISE SOURCE   : TRUCK AND AUTO TRAFFIC
PLANTING   : DECIDUOUS TREES
NOISE REDUCTION : AUTO 20% TRUCK 40%

NOISE SOURCE   : TRUCK AND AUTO TRAFFIC
PLANTING   : CONIFEROUS
NOISE REDUCTION : AUTO 75% TRUCK 80%

NOISE SOURCE   : TRUCK AND AUTO TRAFFIC
PLANTING   : DECIDUOUS
NOISE REDUCTION : AUTO 50% TRUCK 75%

Figure 4.23 Sound abatement will vary with the species selected and its placement. In addition roadway design is also a factor.

complished by the planting of rows of heavy shrubs adjacent to the traffic lanes and constructing a five to six foot (two m) land-form behind the shrubs.

3. *Optimum land-form height will vary for each situation; however, 8 to 10 foot (2.5 to 3 m) heights, when used in combinations with taller varieties of trees, are recommended for general applications provided the noise source is screened from view.*

4. *The noise screen should be placed relatively close to the noise source for maximum benefit and should extend far enough from side to side to assure acceptable sound levels at the protected area.*

5. *Since wind speed and direction affect sound levels at a specific location, the most severe conditions should be used when estimating expected sound levels for design purposes.*

6. *Natural ground configurations, such as hills, ridges, and depressed highways, should be employed to serve as noise screens when planning roadside developments, schools, and residences adjacent to arterial streets in urban areas.*

7. *Existing trees, shrubs, and grass should be left undisturbed, as far as possible, rather than replacing the soft materials with harder reflecting surfaces detrimental to noise control.*

As mentioned earlier, plants can also mask unwanted sounds (Figure 4.24). Plants make their own sounds—the whisper of pines, the rustle of oak leaves, or the quaking of aspens. These are pleasant sounds that tend to make us less aware of more offensive noises. In addition, plants support animals and birds that may make desirable sounds.

Plants can play a role in noise abatement. There are, however limitations to their effectiveness. Although they may reduce noise to acceptable levels, tree and shrub screens, regardless of their size and density, will not completely eliminate sound. Also, a single tree or a few scattered trees will not appreciably reduce noise. Only if trees are massed will they be effective. Trees, shrubs, and other vegetation will aid in noise reduction if used properly, and the advantage will be greater than the psychological aspect of simply screening the noise source from the receiver's view.

Air pollution abatement

The role of trees in reducing air pollution is not well understood, and there is considerable disagreement as to their effectiveness. The types and relative sizes of common air pollutants that affect us are found in Figure 4.25. Most important are those that are either gaseous or particulate.

It is well-known that plants produce oxygen in the photosynthetic pro-

PARTS THAT MAKE SOUND

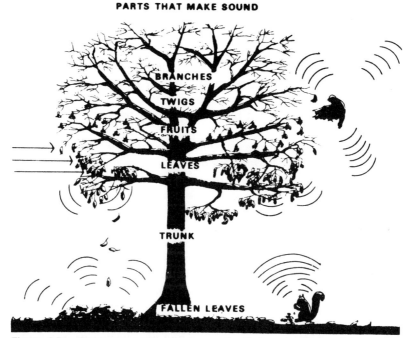

Figure 4.24 Plants can mask noise by creating their own sounds or by enabling accompanying wildlife to do so.

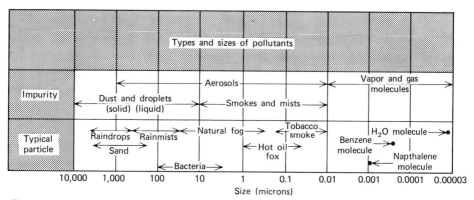

Figure 4.25 Types and sizes of various pollutants encountered in our present-day technological society.

77

cess. Some people have suggested that plants perform an important role in reducing air pollution through the processes of oxygenation (the introduction of excess oxygen into the atmosphere) and dilution (the mixing of polluted air with fresh air). Thus, it is reasoned that when polluted air flows in and around plants and through the freshly oxygenated air, dilution occurs and pollution is lessened (Figure 4.26). Granted that these processes occur, are they significant in abating air pollution? Weidensaul (1973) feels that research data do not necessarily support a major role by plants in this process. He defined an efficient plant air purifier as:

> *one which could reduce the concentration of a given pollutant from an undesirable level at which harmful effects are observed to a level which would not cause injury or damage, without the air purifier (plant) suffering any ill effects.*

Certain plants can absorb specific air pollutants, that is, hydrogen fluoride, sulfur dioxide, and nitrogen dioxide. The pollutant least absorbed, however, is carbon monoxide; and it accounts for roughly one-half the total weight of air pollutants emitted into the air in this country. Species such as sugar maple and yellow birch can readily absorb sulfur dioxide, but they are also easily injured by the gas. Furthermore, it has been estimated that approximately 88 percent of the oxygen produced on the earth through photosynthesis originates in the sea. It has also been estimated that the oxygen produced by an acre of forest land per year represents only 0.03 percent of the total oxygen found over that acre (Weidensaul, 1973). Thus, oxygenation and dilution by plants are probably not at all effective in the abatement of gaseous air pollutants.

Trees, however, are effective in reducing gaseous air pollutants through absorption. A study of ozone pollution and forested areas showed

Figure 4.26 Proposed schematic for air pollution abatement by plants through the processes of oxygenation and dilution.

78

that if an air mass containing 150 ppm of ozone were to stand over a forest for eight hours, the vegetation would absorb approximately 80 percent of it. Taller trees removed more ozone than shorter trees. And the larger and more numerous the leaf stomatal openings, the more effective is the ozone removal (Stevenson, 1970). A recent Russian study has shown that a 1640 ft (500 m) wide green area surrounding factories will reduce sulfur dioxide concentrations by 70 percent and nitric oxide concentrations by 67 percent (Robinette, 1972).

Wind turbulence is a major factor in dispersing gaseous pollutants. Because their presence increases wind turbulence, trees can be used to aid in the disperal of gaseous pollutants if located downwind from the source of pollution.

Particulate air pollutants can be reduced by the presence of trees and other plants in several ways. They aid in the removal of airborne particulates such as sand, dust, fly ash, pollen, and smoke. Leaves, branches, stems, and their associated surface structures (i.e., pubescence on leaves) tend to trap particles that are later washed off by precipitation. Trees also aid in the removal of airborne particulate matter by air washing. Transpiration increases humidity, thus aiding in the settling out of airborne particulates (Figure 4.27). The results of these processes can be readily observed on trees adjacent to factories or along gravel roads.

Trees also often mask fumes and disagreeable odors by replacing them with more pleasing foliage or floral odors or by actual absorption (Figure 4.28). When trees are planted to aid in air pollution abatement, the following guidlines should be used (Bernatsky, 1968):

1. Plantings should be perpendicular to the prevailing winds.
2. Open and permeable plantings should be combined with dense barrier stands.
3. Plantings should be concentric around the pollution source.

Glare and reflection control

Solar radiation affects our visual comfort as well as our thermal comfort. We are surrounded by a myriad of shining surfaces—glass, steel, aluminum, concrete, and water—all capable of reflecting light. We experience discomfort when the sun's rays are reflected toward us by these surfaces. At night, we have to contend with glare from automobile headlights, streetlights, buildings, and advertising signs.

Glare intercepted directly from the light source is termed "primary" (Figure 4.29). Primary glare that is diffused by atmospheric particles makes the light source unrecognizable. This results in a bright haze that can be extremely discomforting.

Secondary glare is reflected light (Figure 4.30). Factors that affect sec-

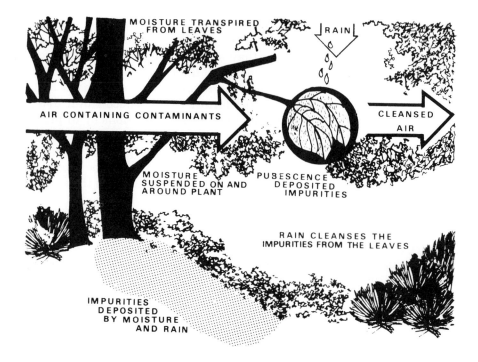

MOISTURE TRANSPIRED
FROM LEAVES

RAIN

AIR CONTAINING CONTAMINANTS

CLEANSED
AIR

MOISTURE
SUSPENDED ON AND
AROUND PLANT

PUBESCENCE
DEPOSITED
IMPURITIES

RAIN CLEANSES THE
IMPURITIES FROM THE LEAVES

IMPURITIES
DEPOSITED
BY MOISTURE
AND RAIN

FILTRATION / AIR WASHER

Figure 4.27 Plants reduce air pollutants through the process of air washing.

ondary glare are: (1) smoothness of the surface; (2) angle of the light path; (3) amount of initial light; (4) air temperature; (5) seasonal and diurnal conditions (position of the sun); and (6) atmospheric conditions.

Discomfort from glare and reflection can be reduced architecturally by awnings, window shades, screens, or by proper building orientation and window placement. We can also wear our polarized sunglasses or purchase tinted windows for our offices, homes, or automobiles.

Plants can be used to screen and soften both primary and secondary glare. Their effectiveness depends primarily on their size and density. Sources of glare must be identified before the proper plants can be selected to control it. The degree of control is also important as it may be desirable to eliminate glare completely or to create a filtering or softening effect.

Plants can block or filter primary glare anytime during the day (Figure 4.29) or night (Figure 4.31). Plants should be selected for proper height and

80

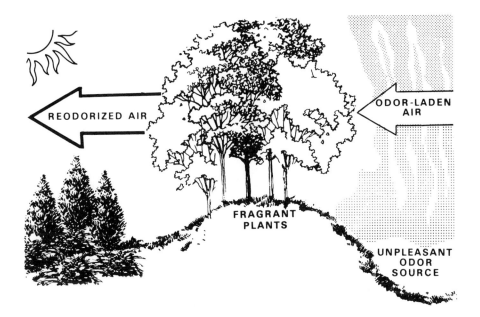

REODORIZATION

Figure 4.28 Trees can reduce unpleasant odors either by absorption of gaseous pollutants or by masking them with their own odors.

foliage density so that they provide protection throughout their lifetime. Plants can be used along the highway to control early morning and later afternoon glare (Figure 4.32). Night light control can be achieved by the proper placement of trees and shrubs around terraces, patios, windows, or even along streets to protect driver vision.

Secondary glare can be controlled by plantings that intercept the primary light source before it reaches the reflector or after it strikes the reflector and travels to the viewer's eye (Figure 4.30).

Traffic control

While adding to environmental esthetics, trees and shrubs may be used to aid in traffic control. This includes not only vehicular traffic but also pedestrian and animal traffic (Figure 4.33). Plants enhance the beauty of an area when used to direct people through it in a definite pattern. Other elements

81

Primary glare.

Figure 4.29 In urban environments trees can be used to intercept primary glare.

Secondary glare.

Figure 4.30 If positioned correctly trees can be used to intercept unwanted secondary glare.

often used to perform the same function (wires, fences, and chains) tend to destroy natural beauty.

Before one considers which plants to use in traffic control, the degree of control desired must be ascertained. Can it be accomplished by ground cover, a hedge, or a belt of trees? Once the type of barrier has been selected, species selection should be based on the following considerations (Robinette, 1972):

1. Ultimate height needed.
2. Spacing or planting density needed.

GLARE
REDUCTION

Figure 4.31 Nighttime glare can be reduced by judicious plant selection and placement.

3. Eventual desired width of the planting.
4. Characteristic of the plant variety.

Some plants are more suitable for traffic control than others because of such characteristics as branching habit, presence or absence of thorns, and stiff or flexible branches. Robinette (1972) has suggested that plant selections should be based on a 10-point scale for each of the following characteristics: thorniness, mature height, spacing, and mature width. His system is as follows:

Thorn and Branching Habit: Since some plant materials are nearly equal in traffic control efficiency, they should be placed on a 10-point characteristic scale. These 10 divisions are:

1. Single-stem—no thorns—flexible branches.
2. Single-stem—no thorns—stiff branches.
3. Multistem—no thorns—flexible branches—open.
4. Multistem—no thorns—flexible branches—less open.

GLARE CONTROL FOR HIGHWAYS

Figure 4.32 The proper placement of trees along highways and median strips can alleviate early morning and late evening glare hazards.

TRAFFIC CONTROL

Figure 4.33 Trees and shrubs can be used to direct or channel pedestrian traffic.

5. Multistem—no thorns—stiff branches—dense.
   Single-stem—thorns—flexible branches.
6. Single-stem—thorns—stiff branches.
7. Multistem—thorns—flexible branches—open.
8. Multistem—thorns—flexible—less open.
   Multistem—thorns—stiff branches—open.
9. Multistem—thorns—flexible—dense.
   Multistem—thorns—stiff—less open.
10. Multistem—thorns—stiff branches—dense.

Plant Height: The plants' ultimate height, when mature, is the next factor to be rated. In rating plants on height, the system extends from 3 in. (7.6 cm) or less, to 5 ft (1.5 m) or more.
   The 10 dimensions are:

1. 0 to 3 in. (0 to 7.6 cm)
2. 3 to 6 in. (7.6 to 15.2 cm)
3. 6 to 12 in. (15.2 to 30.5 cm)
4. 12 to 18 in. (30.5 to 45.7 cm)
5. 18 to 24 in. (45.7 to 61 cm)
6. 24 to 30 in. (61 to 76.2 cm)
7. 30 in. to 3 ft (76.2 to 91.4 cm)
8. 3 to 4 ft (0.9 to 1.2 m)
9. 4 to 5 ft (1.2 to 1.5 m)
10. 5 ft (1.5 m) and higher

Spacing or Density: Spacing is important to consider. Plants, regardless of their characteristics, are ineffective in controlling traffic if they are sparsely spaced, allowing movement through the openings between them. In the rating of plants for spacing, the system extends from greater than 30 in. (76.2 cm) to less than 6 in. (15.2 cm).
   The ratings are:

1. 30 in. (76.2 cm) and wider
2. 27 to 30 in. (68.6 to 76.2 cm)
3. 24 to 27 in. (61 to 68.6 cm)
4. 21 to 24 in. (53.3 to 61 cm)
5. 18 to 21 in. (45.7 to 53.3 cm)
6. 15 to 18 in. (38.1 to 45.7 cm)
7. 12 to 15 in. (30.5 to 38.1 cm)
8. 9 to 12 in. (22.9 to 30.5 cm)
9. 6 to 9 in. (15.2 to 22.9 cm)
10. 6 in. (15.2 cm) and narrower

Width: Plant width is also a major factor in determining the effectiveness of plants for controlling traffic. For example, grass or a ground cover may be an effective barrier if the lawn or planting bed is wide enough; yet in a narrow area, even a medium-size hedge may not be adequate.

In the rating of planting widths the system extends from "1" to "10" as follows:

1. 6 in. (15.2 cm)
2. 9 in. (22.9 cm)
3. 12 in. (30.5 cm)
4. 18 in. (45.7 cm)
5. 2 ft (0.6 m)
6. 3 ft (0.9 m)
7. 4 ft (1.2 m)
8. 6 ft (1.8 m)
9. 8 ft (2.4 m)
10. Wider than 8 ft (2.4 m)

Some plants have a spread or width of greater than 8 ft (2.4 m), making them effective barriers when planted in a single row. Others with less width must be planted in multiple rows.

Summary: Since the relative effectiveness of plants in controlling pedestrian traffic can be rated on the basis of a possible 10 points for each of the four factors, 4 is the lowest possible rating and 40 designates a perfect traffic control plant. The total rating system is:

T-C Number (Traffic Control)	Degree of Effectiveness
4–10	Minimum
10–20	Average
20–30	Good
30–40	Excellent

An example of a shrub with an excellent rating would be *Rhamnus carthartica* or buckthorn. It is a large, well-rounded, and fairly dense shrub that has branches and foliage reaching from the ground to a height of 12 ft (3.7 m) and has a 10 to 12 ft (3 to 3.7 m) spread. It yields a characteristic rating of 9, height 10, density 6, width 10, for a combined total of 35.

Some work has been done concerning the use of plants as effective vehicle barriers. One study was conducted using multiflora rose *(Rosa multiflora)* (White, 1953). A series of crash tests were used to determine this species' ability to absorb and decelerate a vehicle with minimum damage. In tests, it performed quite well at speeds up to 47 miles (75.6 km) per hour. In most instances, roadside plantings should involve resilient plants rather than rigid ones to prevent passenger injury and to minimize automobile damage as much as possible.

Architectural Uses

In building design, materials such as wood, masonry, steel, or concrete are used architecturally as well as structurally. The designing architect asks such questions as: Is privacy needed by the users in a given area? Are there undesirable views that need screening? Is the area too large for comfortable use? Is there a view that can be made more interesting by progressively revealing it? In many situations, trees and shrubs can perform the same architectural functions as do standard building materials.

Each species has its own characteristic form, color, texture, and size. Plants can vary in their use potential as they grow or as the seasons change. Their proper use will vary with the designer and user. Trees, when used in a group, can form canopies or walls of varying texture, height, and density. Some functions can be performed by one tree and others may require many trees. Because they are alive and growing, trees and shrubs are dynamic with regard to their functionality in architectural design.

Since trees and shrubs have architectural potential, they can be used individually or collectively as architectural elements performing the following functions: space articulation (defining space); screening; privacy control; and progressive realization or enticement.

Our perception is based primarily on our function of sight. Space or spatial realization is perceived as the distance to any element that blocks the view (Figure 4.34). Thus, space as perceived in an open park is different from one with many trees. This space realization is further enhanced by textures and shades. Coarse textures and darker shades appear to advance to the viewer, while fine textures and light shades seem to retreat. Trees and shrubs form walls and canopies in landscapes and, along with other architectural components, can be used to enclose, contain, enframe, link, enlarge, reduce, and articulate exterior space. Robinette (1972) discusses these uses along with some examples:

> *Closure is using plants to finish off a space that has been left open. It makes the space more complete and identifiable. Containment is*

Figure 4.34 Trees and shrubs can create a feeling of solitude by their use in breaking up large spaces into smaller ones we are more comfortable with.

providing a small space within a larger space; thus, attention is toward a small, human-scale feeling of the space [Figure 4.35]. Enframement is a technique used to draw attention to the most important space in the area. It focuses attention on a desired view or object and away from the larger space in which the view or object occurs. Linkage is a technique used to join one space with another to make a large area seem smaller and less alien [Figure 4.36]. Enlargement is a method of changing the apparent size of a large space by contrasting it to an infinite space of the skyscape and making it seem smaller in comparison [Figure 4.37]. Reduction involves the placement of plants in an overly large space to make the space smaller [Figure 4.37]. Plants may be used to subdivide or divide space either horizontally or vertically to reduce the apparent size of the space [Figure 4.38]. In space articulation, plants can also be used to subdivide space three dimensionally. A good example of this is the use of plants to accentuate horizontal space [Figure 4.39]. Plants can also be used to break larger spaces into smaller, irregular or rhythmically distinguishable units. Good examples of this are most park designs where different recreation units are subdivided. Trees and shrubs are often used in home and building settings to articulate or define entrances [Figure 4.40]; in functional realization to provide direction [Figure 4.41]; or channel movement.

Define a Space.

Figure 4.35 Trees and shrubs can be used to create unique settings in the process of defining space.

Figure 4.36 Plants can be used to link and unify separate entities.

Perhaps one of the major uses we normally associate with trees and shrubs is screening. This involves not only screening for view but also for privacy. The selection of plant materials for screening has to be judicious since the view is perhaps objectional for only a part of the year; or it may be one that requires continuous screening. Most are well aware of the highway beautification programs of the 1960s aimed at screening objectionable views

ENLARGEMENT

REDUCTION

Figure 4.37 Trees and shrubs can be used to make buildings seem to occupy more space then they actually do, or to reduce open spaces so that they are more pleasant to experience.

VERTICAL SUBDIVISION

HORIZONTAL SUBDIVISION

Figure 4.38 Trees can be used in inner city areas to break up architectural lines and to unify elements.

Figure 4.39 The proper placement of trees can provide a three-dimensional effect in certain architectural situations.

ARTICULATION OF AN ELEMENT
(ENTRANCE)

Figure 4.40 Trees and shrubs can call attention to the location of building entrances.

DIRECTION

DIRECTION

Figure 4.41 Trees and shrubs are especially useful in mall settings to channelize traffic and call attention to entrances.

Screen objectionable views.

Figure 4.42 Trees and shrubs are often used to screen undesirable views.

Create privacy.

Figure 4.43 Trees and shrubs can be used to provide privacy in urban areas.

from the landscape (junk yards, factories, parking lots, cooling towers for air conditioners, service areas and transformer yards, just to mention a few). Screening visually blocks out an unsightly view and replaces it with a less offensive one (Figure 4.42). It hides the unwanted and allows free access to the remainder of the surroundings. Screening can be both negative (blocking ugly surroundings from view) or positive (enhancing surroundings).

Privacy control differs from screening in that it secludes a particular area from its surroundings (Figure 4.43). The difference between the two depends on the point of view and intent of either the viewer or the user. As our population continues to increase, there will be a greater need for privacy control as it is essential for survival. It is needed in such activities as sunbathing, camping, picnicking, reading, relaxation, nature watching, and just plain conversation.

In progressive realization, plants are used to direct the unconscious viewer through the landscape, revealing it a little at a time. A view is usually better if enframed or seen through an opening (Figure 4.44). If a landscape view is partially viewed instead of fully revealed, the anticipation enhances the actual experience. An example is the shadow of a pine branch on a translucent screen. The indirect view is more exciting than a portrait of the branch itself.

Esthetic Uses

Trees and shrubs provide their own inherent beauty in all settings. They are esthetic elements in our surroundings. They can be beautiful simply because of the lines, forms, colors, and textures they project. Trees and shrubs enframe views, soften architectural lines, enhance and complement ar-

Enframe a View.

Figure 4.44 The proper placement of trees can make scenic views even more spectacular because of the window effect they create.

chitectural elements, unify divergent elements, and introduce a naturalness to otherwise stark settings (Figures 4.45 to 4.48). They also produce unique patterns through reflection from glass and water surfaces and can produce beautiful shadow patterns (Figure 4.49). Trees are also dynamic, giving different appearances in the changing seasons and throughout their span of life. They also provide movement and pleasant sounds—the rustling of leaves and the whistle of wind through a canopy. We are attracted to plants because of many of these characteristics. In addition, plants are useful for the berries, nuts, and shelter they provide to birds and animals (Figure 4.50). Studies have shown that wildlife populations are enhanced in urban settings because of trees (Hathaway; 1973, Cauley and Schinner; 1973).

Accent and enframe.

Create background setting.

Figure 4.45 Trees and shrubs are used around homes to accent; enframe; or create background settings.

95

Soften line and mass.

Figure 4.46 Architectural lines can be broken up and their effect softened by proper plant selection and use.

Compliment architecture.

Figure 4.47 Plants can be used to complement modern architectural lines.

Unify architectural elements.

Figure 4.48   The use of trees in downtown areas often aid in breaking up straight lines and unifying diverse architectural designs of varying periods.

Create shadow patterns.

Figure 4.49   Not only do trees act as architectural elements but by their presence as shadow patterns, for example, they introduce other elements.

Williamson (1973) demonstrated in a study in the Rock Creek Park area of Washington, D.C. that sparrows, starlings, and pigeons are adapted to city settings devoid of trees while cardinals, robins, and mockingbirds prefer the wooded park and wooded residential neighborhoods. The latter are more preferred species for most urban dwellers. Williamson (1973) comments that if songbirds find areas lacking trees, shrubs, and lawns unsuitable for living, "why should it be otherwise for humans."

Other Uses

Even though a lengthy list of uses of trees in urban settings have been enumerated, certainly many more uses, including products from the urban forest having economic value, have not been mentioned. Such uses would include places for children to play and in which people can walk and contemplate nature and their own problems, trees used as indicators of historical events and memorials, and substitutes for the natural environment in inner city settings (trees on rooftops and balconies) (Figure 4.51). Trees can also provide a vehicle to evoke memories of other times, places, and feelings because of the view they present or a familiar sound, odor, or touch (Figure 4.52). Needless to say, the city would be a forlorn place to live if it were not for trees.

Attract wildlife.

Figure 4.50   Plants assist our aesthetic enjoyment by enhancing the environment in which our urban wildlife live.

Figure 4.51   In inner cities the contrasting settings in which trees are often found express our basic need for the outdoor environment.

Figure 4.52 All of us have a need for some time to think and reflect on our lives, evoke memories, and commune with nature. Trees and shrubs in urban environments provide appropriate settings.

Note: Some of the material for this chapter—particularly Figures 4.1 to 4.6 and 4.8 to 4.52—was adapted from *Plants/People/and Environmental Quality,* USDA National Park Service in collaboration with the American Society of Landscape Architects Foundation, 1972.

BIBLIOGRAPHY

Bernatsky, A., "The Importance of Protective Plantings Against Air Pollutants," *Air Pollution Proceedings First European Congress Information Air Pollution. Plants, Animals,* Wagenigen, Wagenigen Center for Agricultural Publications and Documents, the Netherlands, pp. 303–395, 1968.

Cauley, Darrel L. and James R. Schinner, "The Cincinnati Raccoons," in *The Metro Forest,* A Natural History Special Supplement, Vol. 82, No. 9, pp. 58–60, 1973.

Cook, David I. and David F. Van Haverbeke, *Trees and Shrubs for Noise Abatement,* University of Nebraska Agricultural Experiment Station Research Bulletin No. 246, 77 pp., 1971.

Cook, David I. and David F. Van Haverbeke, *Tree-Covered Land-Forms for Noise Control,* University of Nebraska Agricultural Experiment Station Research Bulletin No. 263, 47 pp., 1974.

Cook, David I. and David F. Van Haberbeke, *Suburban Noise Control With Plant Materials and Solid Barriers,* University of Nebraska Agricultural Experiment Station Research Bulletin No. EM100, 74 pp., 1977.

Davis, Donald D., "The Role of Trees in Reducing Air Pollution," in *The Role of Trees in the South's Urban Environment,* A Symposium Proceedings, University of Georgia, 1970.

Embleton, T.F.W., "Sound Propagation in Homogenous, Deciduous, and Evergreen Woods," *Journal of the Acoustical Society of America,* Vol. 33, 1963.

Eyring, Carl F., "Jungle Acoustics," *Journal of the Acoustical Society of America,* Vol. 18, 1946.

Federer, C.A., "Effects of Trees in Modifying Urban Microclimate," in *Trees and Forests in An Urbanizing Environment,* University of Massachusetts Cooperative Extension Service Monograph No. 17, pp. 23–28, 1971.

Federer, C.A., "Trees Modify the Urban Microclimate," *Journal of Arborculture,* 2:121–127, 1976.

Hathaway, Melvin B., "Ecology of City Squirrels," in *The Metro Forest,* A Natural History Special Supplement, Vol. 82, No. 9, pp. 61–62, 1973.

Herrington, Lee P., "Vegetation and Urban Physical Environment," in *Proceedings Urban Forestry Conference* State University of New York, pp. 54–59, 1973.

Jensen, M., *Shelter Effect: Investigations into the Aerodynamics of Shelter and Its Effects on Climate and Crops,* 84 p., Copenhagen, 1954.

Kramer, P.J. and T.T. Kozlowski, *Physiology of Trees,* 642 pp., McGraw-Hill, New York, 1970.

Nutter, Wade L., "The Role of Trees in Neutralizing Wastes: A Discussion of Land Disposal Systems for Sewage Effluent and Other Wastewaters," in *The Role of Trees in the South's Urban Environment,* A Symposium Proceedings, University of Georgia, pp. 20–30, 1970.

Owen, Oliver S., *Natural Resource Conservation: An Ecological Approach,* 2nd ed., MacMillan, New York, 1975.

101

Robinette, Gary O., *Plants and Their Environmental Functions,* U.S. Department of the Interior, National Park Service Publications, Washington, D.C., 1972.

Simonson, Wilbur H., "Abatement of Highway Noise with Special Reference to Roadside Design," Highway Research Bulletin No. 110, publication No. 363, *Abatement of Highway Noise and Fumes,* Highway Research Board, National Research Council, 1957.

Sopper, William E., "Effects of Trees and Forests in Neutralizing Waste," in *Trees and Forests in An Urbanizing Environment,* University of Massachusetts Cooperative Extension Service Monograph, No. 17, pp. 43–57, 1971.

Stevenson, Tom, "How Plants Fight Against Air Pollution," *Washington Post,* Sec. H, p. 7, August 2, 1970.

Weidensaul, T.C., "Are Trees Efficient Air Purifiers?," *Arborists News,* Vol. 38, No. 8, pp. 85–89, 1973.

Weiner, Francis M., and David N. Keast, "Sound Propagation Over Terrain," *Journal of the Acoustical Society of America,* Vol. 31, June 1959.

White, Andrew J., *Study of Marginal and Median Tree and Shrub Plantings as Safety Barriers on Highways,* South Lee, N.H., pp. 3–8, 1953.

Williamson, Robert D., "Bird-and-People neighborhoods," in *The Metro Forest,* A Natural History Special Supplement, Vol. 82, No. 9, pp. 55–57, 1973.

5
ENVIRONMENT OF THE URBAN FOREST

The urban forest exists in an environment dominated by people. Thus, the forest must grow in the spaces left after all the structures necessary to urban society have been built. The forest must be molded to fit these spaces as it cannot interfere unduly with streets, sidewalks, parking lots, wires, pipes, and other objects. The forest must also withstand compacted soils and polluted air, and it must be compatible with people, pets, and vehicles. The environment of the urban forest, then, involves site, space and people.

The construction of cities has dramatic influences on existing and future forest sites (Figure 5.1). Grades are changed, drainage is altered, soil is rearranged and compacted, reflective and absorbable surfaces are created, and air circulation patterns are changed. These influences are most often detrimental to the urban forest. They can, however, be beneficial in that buildings and other structures sometimes create favorable microclimates for tree growth.

To illustrate these influences, consider the impact of subdivision development in a naturally wooded area: A substantial part of the forest must be physically removed to make room for houses, streets, driveways, patios, pools, water lines, telephone and electricity lines, sanitary and storm sewers, and gas lines. The sudden removal of strips and patches of a natural forest creates edges at which previously shaded trees are exposed to open sunlight and wind. Excavation and grading cause subsoil to replace topsoil and often drastically alter surface and internal soil drainage. Trees to be retained are often damaged by physical contact with machinery, by root exposure or coverage, and by indiscriminate pruning.

The quality of such development into woodlands is as varied as the number of developers and the regulations under which they operate. In most large urban areas one can find excellent examples of subdivisions having been laid gently into the forest. In these same areas, however, some developers have considered the forest a liability to be removed and the land is leveled.

The spatial and site environment can perhaps be best understood by a discussion of the factors that influence the location of trees in the urban forest. These factors apply both to trees left from urban development into native forests and to the selection of trees for planting.

The first requisite of an urban tree is that it must be able to survive and grow under the conditions of its particular site. It must be adaptable to a particular hardiness zone. It should possess a suitable form for its available space, and it should have a root system compatible with soil space restricted because of concrete, asphalt, and underground utilities. The choice of trees must depend on the limiting factors of the site. The fewer the limiting factors, the greater the choices.

Figure 5.1 Urban construction has dramatic influences on forest sites.

Space

Space is probably the most critical factor in locating urban trees. Space is limited physically by buildings, neighboring trees, overhead wires, curbs, sidewalks, and underground utilities. It is also limited by other spaces appropriated for line of sight vision for traffic signals, signs, street lights, and vistas, and by spaces for vehicle and pedestrian clearance. There are two choices: trees can be selected that when mature will fit available spaces; or attempts can be made to make trees conform by pruning them or otherwise controlling their growth. The former is preferable in cases where trees are to be planted. The latter may well be best in areas of new construction where existing trees may be left. However, these choices are often poorly made, and virtually every city has frequent examples of trees located in spaces much too small for their mature growth. The attempts at conforming such trees to available spaces is perhaps the most costly aspect of urban forestry.

For planting purposes, trees can be divided by mature height into three size classes: (1) small trees, less than 30 ft (9.14 m) when mature; (2) medium trees, 30 ft (9.14 m) to 60 ft (18.28 m); and (3) large trees, 60 ft

105

(18.28 m) and over. Such divisions are not rigid as localized sites might cause differences in growth, particularly with "medium" and "large" trees. However, they are convenient groupings to meet spatial requirements. A sample grouping of popular urban species is given below.

Examples of Tree Species by Size Catagories

Small Trees	
Apricot, flowering	*Prunus armeniaca*
Cherry, "Kwanzan"	*Prunus serrulata*
Crabapple, flowering	*Malus, spp.*
Dogwood, flowering	*Cornus florida*
Hawthorn, Washington	*Crataegus phaenopyrum*
Maple, amur	*Acer ginnala*
Maple, Japanese	*Acer japonicum*
Mimosa	*Albizia julibrissin*
Mountain-ash, European	*Sorbus aucuparia*
Peach, flowering	*Prunus persica*
Pear, bradford	*Pyrus calleryana*
Plum, purpleleaf "Newport"	*Prunus X-blireiana*
Redbud	*Cercis canadensis*
Russian-olive	*Eleagnus angustifolia*

Medium Trees	
Ash, green	*Fraxinus pennsylvanica*
Ash, white	*Fraxinus americana*
Baldcypress	*Taxodium distichum*
Birch, paper	*Betula papyrifera*
Catalpa	*Catalpa speciosa*
Chinese chestnut	*Castanea mollissima*
Ginkgo	*Ginkgo biloba*
Hackberry	*Celtis occidentalis*
Honeylocust	*Gleditsia triocanthos*
Kentucky coffeetree	*Gymnocladus dioicus*
Linden, American	*Tilia americana*
Linden, littleleaf	*Tilia cordata*
Locust, black	*Robinia pseudacacia*
Maple, Norway	*Acer platanoides*
Maple, red	*Acer rubrum*
Maple, sugar	*Acer saccharum*
Pagodatree, Japanese	*Sophora japonica*
Poplar, white	*Populus alba*
Tree-of-heaven	*Ailanthus altissima*
Walnut, black	*Juglans nigra*
Willow, weeping	*Salix babylonica*

Large Trees	
Cottonwood, eastern	*Populus deltoides*
London planetree	*Platanus x-acerifolia*
Maple, silver	*Acer saccharinum*
Oak, bur	*Quercus macrocarpa*
Oak, English	*Quercus robur*
Oak, pin	*Quercus palustris*
Oak, red	*Quercus borealis*
Oak, white	*Quercus alba*
Pecan	*Carya illinoensis*
Sweetgum	*Liquidambar styraciflua*
Sycamore	*Platanus occidentalis*
Tulip poplar	*Liriodendron tulipifera*

Mature height, although extremely important, cannot be the only factor in fitting trees to space. Form must also be considered.

Tree form is an important element in landscape design and should be given careful consideration when fitting trees to available spaces. Trees assume seven basic forms: (1) irregular; (2) vase; (3) oval; (4) pyramidal; (5) columnar; (6) round; and (7) weeping. Many species can be identified by their characteristic form, although varietal differences are sometimes confusing. Form can also be impaired by crowding, storm breakage, or other influences. Recently, much work has been done by nursery workers and others in selecting and breeding trees for specific forms. Fastigate Washington hawthorn, ascending Norway maple, columnar red and sugar maples, and columnar English oak are some popular results of this work.

For confined spaces such as narrow parkways along streets, trees with columnar, oval, and vase forms are best. Columnar trees provide relatively little shade but are often planted close to each other for screening purposes. They are also used to soften or accent lines of tall buildings. Vase-shaped trees have long been popular for street planting as their ascending branches can be allowed to spread above streetside objects and spaces needed for vehicle and pedestrian passage. This quality helped make the American elm such a popular streetside tree prior to spread of the Dutch elm disease.

Pyramidal trees provide rather poor shade as they are narrow at the top. They are best used as specimen trees in the landscape where adequate room is available for low lateral branch development. Pin oak, sweetgum, and baldcypress are examples of pyramidal trees. They are generally not well-suited for streetside planting on other than wide treelawns. Pin oaks are commonly misplanted along streets with the later necessity of removing lower, drooping branches for traffic clearance. (Size, form, and other design elements are discussed in further detail on pages 129–139.)

Soils

Urban forest soils are often drastically altered by construction activity. Topsoil is often removed entirely or covered with subsoil. Sand, chemicals, and waste building materials are frequently incorporated. Many building sites are in fact "filled" ground from rubble and debris. Severe compaction is common and internal drainage is often restricted. Water tables are also often changed.

Engineering specifications for streets, parking lots, and other areas often require intensive soil compaction. Unfortunately, adjacent areas where trees may be planted are frequently also compacted. Compaction also occurs on building sites simply by the presence of heavy construction machinery. Tightly compacted soils are poorly aerated, and gaseous exchange between soil air and the atmosphere is restricted. This results in an unfavorable oxygen–carbon dioxide balance that can inhibit tree root growth. Such soils are also poorly drained internally, with water occupying air spaces and further restricting gaseous exchange. Poor soil aeration can also result from a rise in ground water tables. Water tables are frequently altered by construction activity.

Inadequate soil aeration affects trees indirectly too. Soil ecosystems are altered and favorable soil organisms may be destroyed. Certain damaging fungi thrive in poorly aerated soils because natural control conditions are not present. Root permeability may also be impaired because of excessive carbon dioxide.

Special soil treatments and amendments are often needed to assure plant growth. In extreme situations major treatments are necessary, involving extra excavation of planting sites, construction of drainage systems, and replacement with new soil. Soils can be physically improved by incorporation of sand, peat, or other materials. Organic matter is often needed, but adding it will have little benefit if drainage, fertility, and acidity are not also corrected. Peat moss, stable manure, and compost are commonly used organic amendments. Mineral deficiencies can be corrected by the addition of commercial fertilizers. Soil acidity must also often be altered as it largely governs the availability of nutrients.

Microclimate

The urban forest exists in a microclimate of itself and human structures. The microclimatic factors having the greatest influence on tree growth are air temperature, humidity, and wind. Microclimates can be either beneficial or harmful depending on how much the extremes and duration of heat, cold, wind, and evapotranspiration are influenced.

In general, cities tend to be warmer in both summer and winter than the surrounding countrysides. Wind velocity is less and relative humidity is generally lower. Such generalities can be misleading, however, as cities are not single microclimates. Urban areas are agglomerations of manmade structures, land forms, trees, and other organisms. Each location within an urban setting has its own microclimate, depending on the character and arrangement of the various elements. C.A. Federer, (1971), U.S. Forest Service Meterologist, has identified three broad clases of street-level microclimates: (1) areas with extensive evaporative or transpiring surfaces—parks, wide streets with trees, and the vicinities of rivers or lakes (Figure 5.2); (2) wide treeless streets, squares, and parking lots, open to the sky and very dry (Figure 5.3); and (3) narrow streets and courtyards surrounded by relatively tall buildings (Figure 5.4).

Because of extensive transpiration, Microclimate No. 1 tends to have lower temperatures and higher humidity in the summer. It is also cooler in winter than other areas of the city. Wind velocities are higher because there

Figure 5.2   Street-level microclimate No. 1: areas with extensive evaporative or transpiring surfaces, such as this park in New York.

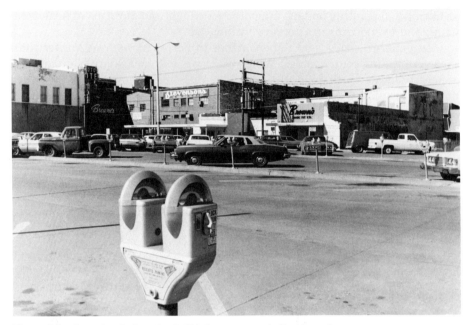

Figure 5.3 Street-level microclimate No. 2: areas open to the sky and very dry such as this parking lot.

are fewer physical barriers. These areas more nearly represent the climate of surrounding countrysides. From a climate standpoint, there would be little advantage or disadvantage for tree growth in these situations.

Microclimate No. 2 has much lower humidity and higher temperatures than other areas. High temperatures tend to be extreme because of excessive radiation. Wind velocities are average to slightly lower than the surrounding countryside. Tree selection is limited here as succulent species often cannot be used.

Microclimate No. 3 has cooler summer temperatures and much greater wind protection than other areas. Winter temperatures are somewhat warmer because of radiated heat from surrounding buildings. A greater variety of tree species can be grown here because of moderated extremes of temperature and wind velocity.

However, there are situations in each area that defy the average. Structures that provide permanent shade, reflected light, or heat radiation create their own mini-microclimates. Also tall buildings and streets often cause a tunneling effect that greatly increases wind velocity. Street direction can have a microclimatic effect, as north–south streets between tall buildings are exposed to midday sun and east–west streets tend to be more shaded.

Figure 5.4 Street-level microclimate No. 3: narrow streets and courtyards surrounded by tall buildings.

Pollution

The urban forest is subjected to varying degrees of pollution. Pollutants can be physical, chemical, and physiological and may be defined simply as foreign substances or influences that adversely affect the growth function of plants. Pollution becomes a matter of concern when tolerable limits of adversity are exceeded. Physical pollutants are those that physically impair plant function, such as heavy dust covering leaf stomata and restricting respiration. Chemical pollutants are chemical in origin and primarily chemical in effect. They may cause physical damage in some cases, but their principal impact is on the chemical processes within plants.

Air pollution

Air pollutants that damage trees are primarily gaseous chemicals, although particulate matter is also often involved. Transportation, electricity generation, and industry are the primary sources of phytotoxic air pollutants. The main air pollutants of the urban forest are: (1) sulfur dioxide; (2) ozone; (3) flourides; (4) ethylene; (5) oxides of nitrogen; (6) ammonia; (7) chlorine and hydrogen chloride; (8) particulates; and (9) herbicides. Of these, sulfur dioxide, ozone, and herbicides are of major importance.

Sulfur dioxide comes mainly from the burning of coal for the generation of electricity and from industries that refine petroleum or metals. Trees and other plants appear to be most sensitive to SO_2 in early summer when leaves are expanding. Sulfur dioxide enters leaves through stomata and reacts with cells, causing injury or death to tissues. Injury may be chronic or severe, depending on pollution levels and the resistance of a particular plant. Ash, aspen, birch, American elm, poplars, and white pine appear sensitive to SO_2, while dogwood, juniper, maple, spruce, and sycamore appear relatively tolerant (Table 5.1).

Ozone is a natural and necessary component of the upper atmosphere. At ground level, however, it can cause injury and death to plants. Ozone is formed by photochemical reactions in sunlight from hydrocarbons and oxides of nitrogen that are emitted primarily by automobiles and other vehicles. Ozone has caused widespread injury and death to ponderosa pine near Los Angeles and is related to the temperature inversion—smog phenomenon of that area. Ash, honeylocust, white oak, white pine, sweetgum, sycamore and tuliptree are sensitive to ozone. Black walnut, gray dogwood, balsam and white fir, maple, red oak, and spruce appear relatively tolerant (Table 5.2).

Airborne herbicides are major sources of plant damage to the urban forest. Used for the control of unwanted vegetation, herbicides such as 2,4-D and 2,4,5-T are often volatilized or particles are carried by the wind. Con-

TABLE 5.1

Relative Sensitivity of
Selected Forest Species to SO_2
(Loomis and Padgett, 1975)

Sensitive	Tolerant
Ash	Black tupelo
Aspen	Boxelder
Birch	Dogwood
Blackberry	Juniper
Carelessweed	Maple
Catalpa	Oak, live
Dewberry	Sourwood
Elm, American	Spruce
Larch	Sycamore
Oak, blackjack	Yellow-poplar [a]
Pine, eastern white	
Pine, jack	
Pine, loblolly (seedlings to 6 ft)	
Pine, Virginia (seedlings to 6 ft)	
Poplar	
Ragweed	

[a]Sensitive spring and early summer.

TABLE 5.2

Relative Sensitivity of
Selected Forest Species to Ozone
(Loomis and Padgett, 1975)

Sensitive	Tolerant
Ash	Birch, European white
Honeylocust	Black walnut
Larch, European	Dogwood, gray
Oak, white	Fir, balsam
Pine, Virginia	Fir, white
Pine, eastern white	Maple
Pine, jack	Oak, red
Poplar	Spruce
Sweetgum	
Sycamore	
Yellow-poplar	

tamination by these chemicals can be particularly troublesome near highways and other public areas where chemicals are used as an economic alternative to mowing or other weed control practices. The urban forests of agricultural regions are often subjected to herbicide drift from aerial or ground application to crop and pasture lands. Redbud and goldenraintree are examples of species that are extremely sensitive to airborne herbicides.

An excellent summary of air pollution and trees (excluding herbicide pollution), including a listing of 43 references, is *Air Pollution and Trees in the East* (Loomis and Padgett, 1975). Much of the previous discussion was based on this publication.

Soil pollution

Soil pollution usually applies to restricted areas and often causes severe problems to trees and other plants. Common soil pollutants are oil, gasoline, manufactured and natural gas, salt, and herbicides. Some pollutants are toxic to plant tissue and cause direct damage. Some are taken systemically through the root system. And others cause indirect damage by displacing oxygen or preventing natural chemical exchanges in the soil.

Soil pollution by herbicides has increased in recent years. A variety of preemergent and postemergent grass and weed killers are now on the market. Although the Environmental Protection Agency required detailed labeling of these chemicals, the labels (including specific directions for use) are often not read, and damage to nontarget plants results. Occasionally even proper use can result in damage, when heavy rains following application concentrate herbicides in low-lying areas within the root zones of trees or other plants. Soil sterilants, used under fences, around signs, parking lot posts, and other areas are often translocated or leached into the root zones of trees. Damage is by systemic intake through the roots.

Rock salt has long been used for melting snow and ice from vehicular and pedestrian ways. Plant damage can be caused by the runoff of salty water and salt absorption via the roots. Damage can also occur from the salt sprayed by passing vehicles and is thus a localized form of air pollution (Lumis, Hofstra, and Hall, 1975). The relative salt tolerance of trees is given in Table 5.3.

Manufactured gas (primarily from coal) contains hydrogren cyanide, carbon monoxide, and unsaturated hydrocarbons. When leaked into the soil, these chemicals can be toxic to plant roots. When used extensively for illumination in the first third of this century, manufactured gas was a significant soil pollutant. Restricted now mainly to containerized use in rural areas, manufactured gas is a minor cause of plant injury. It may, however, cause significant plant injury if it emerges again as a major source of heat energy when natural gas reserves are depleted and the use of coal intensifies.

TABLE 5.3

Relative Salt Tolerance of
Some Selected Trees
(Based on Dirr, 1976)

Species	Salt-Tolerance Rating[a]		
	Good	Moderate	Poor
Ailanthus	*		
Alder, European black			*
Ash, American	*	*	
Ash, green	*	*	
Basswood, American		*	*
Beech, American		*	*
Birch, European white	*	*	
Birch, paper	*	*	
Birch, sweet	*		
Birch, yellow	*		
Buckthorn	*		
Catalpa, northern		*	
Cherry, black	*		*
Crabapples		*	*
Douglasfir		*	a
Elm, American		*	*
Elm, Siberian	*	*	
Fir, balsam		*	*
Hackberry, common			*
Hawthorns			*
Hemlock			*
Hickory, shagbark	*		*
Holly, American	*		
Honeylocust	*		
Hornbeam, American			*
Horsechestnut	*		
Larches	*		
Locust, black	*		
Magnolia, southern	*		
Maple, amur			*
Maple (boxelder)		*	*
Maple, Norway	*	*	
Maple, red		*	*
Maple, silver	*	*	*
Maple, sugar	*		*
Metasequoia			*
Mountain ash		*	
Mulberry, white	*		*
Oak, blackjack	*		
Oak, bur	*	*	*
Oak, chinquapin			*
Oak, English	*		*

115

TABLE 5.3 *(continued)*

Species	Salt-Tolerance Rating [a]		
	Good	Moderate	Poor
Oak, northern red	*		
Oak, pin			*
Oak, swamp white			*
Pears		*	
Pine, Austrian	*		
Pine, eastern white			*
Pine, jack	*		
Pine, mugo	*		
Pine, pitch	*		
Pine, ponderosa		*	
Pine, red			*
Pine, Scotch	*	*	*
Planetree, London			*
Poplars	*	*	
Plum, purpleleaf	*		
Redbud, eastern			*
Redcedar, eastern	*	*	
Serviceberry	*		
Spruce, blue	*	*	
Spruce, Norway		*	*
Spruce, white		*	*
Sumac, staghorn	*		
Tupelo, black	*		
Walnut, black	*		*
Walnut, English	*		*
Willows	*	*	*
Yellow-poplar			*
Yew		*	*

[a]Species with dual entries indicate different findings by various authors.

Natural gas is not believed to be toxic to plant roots (Pirone, 1972). However, it is believed that damage can occur in the vicinity of natural gas leaks from excessive soil drying or by displacement of oxygen. The damages caused by manufactured and natural gas, however, are still confused.

Light pollution

Illumination of urban areas for reasons of comfort and security has increased dramatically in recent years. Since 1950, mercury, metal halide, and sodium lamps have come into common use and have altered the environment of portions of the urban forest. Of particular concern are plants subjected to 24-hour light. In the sense that such conditions may be damaging to plants, light must be considered as pollution. Plant reaction to light is in response to a combination of quality, itensity, and duration interacting with the environment (Cathey and Campbell, 1975). Any factor that would limit growth, such as heat, cold, and drought, could override the effects of light. Plants react differently, but continuous lighting, when other growth conditions are favorable, tends to promote lengthening of branch internodes and expansion of leaf area. Formation and maintenance of chlorophyll are also depressed. The danger of such growth responses is that plants may be more sensitive to air pollution or that growth may be vulnerable to early fall freezes. Amur maple, white and paper birch, sycamore, American and Siberian elms, and flowering dogwood are common urban trees that are sensitive to artifical light (Table 5.4).

TABLE 5.4

Sensitivity of 40 Plants
to Security Lighting
(Cathey and Campbell, 1975)

High
Acer ginnala, amur maple
Acer platanoides, Norway maple
Betula papyrifera, paper birch
Betula pendula, European white birch
Betula populifolia, white birch
Catalpa bignonioides, catalpa
Cornus alba, Tatarian dogwood
Cornus florida, dogwood
Cornus stolonifera, red-osier dogwood
Platanus acerifolia, London planetree
Ulmus americana, American elm
Ulmus pumila, Siberian elm
Zelkova serrata, zelkova

Intermediate
Acer rubrum, red maple
Acer palmatum, Japanese maple
Cercis canadensis, eastern redbud
Cornus controversa, giant dogwood
Cornus sanquinea, bloodtwig dogwood
Gleditsia triocanthos, honeylocust
Halesia carolina, silverbell
Koelreuteria paniculata, goldenraintree
Ostrya virginiana, eastern hophornbeam
Phellodendron amurense, cork tree
Sophora japonica, Japanese pagodatree
Tilia cordata, littleleaf linden

TABLE 5.4 *(continued)*

Low
Carpinus japonica, hornbeam
Fagus sylvatica, European beech
Ginkgo biloba, ginkgo
Ilex opaca, American holly
Liquidamber styraciflua, sweetgum
Magnolia grandiflora, southern magnolia
Malus boccata, Siberian crabapple
Malus sargenti, Sargent's crabapple
Pinus nigra, Austrian pine
Pyrus calleryana, Bradford pear
Quercus palustris, pin oak
Quercus phellos, willow oak
Quercus robur, English oak
Quercus shumardi, shumard oak
Tilia europaea, European linden

Note: Plants have been listed alphabetically and are not grouped in descending order of sensitivity. A high, intermediate, or low rating identifies the relative responsiveness of the plants to security lighting. Plants with low sensitivity are preferred in areas with security lighting.

People

This chapter began by stating that the urban forest exists in an environment dominated by people and that the forest must grow in the spaces that remain after all structures necessary to urban society have been built. This does not mean that urban forests are not important to man or that they are not considered in the design of cities.

Such statement might also suggest that people are a generally negative factor in the urban forest environment. Absolutely not! True, they dig and push and pollute, but they also plant and prune and fertilize and do a half dozen other necessary things to this forest. If human beings and the urban forest are to be compatible, the forest must be managed. The management of the urban forest is considered in Chapter 6.

BIBLIOGRAPHY

Cathey, H. M. and L. E. Campbell, "Security Lighting and Its Impact on the Landscape," *Journal of Arboriculture,* Vol. 1, No. 10, p. 184, 1975.

Federer, C. A., "Effects of Trees in Modifying Urban Microclimate," *Proceedings of Symposium on the Role of Trees in the South's Urban Environment,* USDA Forest Service, p. 26, 1971.

Loomis, Robert C. and William H. Padgett, *Air Pollution and Trees in the East,* USDA Forest Service, 1975.

Lumis, M. P., H. Hofstra, and R. Hall, "Salt Damage to Roadside Plants," *Journal of Arboriculture,* Vol. 1, No. 1, p. 14, 1975.

Pirone, P. P., *Tree Maintenance,* Fourth Edition, Oxford University Press, New York, p. 204, 1972.

6
MANAGEMENT OF
THE URBAN FOREST

This chapter is concerned with the management needs of the urban forest and how these needs are met. There are two forms of management: that which is done *for* the forest to maintain health and vigor; and that which is done *to* the forest to prevent undue interference with the trappings of society. This distinction is significant as indeed much of what is done for the forest is directed toward its betterment. However, a great deal of what is done in the name of management is for other reasons. This is perhaps best illustrated by the percentages of municipal forestry budgets allocated to utility line clearance. Often these percentages far exceed the amount of planting, insect and disease control, and all other practices combined.

As discussed in Chapter 2, the urban forest of even a small city or town might have several thousand owners. All owners, from the smallest private landholders to the largest agency of government, have their own purposes of ownership. And these purposes have a profound influence on the management of the urban forest. Americans have long been staunch defenders of individual property rights, including the right to hold land for whatever purpose they desire. Obviously these rights cannot be absolute as individuals also have a responsibility to society. In the case of land ownership, this responsibility is manifested by statutes or ordinances that either prohibit or require certain things for the benefit of society. For example, there are laws prohibiting debris burning within metropolitan areas and laws requiring property owners to pay taxes to provide a variety of services for society.

It is the responsibility of owners of the urban forest to manage their portions of the forest to the minimum extent acceptable to society. It is the right of property owners to exceed this minimum. The standards vary with time and place. For example, townspeople in one community might tolerate dead trees or poison ivy on a vacant lot whereas in another they would not. They might also have tolerated such a situation 20 years ago and today they might not. The reasons are as complex as the factors that influence human values.

In a typical city the urban forest is managed by a myriad of public and private owners with city government having certain authority over all ownerships. This authority stems generally from police powers for the protection of public health, safety, morals, convenience, and welfare. It allows for the protection of the forest from fire, insects, and disease; it requires control of vegetative growth for public safety; and it provides for certain other areas of management. This authority is usually exercised to the minimum possible extent but offers the only direct opportunity for management of the urban forest as a whole. Thus, management of the urban forest is primarily the responsibility of individual property owners with limited involvement by city government except on city-owned lands. The result is a hodgepodge of species, ages, sizes, and conditions varying from lot to lot, neighborhood to neighborhood, to the edge of the city and beyond. On a whole, it is a situation of contrasts, comparisons, and complete differences, every bit as complex as a natural forest.

The urban forest has three fundamental management needs: planting, maintenance, and removal. We will not attempt to discuss in detail the cultural aspects of these needs as there are many excellent publications on these subjects. (See the list of selected references at the end of this chapter.)* Also, we have included as Appendix IIc the model specifications and standards of arboricultural practice that were prepared for the Atlanta, Georgia area (Sandfort and Nobles, 1976). These are presented as an example of the cultural elements necessary for managing the municipal forest.

We will consider the alternatives for dealing with the management needs of the urban forest, largely from the standpoint of municipal government—their exercise of responsibility to streetside, park, and other public forests, and their influence on the privately owned forest.

Management of parks and other municipally owned portions of the urban forest is generally the responsibility of city government. Responsibility for streetside trees is often less clear and varies from one city to another. It is most often defined by ordinance. However, in many small towns, ordinances are lacking and management is by tradition or policy the responsibility of adjacent property owners. There are three general types of city ordinances concerning streetside trees: (1) those which authorize city governments to assume full responsibility for management; (2) those which make management the responsibility of adjacent property owners but reserve the right of the city government to assume full or partial responsibility; and (3) those which grant full responsibility to adjacent property owners. These ordinances serve as a basis for various management programs.

Planting

Planting is perhaps the most publicly acceptable management need of the urban forest. Most people recognize this need because it is basic, tangible and reasonable. Tree planting is further acceptable since it fosters a satisfying sense of achievement. There is little doubt that we have been influenced by the poets' expression of the nobility of planting trees.

New planting must have high priority; however, at times utility line clearance, dead tree removal, or other necessary and more expensive prac-

*A detailed bibliography of further references is given in John Andresen's *Community and Urban Forestry, A Selected and Annotated Bibliography*, USDA, Forest Service, Southeastern Area, State and Private Forestry, Atlanta, Georgia, 1974.

tices must take precedence. Thus, there is no contradiction with the earlier statement that budgets for utility line clearance often exceed the amount of money spent for planting, insect and disease control, and all other practices combined. There are three primary management considerations regarding planting in the urban forest: composition, location, and design.

Species composition control

Experience with Dutch elm disease has recently brought into sharp focus the need for controlling the composition of the urban forest. The aftermath of the disease in communities where American elms once made up as much as 90 percent of the total tree population is tragic. In communities with lesser percentages of elms, the impact has obviously been less severe. This experience has led many municipal forestry departments to adopt a policy of species diversification so that no single species makes up more than 10 or 15 percent of the total population. The wisdom of such a policy is difficult to question provided that species concentrations and age classes are also considered.

The most direct way of controlling species composition is for all streetside, park, and other public area planting to be done by crews of the municipal forestry departments. The second most direct method is for planting to be contracted with private firms. In both cases, municipal government has control of the planting operation; in fact, this is the situation in most larger American cities. These operations are usually based on long-range master planting plans that consider species, site, and social factors. In smaller cities and towns, streetside planting is often the responsibility or option of adjacent property owners. In such cases, composition is often controlled by less direct means such as planting permits and official species lists. These are prescribed by ordinance but often suffer from inadequate enforcement.

An even less direct method, often used in small towns, is the wholesale purchase of planting stock by a department, board, commission, or other organization. Such purchases are made on the basis of orders by property owners from a selected species list. The trees are sold at or near cost and may be planted by city crews, civic organizations, or property owners themselves. The species list usually includes several choices by size classes (small, medium, and large trees). In this way, composition can be controlled to a degree and spatial factors can also be taken into account. The species offerings are usually changed from year to year for further diversity.

Species composition can be controlled to an extent on private property by ordinances that prohibit the planting of certain species. Such prohibitions usually result from undesirable characteristics such as "cotton" from cottonwoods, messy fruit from certain varieties of crabapples, or the offensive order of ginkgo fruit. Composition can also be influenced by encouraging the planting of certain species; this is done through news media releases by municipal forestry departments, often in cooperation with local nurseries.

Location

There are two aspects to the challenge of locating new trees and related plants in the urban environment: (1) to locate plants for minimum interference with the objects and workings of society; and (2) to locate them for maximum environmental enhancement. This challenge is perhaps best illustrated by the selection and design of streetside plantings. Spatial factors were discussed in Chapter 5. While these factors influence all planting in the urban forest, they are particularly critical to streetside trees and involve potential interference with curbs, sidewalks, driveways, fireplugs, street intersections, traffic signals, signs, streetlights, overhead wires, underground utilities, buildings, and existing trees.

Four general streetside situations can be identified: (1) parkways or treelawns between curbs and sidewalks—these are generally found in older residential areas but often extend into business districts and other areas; (2) treelawns not defined by sidewalks—as in newer residential areas; (3) sidewalks extending from curbs to buildings—generally in business districts; and (4) streetsides with no well-defined treelawns—mainly in strip developed commercial areas along major streets. The tree planting challenge varies greatly between these situations and warrants further discussion.

Treelawns Between Curbs and Sidewalks: Rectangular platting was the traditional design of American cities until the early twentieth century. This design was influenced largely by our rectangular system of land survey, which offered a convenient base for further division into blocks and lots. Departures from this design resulted generally only when topographic or other landscape features were too imposing. Sidewalks adjacent to streets filled an obvious need in residential areas in pre-automobile days. It can be argued that sidewalks were placed well away from streets simply to provide safety for pedestrians (or perhaps to protect them from splashing by water and mud) or that they were deliberately so located to provide a lawn for trees. In either case, these areas were heavily planted to trees, which have since competed with utilities, signs, lights, and other objects.

Original trees were often planted in the center of the treelawn with strict regimentation by straight row and spacing (Figure 6.1). Spacing was most often too close, perhaps reflecting a lack of appreciation for mature size. Close spacing was also a result of narrow lots with property owners often wanting two trees at the front of 40 to 50 ft (12.19 to 15.24 m) lots.

125

Figure 6.1 Parkways, or treelawns, between curbs and sidewalks with trees planted in straight rows are common in older residential areas.

New planting means primarily individual tree replacement, since opportunities for design considerations such as form, texture, color, and scale are limited. Exceptions are areas where extensive losses from Dutch elm disease or other causes have occurred and have prompted large-scale replacements.

Treelawns Not Defined by Sidewalks: Modern subdivisions are products of our automobile-oriented society. They are characterized by wide curving streets, few sidewalks, large lots, and houses set well back from the streets (Figure 6.2). These areas often allow departure from the traditional single row of streetside trees and provide opportunities for informal design. There are generally fewer obstructions to trees, as lawn spaces are larger and utility lines are frequently buried. Tree planting is often controlled by subdivision regulations that require a specific number of shade trees per lot. Such regulations often also prohibit tree planting within certain distances of street curbs. However, in subdivisions that do not have such regulations, streetside trees are planted by developers and property owners and through planned programs administered by city forestry departments. These programs vary from specific design input by landscape architects to crews being sent out with general spacing instructions.

126

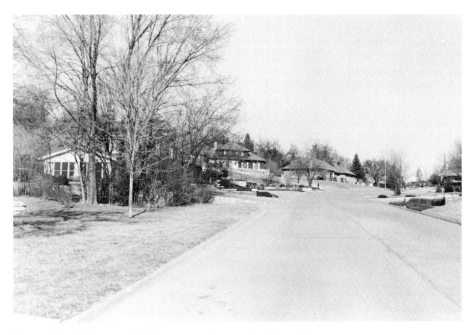

Figure 6.2 Modern subdivisions are characterized by wide curving streets, few sidewalks, and houses set far back from the street.

Design is sometimes governed by maintenance considerations. Maintenance is the primary rationale for lining individual streets with a single species. This practice is based largely on the idea that insects and diseases specific to individual species can be more efficiently controlled. Such plantings are further excused on the premise that repetition of a single species provides unity and harmony. It is also often thought logical to line streets named after trees with that tree. Thus, Maple Street ought to have maple trees along it. The main reason, however, is maintenance even though there is little evidence that maintenance costs are, in fact, reduced. The case against this practice is that site differences are often ignored and that repetition is frequently monotonous. The strongest argument, though, is that if an effective control capability is not maintained, insect or disease epidemics could denude entire streets. It is perhaps unrealistic to assume that such a capability can be maintained throughout the lifespan of the trees.

Business Districts: Business districts, with sidewalks extending from curbs to buildings, are among the most difficult areas for tree planting. Spatial and site problems are most severe and people impact is greatest. If properly located, however, trees can have a very favorable influence on the visual environment of these areas (Figure 6.3). Trees can unify architectural elements, "soften" hard building materials, provide color and character, and create seasonal change and variety. Perhaps no other operation can do more for less cost than the planting of trees.

Streetside trees in business districts must be carefully located. They should not be used in front of major store entrances or display windows but may be used in front of areas between windows or where buildings join. Trees must also not obscure advertising signs or marquees. Automobile parking arrangements must be considered. For angle parking, trees must be located a minimum of 30 in. (76.2 cm) from curbs to prevent damage by car bumpers. They should also be located directly in front of parking spaces so that they do not interfere with pedestrian movement between cars. Obviously above and below ground utilities, parking meters, and other physical features must also be considered.

If careful attention is paid to all site factors, trees can often be planted in sidewalk wells. This method is generally preferred in that greater soil volume is available for root development. In situations where underground obstructions prohibit sidewalk wells, containers and raised beds are often used. Design, location, species selection, and maintenance are extremely

Figure 6.3 Trees can be grown successfully in business districts and can have a very favorable influence on the visual environment.

important. Restricted soil volume is the main problem and frequent watering is called for. Raised planters are also convenient places for litter disposal, and daily cleanup is often necessary. If properly designed and a strong commitment made to maintenance, containers and beds can support trees and other plants beautifully. If not, they will rarely be successful.

Species and variety selection are very important as trees must conform to available space. Trees with upright form are most commonly used as there is limited space for lateral branch spread. Selection and location must be done by competent personnel fully cognizant of all factors. Such work is often done by qualified landscape architects. In some cities such projects are funded by store owners, business organizations, or other sources. Generally, however, business district planting is the responsibility of city forestry departments.

Strip Developments: Commercial strip developments along major streets are extremely difficult planting situations. Such areas are often a profusion of driveways, signs, poles, and wires badly in need of trees to enhance the visual environment but with few logical places to plant them (Figure 6.4). Commercial considerations simply take precedence over trees along such streets. As with business district plantings, proper location is extremely important, requiring that all factors be considered.

Design*

The street corridor must be considered a volume or a space and not simply an elongated or lineal ground plane. A successfully designed streetside landscape will be open where pleasant views or safe vision is desired; closed where visual screen is needed; and varied in form, size, texture, and color for interest. Spatial variety is important in preventing driver fatigue, maintaining driver alertness, and emphasizing danger zones. It also helps in developing a satisfactory visual–sensual experience. Spatial variety must, however, be properly designed. Too much variety leads to disorder, a lack of harmony, and continuity, while too little variety results in monotony. The ideal street corridor will be scientifically engineered and artistically formed of expanding and contrasting spaces in which adequate variety exists. Motorists and pedestrians should move safely and freely through the corridor, enjoying a streetscape designed to keep them relaxed, happy, and alert.

A street corridor space, whether occurring naturally or intentionally designed, will be enclosed by base, vertical, and overhead planes (Figure 6.5). It is a three-dimensional volume limited only by the relationships of

*These sections on design, pp. 129–139, were prepared by James J. Nighswonger, Landscape Architect, Department of Forestry, Kansas State University.

Figure 6.4 Strip developments are badly in need of trees to enhance the visual environment, but there are few logical places to plant them.

these three elements of space enclosure. In the street corridor the space is usually experienced while driving, riding, or walking. To the viewer it will be a continually changing space primarily affected by changes in the vertical plane.

The base plane within the street corridor space is usually consistent in color and texture within a given area. It may be comprised of concrete, asphalt, brick, gravel, grass, or combinations of the same. Lack of variety in this base plane induces monotony, boredom, and fatigue. The overhead plane likewise is not readily perceived as variable when comprised of sky or cloud cover. More variety and interest exist, however, when this plane is formed by a broken tree canopy that creates light and shadow patterns within the corridor and a more highly defined enclosure.

The most variety and interest occur within the vertical plane. This portion of the three-dimensional enclosure of space is also the area where trees and shrubs have their greatest influence. Therefore, street trees, buildings, walls, solid fences, vertical land forms, and other objects that create vertical enclosures are the most significant parts of the space. In the creation of this vertical enclosure the importance of the proper use of street

130

Figure 6.5 A street corridor space will be enclosed by base, vertical, and overhead planes.

trees with respect to form, size, texture, and color cannot be overemphasized!

Designing the vertical enclosure

The vertical enclosure created by vegetation or other objects provides visual control. Everything that occurs within the enclosure is a part of the visual function of that space and must be taken into account. A desirable object can be emphasized and, conversely, an unattractive object negated by manipulating the vertical enclosure (Figure 6.6). Strong contrasts in form, size, texture, and color, or combinations of the design elements will create interest and lead the viewer's eye to a desired object (Figure 6.7). By the same token, repetition of any one of the design elements may tend to negate an associated object (Figure 6.8).

An object outside the vertical enclosure of the street space can be introduced into the space visually. A distant mountain or meadow, a lake, a building, or any other pleasing feature can become a part of the visual scene when openings in the vertical enclosure are designed that permit viewing and provide enframement of the outside object.

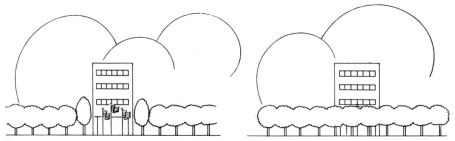

Figure 6.6 Manipulation of the vertical enclosure can emphasize or negate an object.

Figure 6.7 Strong contrasts in texture and color will attract viewer attention to a desirable object.

Figure 6.8 Repetition of the design elements, (form, size, texture, and color) will negate an associated object.

132

Generally strong contrasts within the vertical enclosure should be avoided. Repetition and subtle changes in form, size, texture, and color are desirable. Exceptions to this principle occur at major street intersections or at any other area where alertness and viewer attention are desired (Figure 6.9).

Design elements

Street trees when properly used perform limited engineering functions such as sound control and filtering polluted air; their architectural functions such as softening building lines provide a visual screen or privacy; and their climatological functions provide shade and wind control. Any of these purposes alone may be reason enough to plant trees along street sides. In reality, trees provide a combination of these functions in any setting, thus contributing substantially to human comfort and enjoyment.

However, in order to select and design street tree plantings properly, esthetic functions and art principles must receive consideration. The terms such as sequence, repetition, rhythm, unity, emphasis, and scale are basic to good street tree design. Also the four elements—form, size, texture, and color with respect to tree chracteristics—must be understood by the designer.

Form: All trees have a characteristic form or shape under normal growing conditions. The form of some varieties changes as a tree develops from its juvenile size to maturity; however, the designer should be most concerned with mature form since that is the characteristic form. A tree's form is created by its outline, branch and twig structure, and habit of growth. Form is such a prominent characteristic of many species that a tree can be identified from it often from several blocks away (Figure 6.10). Of the four tree characteristics, form is the strongest design element and must be considered in any well-designed group planting or streetside landscape. The most suitable forms for streetside situations include round, oval, upright oval, fastigate, or irregular as compared to pyramidal and weeping forms. Pyramidal or weeping forms are seldom suitable in streetside applications. Such trees occupy space often needed for vehicular and pedestrian movement (Figure 6.11). They also create visual obstruction and will dominate in the streetside landscape when they are foreign to the characteristic landscape.* Pyramidal forms accent, especially when used in association with rounded, oval, irregular, or weeping shapes. For these reasons trees assuming a characteristic pyramidal form are best used in park or large open-space development or, in some instances, in

---

*For our purposes the term "characteristic landscape" refers to the predominate environmental character of a specific area as influenced by a particular tree character and composition that dominates.

133

Intersection planting
treatment

Figure 6.9 Major street intersections can be emphasized by strong contrasts in the vertical enclosure. This intersection is emphasized by abrupt changes in tree size, color, and texture.

134

IRREGULAR   VASE   OVAL   PYRAMID   FASTIGIATE   ROUND   WEEPING

Figure 6.10   Major characteristic tree forms that occur in natural and cultivated species.

Figure 6.11   Trees with pyramidal or weeping forms may occupy the physical and visual space needed for the safe movement of wheels and people.

wide boulevard plantings where their low branching habit and density can reduce headlight glare and provide a visual screen without occupying the physical space needed for vehicles, pedestrians, or visual access.

Size: All trees, given normal growing conditions, can be expected to attain a certain ultimate size. As a design element, size is probably next in importance to form—and size is definitely the most misused element in streetside landscapes.

    The layperson will frequently select a tree on the basis of how well he likes a certain species and give little regard to how large it will grow. Thus

135

we commonly observe trees growing into overhead utility lines, breaking sidewalks and curbs, obscuring views, creating traffic hazards, and growing out of scale with respect to their surroundings.

For design purposes, trees can be grouped into three size categories: small, medium, and large, as discussed in Chapter 5. These are illustrated in Figure 6.12. In the past, communities throughout much of the country had streets that were lined and canopied by large elms, oaks, maples, and other species. This concept often resulted in beautiful, well-defined spaces that many people fondly remember (Figure 6.13). The modern-day street scene has changed, however. Driving surfaces on streets and boulevards are much wider; utilities both above and below ground are more numerous; curb cuts, drives, and sidewalks occur more frequently, all resulting in reduced space for trees (Figure 6.14). Consequently large growing trees seldom have a place along the street today. Even medium trees grow too large for some situations. Small and medium growing trees should therefore comprise the basic landscape in most modern street corridors.

Texture: The term texture, when describing tree characteristics, refers to visual and not tactile texture. The concern is thus for the visual texture of a tree or a group of trees and the relationship to other plants in the same visual space. Texture may be described as coarse, medium, or fine (Figure 6.15). However, this description is relative. A plant's texture can best be described as coarse when compared to another plant that possesses a medium or fine texture and vice-versa.

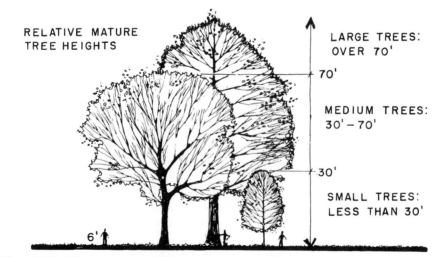

RELATIVE MATURE
TREE HEIGHTS

LARGE TREES:
OVER 70'

70'

MEDIUM TREES:
30' – 70'

30'

SMALL TREES:
LESS THAN 30'

6'

Figure 6.12   Size categories of mature trees for design purposes.

Figure 6.13 Streets canopied and lined by large trees are attractive. well-defined visual spaces.

A tree's texture is created by foliage and twig size primarily, with bark characteristics also playing a part. Since foliage size is the most important factor, texture relationships with decidious trees are most significant during the growing season.

When considering texture in a plant composition, uniformity and continuity are important. Subtle change in texture is appropriate and will add interest to the street space. On the other hand, abrupt textural changes will accent or create dominance; thus abrupt change should be designed only when dominance is desired. For example, in a grove of honeylocusts (fine texture), a catalpa (coarse texture) will stand out or dominate. Likewise a sycamore, London planetree, or basswood will dominate when used with fine-textured trees as part of a design.

Color: Color is a fourth design element. Again, uniformity with subtle change is important when considering color combinations. Various shades of green predominate the summer scene in any tree grouping. The shade or tint differences will vary with species and varietal changes, health or physical condition of the plant, soil or nutrient change, age of the foliage, and other factors. All greens that occur in nature generally blend well with one excep-

137

Figure 6.14 Competition for space along the modern-day street often leaves little room for trees, especially larger sizes.

tion; yellow-green foliage may dominate if its intensity is strong. Generally the designer should avoid blues, purples, reds, and other colors when they are not common in the characteristic landscape. Plants assuming such contrasting colors will attract attention. As before, if the purpose is to accent or attract attention, then color contrast is another device available to accomplish this objective.

Fall colors—reds, browns, yellows, and greens—often blend well with one another because they are related or analogous. High intensity can still result in dominance even in a related color, however. A knowledge of complementary and analogous colors, intensity, shades, and tint is important when designing with color, whether working with paint or plants.

Coarse   Medium   Fine

Figure 6.15 Relative foliage textures as perceived visually.

Putting it all together

The use of form, size, texture, and color in the development of esthetically pleasing and functional spaces is the key in street tree design. Many of the factors involved have been discussed in this chapter; however, some additional comments should be made.

Seldom will the designer utilize all four of the design elements at one time in concept development, but all four must be considered. To achieve design continuity, repetition of elements is basic. For example, careful selection and spacing of trees with respect to size, form, and color, or size, form, and texture are common approaches. The common denominators should usually be size and form (Figure 6.16).

Also, it is best to utilize plants in odd-numbered groupings, for instance, in groups of 3, 5, 7, or 9, when informality or "naturalness" is desired in a design.

Exceptions to the above guidelines occur when emphasis or viewer attention is desired. In such cases, the more variety or change from the characteristic landscape the stronger the emphasis. For example, in a composition where medium-sized trees, round in form, green in color, and fine in texture predominate, plants that are large, pyramidal, bright red, and coarse will seem to shout out for attention. In addition, the use of even numbers of dominating plants at both sides of a desirable view or dangerous area where viewer alertness is important will create even stronger emphasis.

Maintenance

From a management perspective, maintenance of the urban forest may be defined as the implementation of practices necessary for reasonable health, vigor, and compatability with the urban environment. Maintenance in-

Figure 6.16 A well-designed interesting street corridor resulting from repetition without monotony, and subtle change in size, form, and texture.

volves all practices between planting and removal. These practices can be grouped into three categories: (1) growth control; (2) damage control; and (3) insect and disease control. There is some overlapping of these categories. For example, certain growth control practices can prevent damage and influence disease control. This overlapping is considered in the following discussion. We will discuss maintenance generally from the standpoint of private property owners and more specifically of municipal governments.

Growth control

There are two types of vegetative growth control practices in the urban forest: those that retard or redirect growth, and those that enhance growth. The first category primarily involves pruning, although some work with chemical retardants is also included. In the second category are practices such as irrigation, fertilization, and control of competing vegetation

Pruning: Pruning is one of the most important management practices in the urban forest. It may be done for the following reasons:

• Reduction of hazards to life and property
• Clearance of utility lines or other subjects
• Development of structural strength, shape, and form
• Appearance
• Production of fruit
• Exposure or enhancement of vistas

Proper pruning is a specialized practice requiring knowledge of plant growth and response. This knowledge is frequently lacking, however, and one can find abundant examples of improper pruning in virtually every city. Pruning is often thought to entail only the removal of lower tree branches, or worse, the near complete removal of tree crowns. Topping, or modified pollarding, is most often practiced in the central and western United States, particularly where Siberian elms abound. Topping is the indiscriminate removal of a tree's crown, leaving large branch stubs vulnerable to decay and resulting in a profusion of adventitious branches (Figure 6.17). The reasons for such improper pruning are based largely on the fear that during storms tall trees will fall on houses or other property. Topping has been done often enough also so that it appears to be the correct thing to do. However, it is a tragedy of many cities and towns that large sums are expended on topping in this misguided belief. This belief is often encouraged by contractors who either know no better practices or find topping the most profitable. This indictment of topping reflects our strong feelings and does not obscure the recognition that it may be necessary as a last resort in cases where trees

Figure 6.17 Topping is the indiscriminate removal of a tree's crown. Tragically, large sums of money are expended on this destructive practice in the misguided belief that it is the proper thing to do.

have suffered severe storm damage. In such cases, detrimental effects can be reduced by making slanting cuts with branches or buds at the peak. As a normal practice, however, topping is simply not justified.

Pruning of street and park trees may be contracted to commercial arborists or done by municipal crews. In many cities where forestry program budgets are limited, priorities for pruning are necessary. These priorities are usually established according to area. For example, pruning of trees in a centrally located park would probably be more important than pruning of streetside trees in an industrial area. Priorities must also be based on considerations of safety, tree value, species, and size. Pruning for safety is obviously needed to eliminate hazardous branches, to clear sight lines for traffic, and to reduce cover for criminal activities in parks and other areas. There is little doubt that much pruning in the urban forest is made necessary by the improper selection and location of trees. There are, however, few trees that do not require pruning at some times during their lifespan. Pruning of young trees to develop structural strength and good form should be given a high priority; this can prevent more expensive pruning much later.

In spite of the wishes of many people, the placement of all power lines underground is unlikely and line clearance will continue to be an important and expensive pruning job in the urban forest. Line clearance is usually the responsibility of power companies or municipal utility departments. Clearance specifications are prescribed for various types of lines, and tree limbs and other obstructions must be removed. Utility line easements allow entry on private lands for line clearance and other maintenance. City ordinances and easement regulations often prohibit tree planting beneath wires or prescribe certain low-growing species.

Proper utility line clearance requires a knowledge of tree species, growth characteristics, and response to pruning. Directional pruning is often practiced, particularly for species with ascending branches. Paths for lines can be cleared through trees or branches can be trained to grow away from lines (Figure 6.18). Such methods are not practical, however, for trees with strong terminal branching habits, and drop crotching and topping may be the only recourse (Figure 6.19). The quality of utility line clearance pruning has increased in recent years largely as a result of environmental awareness, corporate image concern, and efforts of the Utility Arborist Association, an affiliated association of the International Society of Arboriculture.

In an effort to reduce costs of manual pruning, considerable work has been done with chemical growth inhibitors. Such chemicals either directly prevent cell division in terminal buds or influence hormones that affect growth. Some growth-retarding chemicals are currently on the market, and these products are useful under certain conditions. However, much research remains to determine the practical application of "chemical pruners."

Growth Enhancement: Increasing growth by practices that maintain plant health and vigor is a necessary management need of the urban forest. These practices may directly or indirectly influence plant growth and may involve irrigation, fertilization, soil aeration and amending, thinning and release, and grass and weed control. The intensity of application of these practices depends largely on the functional value of individual trees or groups of plants. There is often a conflict between growth enhancement and the need to restrict growth. This conflict can be moderated if health and vigor can be enhanced, and increased growth can be redirected.

Damage control

Control of tree damage involves prevention and repair. Much damage can be prevented by judicious pruning and, as suggested in the discussion of topping, much damage can be done by improper pruning. Damage prevention involves reducing the likelihood of physical damage and preventing of wood decay. In addition to pruning, these measures include construction and grade change precautions, cabling and bracing, wrapping, treatment of

143

Figure 6.18 Paths for utility lines can often be cleared through trees, and branches can be trained to grow away from lines.

144

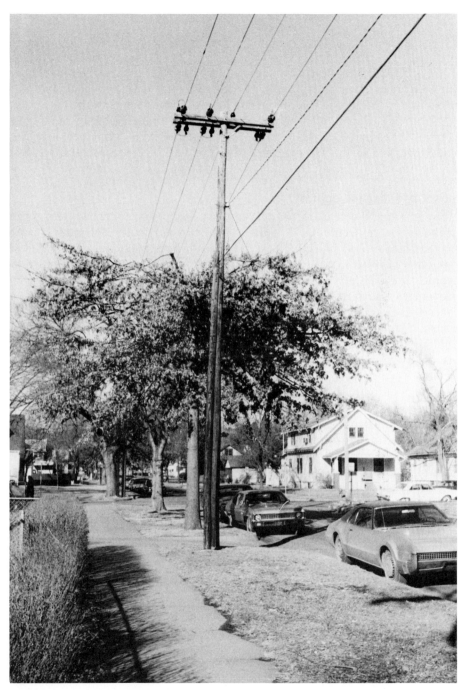

Figure 6.19 Trees with strong terminal branching habits, such as pin oaks, offer little recourse other than topping to drop crotching under utility lines.

pruning cuts, mulching to discourage damage by lawnmowers, construction of physical barriers, posting of signs, and policing. Damage repair includes the treatment of cavities, breakage, and other wounds. The objective is to prevent decay and put wounds in the best condition for closure.

Damage control must be integrated with all management practices as it involves correct location of trees, proper pruning, maintenance of health and vigor, and insect and disease control, as will be discussed. It also must involve information, education, and enforcement by responsible officials.

Insect and disease control

Many insect and disease situations can be tolerated as a natural part of the urban forest environment. A point at which a particular outbreak can no longer be tolerated is difficult to determine, both from the standpoint of reduction of health, vigor, and function of the trees, and its annoyance to people. The difficulty is compounded since often control measures must be preventive and initiated well in advance of the actual damage. Effective control involves several elements: (1) knowledge of insect and disease life cycles; (2) monitoring; (3) decision making; (4) physical capability for control application; and (5) legal authority for action. These ingredients must operate also within the climate of public attitudes concerning the use of pesticides. Fortunately, for control purposes, most insects and diseases are specific to individual tree species or varieties. Occasionally however, insects are less discriminating, particularly when they are at high population levels. Recent gypsy moth outbreaks in eastern states attest to this.

A basic management approach considers the tree insects and diseases that can be controlled on an individual tree basis and those that require control measures applied to the entire tree species population. Thus, the critical question is whether a particular tree can be protected within tolerable limits by control measures applied to it alone. If individual trees can be protected, priority systems can be set up for control application. Obviously, such decisions must also consider the impact of insect or disease attacks on the health and vigor of individual trees.

Legal authority for insect and disease control programs has been clearly established in most states. State statutes authorize municipalities or other local units of government to levy taxes to pay for control of epidemic pests and diseases and to allow enactment of local ordinances to carry out such programs. The exercise of such authority is perhaps best illustrated by efforts to control Dutch elm disease.

Dutch elm disease is a fungus affecting the water-conducting vessels of elm trees. It is spread primarily by elm bark beetles but is also transmitted by root grafts of adjoining trees and to a minor degree by unsanitary pruning tools. The main vector, however, is the European bark beetle, and most control measures have been directed toward reduction of beetle populations. Recent developments of soluble fungicides and systems for their applications offer promise for a more specific control of the fungus. Elm bark beetles breed in dying elm trees and infect other elms mainly by feeding in twig crotches. Control measures are spraying, sanitation, and prevention of transmission through root grafts. Spraying involves the application of insecticides to destroy the feeding beetles. Sanitation is the removal and destruction of breeding wood. Prevention of transmission through root grafts is primarily by chemical barriers. To be effective, Dutch elm disease programs require: (1) adequate public financing; (2) legal authority and systems for the designation and condemnation of breeding trees on all public and private property; (3) physical capability for timely spraying and tree removal; and (4) a continuing commitment. Numerous cities have demonstrated that as long as the program was diligently followed, elm losses could be held to a very small percentage of the total population. A continuing commitment is extremely difficult, however, in a climate of tight budgets, environmental concerns, and public attitudes. Cannon and Worley (1976) found that some communities temporarily suspend control programs during a period of temporary financial stress only to find that they could not regain control of the disease situation later. They also observed that the communities that experienced the fewest elm losses had well-founded control programs, conscientiously applied, and sustained over the years.

Concern over widespread use of chemical sprays plus the high costs of materials and applications have prompted increased interest in alternative methods of insect and disease control. Integrated control programs are being developed. A model program, developed by William and Helga Olkowski of the Department of Biological Control, University of California, Berkeley, has received widespread attention. In effect in the city of Berkeley, this program considers the management of insects and diseases as the management of ecosystems. An intensive study of problem situations is required. Often insect problems can be solved by biological controls involving the introduction of natural enemies or the creation of conditions favorable for natural enemies. Certain leaf-eating caterpillars are safely and selectively controlled by spray applications of *Bacillus thuringiensis,* a bacterial enemy of lepidoptera larvae. Additional treatments are water sprays and selective pruning to physically remove insects and sticky adhesives to trap insects. Chemical sprays are also used but in greatly reduced amounts, a result of careful monitoring and optimum timing of applications. A strong effort has also been made to inform citizens of the program. In operation since 1972, the program has resulted in lower pest management costs, fewer citizen complaints, the elimination of secondary pest outbreaks, and a reduction of environmental contamination (Olkowski and Olkowski, 1975).

147

Removal

Removal (which includes utilization and disposal) of materials from the urban forest is an important management need. Materials that must be removed are dead trees, hazardous trees (physically hazardous and those that harbor potentially epidemic insects and diseases), overcrowded trees, pruning debris, storm debris, stumps, leaves, and obnoxious fruits.

As with other management practices, the removal of materials from the urban forest must be authorized, planned, and funded; such a plan must be flexible enough to deal with emergency situations such as storms or other disasters. Authority for material removal is generally an exercise of police powers that provide for the safety and convenience of residents. Most removal work can be planned. Plans are based on inventories, inspections, and past records.

In most cities, annual inspections are made of all public trees; dead, dying and hazardous trees are designated and recorded. In cities having Dutch elm or other disease control programs, dead and hazardous trees on private property are also designated. Owners are notified and are given a reasonable time for removal. In most situations, if such trees are not removed within the designated time, they are removed by the city and the cost charged against property taxes.

The bulk and weight of wood materials to be removed often necessitates on-site processing. Twigs and branches can be conveniently reduced by chipping. Larger portions of tree trunks can also be chipped but require bigger and more expensive machines. Wood chips may be used in the manufacture of particle board, roofing materials, and paper products. They also make excellent mulching material and are often used as animal bedding and poultry litter. The search for such uses has intensified because laws passed in recent years have prohibited the burning of wood wastes for air pollution reasons.

The problem of disposal of forest debris is illustrated in Chicago where it is estimated that about 295,000 elms with a minimum trunk diamter of 20 in. (50.8 cm) will have died of Dutch elm disease between 1968 and 1978. It is also estimated that removal costs will have amounted to about $24 million during this period (Hartman, 1973). In an effort to utilize elm wood and partially to offset the cost of removal, the Bureau of Forestry has purchased a chip-harvesting machine and arranged to supply chips to a roofing shingle manufacturer. In 1972, an estimated 15 to 20 percent of the wood from the 21,000 trees that were removed were turned into chips and sold, grossing $22,000. The Bureau has also explored the possibility of sawlog utilization and disposal by burning for energy production.

Many cities are attempting similar programs, the feasibility of which is

148

limited by several factors: (1) the expense of harvesting and processing machinery; (2) an insufficient volume of wood; (3) limited markets for products; (4) the attitudes of city officials; and (5) the fear of metal objects in trees.

The conversion of debris into products from the urban forest has led Chicago urban foresters to an interesting theory and perhaps to a future reality. Why not develop for the urban forest a sustained yield system in which not only dead trees but mature trees are harvested as well? Such a system would produce revenues from harvested products that would pay for forestry program costs—planting, maintenance, and removal. This theory is based largely on the logic that maintenance costs increase sharply as trees become overmature and eventually have to be removed anyway. Why not remove them at the optimum time when dollar value can be maximized?

The obvious problem with this approach is that large old trees have a greater value (utility) to residents by their presence than the value of their products. Many people would view the sight of large live trees being cut as offensive and some would consider it intolerable.

Collection and disposal of leaves can be troublesome and expensive operations in municipal forestry programs. In recent years, rapid advances have been made in collection and handling systems. Portable shredder-compactors with powerful vacuums for collection are now in use. The city of Webster Groves, Missouri operates a leaf compost center where leaves are shredded and composted for use in various city planting projects. Compost material is also placed in convenient pickup locations in parks and is eagerly sought by city residents.

Recent fossil fuel shortages have focused attention on wood as an alternative energy source. There has been a sharp increase in the demand for fireplace and other fuelwood from the urban forest. Technology is also rapidly developing for industrial, municipal, and institutional heating plants that utilize garbage and solid wastes from urban areas. The combustible fraction of municipal solid waste is 80 percent. The amount of urban forest wood material varies greatly by city but often constitutes a significant part of this total. For example, in 1976 the Shawnee County, Kansas (county population, 173,418 including Topeka) landfill disposed of 18 million pounds (8.1 million kilograms) of tree debris. If utilized for fuel, this would have yielded over eight billion BTUs. The energy potential of waste wood is significant, with one ton of dry wood producing about 17 million BTUs. This is equivalent to approximately 13,000 c ft^3 (390 m^3) of natural gas, 0.54 tons (0.49 t) of coal, or 2 barrels of oil (Arola, 1976). Table 6.1 shows comparative BTU yields per cubic foot of oven dry wood for various species. The University of Kansas is designing a plant to supply the total heating needs of the university from garbage and wood materials. Wood will be supplied from

149

TABLE 6.1

Conversion of Green Weight to Oven-Dry Weight and BTU per Cubic Foot

| Species | Specific Gravity | | Solid Wood in Pounds | aBTU/Green |
	Green	Oven-Dry	O.D. Wt/Green C.F.	(C.F. × 10⁹)
			(0.45 kg)	
Osage orange	0.76	0.84	47.4	408
Black locust	0.66	0.71	41.2	354
Hickory	0.64	0.78	39.9	343
Post oak	0.60	0.79	37.4	322
Pecan	0.60	0.76	37.4	322
Honeylocust	0.60	0.67	37.4	322
Mulberry	0.59	0.69	36.8	316
Bur oak	0.58	0.76	36.2	311
Red oak	0.56	0.74	34.9	300
Sugar maple	0.56	0.67	34.9	300
Green ash	0.53	0.65	33.1	285
Black walnut	0.51	0.56	31.8	273
Kentucky coffeetree	0.50	0.57	31.2	268
Hackberry	0.49	0.56	30.6	263
Red elm	0.48	0.57	29.9	257
White elm	0.46	0.55	28.7	247
Sycamore	0.46	0.54	28.7	247
Redcedar	0.44	0.49	27.5	236
Soft maple	0.44	0.52	27.5	236
Catalpa	0.38	0.42	23.7	204
Cottonwood	0.37	0.43	23.1	199
Red alder	0.37	0.43	23.1	199
Willow	0.36	0.41	22.5	194

a Heat yield calculated by reduction of green (fresh) volume to 0% moisture, then taking weight □ 8600 BTU to obtain yield/cubic foot of green material.

Source: Gary G. Naughton, "University of Kansas Energy Forest Third Interim Report," Kansas State University, June, 1976 (unpublished) nearby urban areas and will also be grown specifically for the heating plant on university lands. Technology for development of this fuelwood production and utilization system is being furnished by the Department of Forestry at Kansas State University, a sister institution.

BIBLIOGRAPHY

Arola, Roger A., (Data presented at seminar, "Use of Wood Residues for Fuel," June 1976, Madison, Wisconsin).

Cannon, William N., Jr., and David P. Worley, *Dutch Elm Disease Control: Performance and Costs,* Forest Service, USDA, Research Paper NE-345, Upper Darby, Pa, 1976.

Hartmann, Frederick, *The Chicago Forestry Scheme,* A Natural History Special Supplement, November 1973.

Olkowski, W. and H. Olkowski, "Establishing an Integrated Pest Control Program for Street Trees," *Journal of Arboriculture,* Vol. 1, No. 9, pp. 167–172, 1975.

SELECTED READINGS

Brown, George E., *The Pruning of Trees, Shrubs and Conifers,* Faber and Faber, London, 1972

Christopher, Everett P., *The Pruning Manual,* MacMillan, New York, 1964.

Fenska, Richard R., *The Complete Modern Tree Experts Manual,* Dodd Mead, New York, 1964.

Pirone, P. P., *Tree Maintenance,* Fourth Edition, Oxford University Press, New York, 1972.

7
MONETARY
VALUES OF
THE URBAN FOREST

In Chapter 4 we described the benefits of trees in urban areas. However, it is one thing to list these benefits and quite another to assign monetary values to them. In many cases the values are intangible and thus difficult to determine monetarily. Yet urban trees do have value both from an individual and community standpoint. Kielbaso (1971) in an article titled "Economic Values of Trees in the Urban Locale" has listed eight aspects in deriving tree values: (1) alternative values; (2) city assets; (3) maintenance values; (4) timber values; (5) property values; (6) legal values; (7) evaluation formulas; and (8) replacement costs.

Alternative Values

Certainly trees must have some value or society would not spend money planting and maintaining them. Instead these funds would be invested in some other manner, for example, bank, savings and loan, stocks, and bonds. These are what are termed alternative values. Specifically, the planting and maintenance of trees in urban areas indicate the value placed on them. For example, Washington Square, a tree-covered park in Philadelphia, has an assigned property value equal to the value of the 20-story Penn Mutual Building adjacent to it (Kielbaso, 1971). Central Park in New York City is another similar example. It does not produce revenue and it costs a considerable amount to maintain the plants within its boundaries, yet New Yorkers have decided that the park is worth the cost. Even despite the recent and continuing economic problems in New York, this attitude is probably unchanged.

City Assets

Given the foregoing, trees must represent an asset to a city just as streets, sewers, water lines, schools, and hospitals do. The following combination of tables from Dressel (1963) and Kielbaso (1971) shows the value of trees in urban areas as determined by a survey of city foresters (Table 7.1).

As shown in Table 7.1, cities vary in assigning value to trees. If the average table value of $187 per tree is applied to the estimated 32.25 million street trees in the United States (Tilford, 1957), it gives a total value of around $6 billion. The main purpose for establishing the value of the street trees is to confirm to the city government and the taxpayers that trees represent a considerable investment that justifies the funding of a continuing management program.

TABLE 7.1

Street Trees as City Assets
(Combined from Dressel (1963)
and Kielbaso (1971))

City	Date of Survey	Estimated Tree Value	Number of Street Trees	Dollar Value Per Tree
Dearborn, Mich.	1958	$15,000,000	100,000	150
Detroit, Mich.	1970	60,000,000	300,000	200
East Orange, N. J.	1963	4,365,320	27,000	175
Newark, N. J.	1949	6,000,000	60,000	100
Iowa City, Iowa	1960	4,193,560	8,594	488
Greenwich, Conn.	1932	12,000,000	60,000	200
Palo Alto, Calif.	1956	6,000,000	30,000	200
Washington, D. C.	1965	25,000,000	350,000	71
Lincoln, Neb.	1966	6,000,000	60,000	100
			Average	$187

Maintenance Values

Maintenance costs are another way of determining street tree values, for example, planting, pruning, feeding, irrigation, disease, and insect control. A 1965 survey reports per capita maintenance expenditures for street trees, ranging from less than one cent per tree to $6.16, with an average of $2.47 per tree (Table 7.2) (Hatcher, 1965). These expenditures were divided as follows: planting, 14 percent; spraying, 14 percent; pruning, 32 percent; removal, 32 percent; and preventive maintenance, 8 percent. If this money were invested in a bank instead of a tree program and an annuity principle applied, the value of the trees could be estimated at different periods as shown in Table 7.3 (Kielbaso, 1971).

The values shown in the tables represent normal tree care. Such values can increase tremendously during insect or disease outbreaks. For example, Lincoln, Nebraska, initially appropriated $135,000 to protect its elms from Dutch elm disease at a cost of $2.25 per tree. This was followed with additional appropriations of $90,000 ($1.50 per tree) for the next five years. Similar situations were common in many cities as Dutch elm disease advanced westward.

Planting and removal costs also indicate tree values. New York City spends $750,000 annually to plant 5000 trees ($150/tree) (Schiff, 1969). In 1955, Richfield Oil Company spent $20,000 to plant 13 trees in the

155

TABLE 7.2

Street Tree Budget Information for
Selected Cities (from Kielbaso, 1971)

City	Number of Trees	Budget	Dollars/ Tree	City Population	Dollar/ Capita	Date Year
East Orange, N. J.	27,000	$ 102,881	3.80	90,000	1.14	1965
Richmond, Va.	250,000	168,000	0.67	219,000	0.76	1965
Wooster, Ohio	2,595	3,800	1.49	18,000	0.21	1965
Washington, D. C.	350,000	980,000	2.80	764,000	1.28	1965
Minneapolis, Minn.	350,000	1,049,000	3.00	483,000	2.17	1969
Palo Alto, Calif.	50,000	50,000	1.00	41,000	1.22	1956
Long Beach, Calif.	240,000 app.	649,162	2.70 app.	344,000	1.88 app.	1969
Lansing, Mich.	33,000	324,000	9.80	108,000	3.00	1970
Detroit, Mich.	300,000	2,200,000	7.30	1,670,000	1.30	1970
Midwest Average [a]			2¢—2.47—14.82		1¢—0.86—6.16	

[a]From Hatcher, 1965.

TABLE 7.3

Annuity Values for 30 and 50 Years at 5% Interest
for Selected City Forestry Programs
(from Kielbaso, 1871)

City		Budget Information	Total Program Value		Individual Tree Values		
			30 Years	50 Years	Expenditures Per Year	30 Years	50 Years
East Orange, N. J.	1965	$ 102,881	$ 6,831,300	$21,502,129	$3.80	$252.32	$ 794.20
Richmond, Va.	1965	168,000	11,155,200		.67	44.49	140.43
Washington, D. C.	1965	980,000	64,972,000		2.80	185.92	585.20
Wooster, Ohio	1965	3,800	252,320		1.49	98.94	311.41
Detroit, Mich.	1970	2,200,000	145,200,000		7.30	481.80	1,525.70
Lansing, Mich.	1970	352,000	23,372,800		9.89	646.80	2,048.00
Minneapolis, Minn.	1969	1,049,000	70,313,600		3.00	199.20	627.00
Palo Alto, Calif.	1956	50,000	3,320,000		1.00	66.40	290.00
Midwest Average [a]	1965				2.47	164.01	516.23

[a]From Hatcher, 1965.

157

downtown area of Los Angeles ($1525/tree). Other examples are given in Table 7.4. The first part of the table lists the numbers of trees planted in several cities surveyed in 1970. Current planting costs average around $50 per tree. The second part lists tree removals. At an average cost of $75 per tree, the total value of trees removed in these cities would exceed five million dollars.

Timber Values

If we were to use forestry in its traditional sense, the urban forest value would be expressed in terms of sawtimber, veneer, and other products. It has been estimated that 100,000 board feet of saw timber could be harvested on a sustained annual basis from Boston, Massachusetts (Foster, 1965). Obviously, in the urban areas of North America the amenity values of trees make this approach difficult. It should be noted that trees are an asset that tend to increase in value over time. They do, however, become a liability at death because they have to be removed. This liability could perhaps be partially offset by a sustained yield management program. This liability can be further offset by the utilization and sale of chips, firewood, and other products. However, this is not always feasible and depends on local market conditions.

Property Values

Most people consider that trees do enhance property values. However, there are those who assign a negative value to trees as their presence means the raking of leaves and problems in lawn maintenance. Tree value is manifested by the final agreement made between buyer and seller. Is the buyer willing to pay more for a wooded lot as compared to a treeless one? Tree values are hard to assess in these situations as it is difficult to separate tree values from the rest of the property (land and improvements).

Kielbaso (1971) contacted a bank appraiser concerning tree values in subdivisions. The appraiser suggested that "off the record" he might value a lot with trees at up to $10 per front foot more than a lot without trees. However, he could not be definitive because there is much risk involved. Kielbaso (1971) suggests that it really boils down to two factors: high grade buyers (higher income bracket) and risk. He suggests that people with high incomes are more willing to pay for the amenities trees provide and banks are more willing to risk their money on such affluent individuals.

158

TABLE 7.4

Shade Tree Projects of Selected Cities
(from *Weeds, Trees, and Turf Magazine,*
December 1970)

Tree-Planting Projects [a]	
21,400—Milwaukee, Wis.	2,255—Richmond, Va.
6,714—Baltimore, Md.	1,731—New Orleans, La.
5,213—Toledo, Ohio	1,478—Dayton, Ohio
4,083—Rochester, N. Y.	1,343—Pontiac, Mich.
3,297—Cleveland, Ohio	1,272—Portsmouth, Va.
3,141—Flint, Mich.	1,117—Minneapolis, Minn.
2,567—Aurora, Colo.	1,084—Philadelphia, Pa.
2,457—Detroit, Mich.	1,080—Tonawanda, N. Y.
2,364—Midland, Mich.	1,000—Buffalo, N. Y.
Tree-Removal Projects [b]	
15,737—Milwaukee, Wis.	2,228—Flint, Mich.
10,623—Detroit, Mich.	2,043—Cleveland, Ohio
5,120—Des Moines, Iowa	1,868—Lincoln, Neb.
5,000—Buffalo, N. Y.	1,641—Toledo, Ohio
4,906—Rochester, N. Y.	1,550—New Orleans, La.
3,500—Topeka, Kansas	1,500—Richmond, Va.
3,500—Omaha, Neb.	1,473—Philadelphia, Pa.
3,250—St. Louis, Mo.	1,375—Akron, Ohio
2,983—Dayton, Ohio	1,350—Monmouth City, N. J.
2,790—Wichita, Kansas	1,023—Evanston, Ill.
2,708—Baltimore, Md.	

a = number of trees planted in 1970.
b = number of trees removed in 1970.

Kielbaso (1971) gave the following examples of indirect methods to ascertain the property values assigned to trees in urban areas: (1) Gould (1970) reported that property values in the northeastern United States seemed to vary with the amount of forest and open space and that the best of the suburbs had almost 100 acres of forest or open space per 1000 people; (2) Edlin (1963) reported a situation of urban dwellers opting to preserve a 10-acre woodland adjacent to their property primarily because they feared a loss of market value if the woods were to be removed; (3) Purcell (1956) reviewed some prime property subdivisions in Toronto in which small or-chard trees aided in selling the homes. One developer valued the trees at $300 each and planned his streets to utilize a maximum of them; and (4) national realty officials have adopted increased values for homes having

159

sound tree plantings (Johnson, 1956). Kielbaso (1971) mentions also a home with a 300-year-old elm being sold. A $24,000 offer was made prior to a hurricane that destroyed the tree. The undamaged home eventually sold for $15,000 after the hurricane. Thus, it could be concluded that tree was worth $9000 to the property value.

Dr. Brian Payne of the U.S. Forest Service has found that trees may increase property value by as much as 20 percent, with average increases of 5 to 10 percent. This translates to increases of $3000 to $7000 in value. The data were obtained by showing photographs of architecturally similar houses, with and without trees, to realtors and asking them to estimate selling prices (Payne, 1975). In another study of a similar nature, seven simulated combinations of amount and distribution of tree cover for a 12-acre tract of unimproved residential land were presented to professional appraisers for value estimation. Arrangements with trees were valued higher than those without trees and scattered tree arrangements were valued higher than dense cover arrangements (Payne and Strom, 1975).

As can be seen, trees do have value in real estate. However, the actual value is subject to discussion and varies from region to region with realtors, developers, and individual buyers and sellers.

Legal Values

Probably the area most wrought with difficulty in assigning the worth of trees is that of legal values, that is, court suits, income tax deductions, and insurance casualty loss claims. Recently we have seen some trends toward the viewpoint that trees should have legal standing or legal rights. Indeed there is a book by Christopher D. Stone titled "Should Trees Have Standing—Towards Legal Rights for Natural Objects" (1974). In the past, an unwillingness to attach values to trees contributed to society's general disregard of trees. This is evidenced by settlements that insurance companies award for tree damage and the general attitude of the Internal Revenue Service toward tree values. However, as evidenced by the recent environmental movement, people are more concerned about trees and their legal values. This has caused insurance claims adjusters, Internal Revenue Service agents, and municipal officials to become more aware of tree values. Below are some examples of tree appraisal situations that have been reported in the Rochester, New York area over the past several years (Micha, 1975):

- Tree damage to loss to vehicular accident
- Sudden tree loss due to high wind

- Presurvey of trees prior to gasline installations
- Presurvey of trees prior to underground electrical installations
- Presurvey of trees prior to sewer and water-line construction
- Overencroachment during construction
- Presurvey of trees prior to road widening
- Trees damaged or destroyed by lightning
- Timber theft
- Poor pruning practices
- High water tree loss
- Chemical injury to trees and plants
- Property survey to determine tree values prior to home construction
- Tree damage and loss due to fire

If one were to survey other cities, other situations could certainly be found, but it does point out the increasing concern of landowners for tree values. In terms of such appraisals, let us look at the normal channels in which legal values for trees are ascertained and hopefully awarded; that is, insurance companies, the Internal Revenue Service, and the appraisal process and the courts.

Insurance settlements

Insurance agencies regularly deal with casualty losses to trees. One of the first problems that enters into such a discussion is what is a casualty. As defined by the Internal Revenue Service, "a casualty is the complete or partial destruction of property resulting from an identifiable event of a sudden, unexpected or unusual nature." Loss of death of a tree due to lightning or a tornado is a casualty. But what about Dutch elm disease? An elm killed by Dutch elm disease is just as dead as if it were struck by a tornado and certainly is a loss to the property; however, it is not a casualty as it did not happen suddenly. The same holds true for all other diseases or insect attacks.

Casualty loss statements in all insurance policies are essentially the same. The various insurance companies do not usually dictate the terms of their policies nor do the state insurance commissions. As a whole, there are about three or four insurance service organizations that write the policies for all the rest of the insurance companies in the nation (Gustin, 1975). Thus, the policies from all the companies tend to be similar and read as follows (Gustin, 1975):

> *This company shall be liable for loss to trees, shrubs, plants, and lawns (except those grown for business purposes) only when the loss is caused by fire, lightning, explosion, riot, civil commotion,*

161

malicious mischief, theft, aircraft or vehicle not operated by an occupant of the premises. The Company's liability in any one occurrence under this provision shall not exceed in the aggregate for all such property 5 percent of the limit of liability of Coverage A nor more than $250 on any one tree, shrub or plant including expense incurred in removing the debris.

Most companies do have some type of deductible clause ($50 to $100) and thus for any one tree the actual amount collectible for a casualty could be as low as $150. If a large tree were involved, it may well cost in excess of $250 to simply remove the tree, let alone replace it. In addition, it does not matter if you have a valuable rare tree or if you live in California, Kansas, or New York, the limit is still the same. Insurance companies indicate that the number of claims for tree losses are few (Gustin, 1975). The limit of $250 was established in 1954 and has remained the same since. Any policy change has to involve the Board of Directors of the Insurance Service Organization and they meet only once every six years (Gustin, 1975). The International Society of Arboriculture and the American Society of Consulting Arborists are attempting to persuade the insurance industry to increase liability coverage under the casualty clause to $500.

Internal revenue service

Claiming casualty losses as income tax deductions is a much more complex procedure with many variables. Among these are: (1) rulings of a similar nature involving trees and shrubs that may be referred to by IRS personnel when reviewing a casualty loss claim; (2) the attitudes of reviewing officials toward trees and their legal standing or value; and (3) how closely the individual return is reviewed.

The IRS publication, *Tax Information on Disasters, Casualty Losses and Thefts,* makes the following points in reference to trees and shrubs:

Damage to trees and shrubs. If ornamental trees and shrubs on residential property are damaged or destroyed by a casualty, you may have a deductible casualty loss. To claim a deduction, you must establish that there has been a decrease in the total value of the real estate. A different rule applies in cases of such damage to property used for business purposes.

Disease. The loss of trees, shrubs, etc., on property used for residential purposes, as the result of disease, or fungus spread by beetles, insects, worms, etc., are not deductible as casualty losses.

Proof of Loss:

You must be able to prove that you actually sustained a casualty or theft loss and the amount of the loss that is deductible. You should be prepared to show:

1. *The nature of the casualty and when it occurred (in the case of theft, when it was discovered).*

2. *That the loss was the direct result of the casualty (or in the case of theft, that the property was actually stolen).*

3. *That you were the owner of the property.*

4. *The cost or other basis of the property, evidenced by purchase contract or deed, for example, (improvements should be supported by checks, receipts, etc.).*

5. *Depreciation allowed or allowable, if any.*

6. *Value before and after the casualty, for example, decrease in fair market value.*

7. *The amount of insurance or other compensation received or recoverable, including the value of repairs, restoration, and cleanup provided without cost by disaster relief agencies.*

If the preceding material is read carefully, three important factors stand out when computing the amount of a casualty loss for IRS purposes. These are:

1. The *decrease* in *fair market value* of the property as a result of the casualty.

2. The *adjusted basis* of the property.

3. The *amount of insurance or other compensation* you received or expect to receive as a result of the casualty.

In general, the amount of loss is the decrease in fair market value, limited to the adjusted basis, and reduced by any insurance or other reimbursement.

The problem of insurance compensation is straightforward. However, what is meant by *decrease in the fair market value* and *adjusted basis of property*?

Decrease in the Fair Market Value: This is the difference between the value of the property immediately before and immediately after the casu-

163

alty. It is not necessarily the cost of replacing or repairing the property and most certainly does not reflect any sentimental value. The loss has to be based on intrinsic value, apart from any sentimental or replacement value. The difference between the fair market value of the property immediately before and immediately after the casualty should be established by contacting an experienced and reliable appraiser. Any fees involved in this appraisal may be deducted as an expense of determining the tax liability but not as a part of the casualty loss deduction.

Adjusted Basis of Property: Most property is acquired by purchase. The amount paid for it is termed its "basis." However, if the property has been subjected to depreciation, previous casualty losses, or other recovery adjustments, the "basis" of the property must be reduced to reflect these amounts. Conversely, any expenditures for capital improvements should be added to the "basis." The end result is what is termed the "adjusted basis."

IRS $100 Limitation: In the computation of deductions for personal casualty losses the IRS requires that $100 be deducted from the final total loss value. For example, if the total loss is $2100 the actual amount you are allowed to claim is not $2100 but $2100 minus the $100 limitation, or $2000.

Below are two examples of casualty loss deductions. One involves personal casualty loss deduction, the other a business casualty loss deduction. Both involve landscape plant considerations.

Personal Casualty Loss Deduction: Different rules apply when determining the amount of personal casualty loss deduction in the case of real property (house and landscaping) and personal property (furniture, car, etc.).

In determining a loss to real property, all improvements, such as buildings and ornamental trees are considered an integral part of the realty, and a single casualty loss for the entire property is determined. The amount of loss deductible is computed by comparing the decrease in the fair market value of the entire property with its adjusted basis. The loss for tax purposes is the lesser of these amounts. From this amount you must subtract any insurance reimbursements, and finally the $100 limitation must also be deducted. For example:

You purchased a house several years ago paying $3000 for the land and $15,000 for the building. You also paid $1000 for landscaping. In June the residence was completely destroyed by fire. Competent appraisers determined that a fair market value immediately before the fire of $22,000 but only $5000 after the fire. Shortly after the fire, the insurance company paid you $15,000 for the loss of your residence. Your casualty loss would be computed as follows (IRS, 1976, pages 4 and 5):

1.	Value of the total property before the fire	$22,000.00
2.	Value of the total property after the fire	5,000.00
3.	Decrease in value of total property	$17,000.00
4.	Adjusted basis of entire property (land, building, and landscaping)	$19,000.00
5.	Loss sustained (lesser of 3 or 4)	$17,000.00
6.	Less insurance recovery	15,000.00
7.	Casualty loss before application of $100 limitation	2,000.00
8.	Less $100 limitation	100.00
9.	Casualty loss deduction	$ 1,900.00

However, what about damages to trees and shrubs? For example, you have paid $3000 for land and $30,000 for a new home. In addition you have spent $1250 landscaping, which includes $1000 for a 6 in. caliper, 25 ft tall blue spruce. A windstorm completely destroyed the blue spruce tree but left the house and remaining landscape plants unscathed. How would this casualty loss be calculated? The IRS has stated that trees and plants are considered an integral part of the property and no determination of fair market value of the house, land, and trees can be made separately. This presents a dilemma. However, there is a bright spot—read carefully the following excerpt out of the IRS booklet (page 5) on casualty losses.

If a storm damages trees or shrubs on property held for personal use (real property), the loss is the actual decrease in the value of the property as a whole. The cost of repairing the damage to the property may, in any particular case, serve as evidence of the overall loss to the property. However, the loss may not exceed the amount necessary to restore the property to its value just before the casualty.

Thus, replacement costs are acceptable as evidence of decrease in value. For example, a qualified appraiser valued the total property at $39,000 before the storm. This example is assuming some appreciation, which has been the rule for most homes in recent years. A nurseryman estimates replacement cost at $1500 for the blue spruces.* Your casualty loss deduction would be as follows:

1.	Value of the real property before the storm	$39,000.00
2.	Value of the total property after the storm, $39,000 − $1500	$37,500.00
3.	Decrease in the value of the total property	$ 1,500.00
4.	Adjusted basis of the entire property $3000 + $30,000 + $1250	$34,250.00
5.	Loss sustained (lesser of 3 or 4)	$ 1,500.00
6.	Less insurance recovery ($250 per tree)	250.00
7.	Total loss	$ 1,250.00
8.	Less $100 limitation	100.00
9.	Casualty loss deduction	$ 1,150.00

As we will discuss later, the problem of shrub and tree losses focuses mostly on how the loss is arrived at, that is, replacement costs versus individual shade-tree evaluation formulas.

Business Casualty Loss. Fortunately for businesses, the IRS is a little more lenient in claiming losses to landscape plants. With business property, the fair market value involves the individual items of property destroyed. Thus, if a business property loses ornamental plants or trees, the amount of the deduction is by reference to the volume of the plants lost and does not involve any change in the value of the entire property (Gustin, 1974). As stated by the IRS manual (page 5):

> A casualty loss to the business property or to property held for the production of income is determined by reference to the identifiable property damage. Thus, if damage occurs to a building and trees, the decrease in value is measured by taking each into account separately, with separate losses being determined for each.

For example, three years ago you purchased a house for rental purposes paying $3000 for the land and $15,000 for the building. You also paid $1000 for landscaping. For those years you were allowed total depreciation of

*This evaluation could also be done by an urban forester, horticulturist, or arborist.

$1125 for the building and $150 for the landscaping. In June, the house was completely destroyed by fire and severe damage was inflicted on the landscaping.

Competent appraisers determined that the trees and shrubs were worth $1500 before the fire but only $1000 after the fire. The trees and shrubs were not covered by insurance but the house was insured for its fair market value. Shortly after the fire, the insurance company paid you $17,500 in full settlement of its liability.

The gain or loss from the fire is determined as follows (IRS, 1976, p. 5):

		Building	Trees and Shrubs
1.	Value before fire		$1,500
2.	Value after fire		1,000
3.	Decrease in value		$ 500
4.	Adjusted basis	$13,875	$ 850
5.	Loss for trees and shrub decrease in value		$ 500
6.	Less insurance recovery	$17,500	None
7.	Gain from fire insurance proceeds on building	$ 3,625	
8.	Loss from fire damage to trees and shrubs		$ 500

As shown thus far in this section on legal values, it is not impossible to collect insurance payments or deduct tax losses for the casualty loss of trees and shrubs. However, it is important to understand the regulations in order to do so competently. With the material just discussed as source material and with their professional background, urban foresters are qualified to make the necessary appraisals. With time, insurance and IRS regulations will change and all should be reviewed and kept up to date for accurate appraisal.

Litigation and condemnation

Often foresters and arborists are asked to estimate tree values in condemnations and civil suits. Condemnation, according to the IRS, is "the exercise of a legal power of the Federal Government, a State Government, or political subdivision, to take privately owned property for any public use, upon an award and payment of a reasonable price for the property."

These usually involve city improvement projects, for example, new streets, parks, sewer lines, and water lines. They may also involve commercial utility firms rights-of-way (e.g., power and light companies and natural gas companies). Land having trees may be condemned, thus forcing an evaluation of the timber in addition to the land. In other cases, this may involve only the value of the trees removed. The evaluation procedure used depends on the use of the property. In some cases, forest timber evaluation procedures are appropriate. Where esthetic benefits of trees in urban areas or around rural homes are of paramount importance, the International Society of Arboriculture Shade Tree Evaluation Formula is used. The use of this formula is discussed later in this chapter.

In recent years the number of civil suits involving trees has increased substantially. This reflects the increasing concern for the legal values of trees and attempts to attach monetary values to what were previously considered intangible benefits. Such suits most often involve construction activities, herbicide drift, vandalism, and improper tree maintenance activities. A common factor in all of these suits is an appraisal of damage, which requires the professional expertise of a forester or an arborist using timber or shade tree evaluation procedures. Many suits end up in court, require additional testimony from the professional involved, and litigation may be prolonged for years. Kielbaso (1971) and Peters (1971) have presented information regarding litigation, IRS, and insurance settlements. Kielbaso (1971) in regard to litigation has stated:

> *Through time and many appealed cases, the following principles appear noteworthy:*
> **1.** *Most cases involving tree values are determined by measure of property value before and after tortious acts (this is most common, but not prescribed).*
> **2.** *Under appropriate circumstances, justice may dictate that the decision be based on the value of the tree or the reasonable cost of a reasonable restoration:*
> **a.** *The owner of an estate is entitled to have it in such condition as he wants.*
> **b.** *If an owner holds for a purpose, be it his own use or sale, he is entitled to compensation although the damage does not impair general market value.*
> **c.** *But an ornamental shade tree, upon land available for dwelling-houses, has a very different relation to the land, and may give it a special value.*

Kielbaso (1971) in citing cases under each of the above categories made the observation that:

Perhaps the point to note is that in the more recent cases the courts have been awarding damages for trees other than the property market-value reduction. They have even approached esthetics and even sentimental values, although this terminology is carefully avoided.

For the professional doing the evaluation for litigation the process more often than not is more complex than applying a simple formula. Often other factors come into focus such as woodland values versus residential values, simple shade tree evaluation versus replacement costs, cleanup costs, and site restoration costs.

Evaluation Formulas

As mentioned earlier the assigning of dollar values to shade and ornamental trees is important for a variety of reasons: determining city tree assets for budgetary purposes; insurance compensation for casualty losses; income tax deductions; condemnation; and litigation. The use of established shade tree evaluation formulas is very common and an accepted methodology in all of these except for income tax deductions. However, replacement costs can be applied in the case of IRS casualty loss deductions.

Shade tree evaluation formulas have evolved over the past century. One of the first involved an arbitrary system of valuation of $5 to $150 per tree. It was used to ascertain damage caused by horsedrawn carriages. In 1901, a professor at the University of Michigan devised a formula for shade tree valuation using a set figure of $15 plus compound interest at four percent for 25 years. This was known as the Roth Method. Sometime later a circumference method was devised that assigned an arbitrary value of $5 per circumference inch. This was followed by a diameter inch on a sliding scale and later a basal square foot and basal square inch method set values at $75 per square foot and 75¢ per square inch. The earliest generally accepted method was developed in the early 1900s by Dr. George Stone of the Massachusetts Agricultural College. His formula used as critical factors the size, location, and condition of trees. Dr. Stone later worked with Dr. E.P. Felt of the Bartlett Research Laboratories in an attempt to improve evaluation procedures. The result was the Felt method, which assigned a value of $1 per square inch of basal area at diameter breast height (dbh) and allowed for species, condition, location, and residential land values. The Felt formula was widely accepted and used by those in arboriculture for many years. In 1969, the Felt method was revised by O.W. Spicer for use by the

Bartlett Tree Experts Co. (Spicer, 1969). This is known as the Felt–Spicer Formula. It takes into account the following factors for computing tree values: size, species, basic value, location, condition, fluctuating land values, and the changing purchasing power of the dollar (inflation). The basic value is computed by determining the diameter of the tree and using the formula [$R^2 \times$ (cost of living index) = basic value in dollars] where R^2 is the radius of the tree at dbh squared. The base value is then adjusted up or down by the application of a species factor, condition factor, location factor, and an assessed property evaluation factor. The primary arguments against this method are that it is somewhat discriminatory to use assessed property values and that it also requires the additional expertise of a land assessor. Most foresters and arborists feel that a tree should have a value of its own separate from the value of the property involved.

Perhaps the most widely accepted method for shade tree evaluation is the one developed jointly by the International Shade Tree Conference (ISTC) and National Arborists Association (NAA). The method was first developed in 1951 and was accepted and published in 1957. Basically the ISTC Formula as originally devised was as follows:

Value of tree = basic value × species factor × condition factor

The basic value was determined by measuring the diameter of the stem at a point 4.5 (1.37 m) ft above the ground (dbh). This was then converted to square inches and multiplied by $5. Since 1957 the dollar value has been revised three times to account for inflation, and it now stands at $10 per square inch.

Species factor was based on local experience with various species in certain well-recognized geographic regions. It was expressed in five percentages classes of 100, 80, 60, 40, and 20.

Condition factor was also expressed in five classes: 100, 80, 60, 40, and 20 percent. In this matter, considerations of age, location, disease, and so on were to be weighed.

Very recently the ISTC formula was revised and refinements added (ISA, 1975). The previous formula was not without fault. It presented no procedure for evaluating shrubs, underestimated values for smaller trees, and overestimated values for large trees. The new formula stresses the professional aspects of shade tree evaluation (Chadwick, 1975). It also incorporates new guidelines to allow for replacement values to be used for shrubs and for small trees under 12 in. (30.48 cm) in diameter. This is normally done by consulting with nurseries that can supply the appropriate stock of a given species in the size desired. It also considers such factors as availability, area problems, removal costs of casualty trees, and guarantees. Normally, the value exceeds the $10 per square inch category used in larger

170

trees. The actual calculation for trees and shrubs under 12 in. in diameter is as follows:

Tree value = basic replacement cost × species factor × condition factor × location factor

The basic value is computed using tree caliper to determine the basal area in square inches. This is done by applying the American Standards for Nursery Practice in caliper measurements: for trees up to 4 in. in caliper the basal area is computed using tree caliper measurements at 6 in. above the ground and 12 in. above the ground for those over 4 in. in caliper; and a location factor has been added in five classes of 100, 80, 60, 40, and 20 percent. This percent class is judged from architectural, engineering, climate, and esthetic benefits that take into account such functional values as shade, screening, sound, and climate amelioration. It can also be extended for use on trees in park settings.

Trees that range from 13 to 40 in. (33.02 to 101.6 cm) are evaluated by the following formula:

Tree value = basic value × species factor × condition factor × location factor

Size in these larger trees is based upon cross sectional area in square inches at diameter breast height or 4.5 ft (30.48 cm) above ground level. Another revision in trees of the 13 to 40 in. (33.02 to 101.6 cm) category involves evaluation of multiple stem specimen trees.

Evaluation of shade trees above 40 in. (101.6 cm) in caliper are left to the judgment of the professional involved. Specifically this is designed to eliminate the problem of the excessively high values that such trees generate by strict application of the formula. It allows for the professional judgment of foresters, arborists, and horticulturists on an individual case basis, using the knowledge and experience that qualifies only them to make such determinations.

It is hoped that with the revisions noted, the new formula of the ISTC (now the International Society of Arboriculture) will become a standard method to be used in the computing casualty losses for not only the insurance industry and the courts but the Internal Revenue Service as well.

Bibliography

Chadwick, L. C., "ASCA Recommendations for Modification of the ISTC Shade Tree Evaluation Formula," *Journal of Arboriculture,* 1(2):35–38, 1975.

171

Dressel, K., "Street and Park Evaluation," in *Proceedings of Midwest Shade Tree Conference,* 18:105–112, 1963.

Edlin, H., "Amenity Values in British Forestry," *Forestry,* 36:65–89, 1963.

Felt, E. P., *Our Shade Trees,* Orange Judd Publishing Co., 1942.

Foster, C., "Forestry in Megalopolis," *Proceedings of Society of American Foresters Meeting,* 65–67, 1965.

Gould, E., "Values, Trees and the Urban Realm," *Symposium on Trees and Forests in an Urbanizing Environment,* University of Massachusetts, Amherst, pp. 79–91, 1970.

Gustin, Guy, Jr., "Viewpoint of IRS and Insurance Agencies on Shade Tree Values," *Journal of Arboriculture,* 1(3):58–60, 1975.

Hatcher, O., "Scope of Shade Tree Care in Region 5 of the International Shade Tree Conference," *Proceedings of International Shade Tree Conference,* 41:114–119, 1965.

Internal Revenue Service, *Tax Information on Disasters, Casualty Losses, and Thefts,* Publication 547, 1976.

International Society of Arboriculture, *A Guide to the Professional Evaluation of Landscape Trees, Specimen Shrubs and Evergreens,* 1975.

Johnson, I., "Planning and Implementing a Municipal Street Tree Program," *Proceedings of International Shade Tree Conference,* 32:219–229, 1956.

Kielbaso, J. James, "Economic Values of Trees in the Urban Locale," *Symposium on the Role of Trees in the South's Urban Environment,* pp. 82–94, 1971.

Micha, Frederick, R., "Trees Should Have Standing," *Journal of Arboriculture,* 1(4):78–80, 1975.

Payne, Brian R., "Trees Could Make A Difference In The Selling of Your Home," Northeastern Forest Experiment Station, Forest Science Photo Story No. 26, 1975.

Payne, Brian R. and Steven Strom, "The Contribution of Trees to the Appraised Value of Unimproved Residential Land," *Valuation,* 22(2):36–45, 1975.

Peters, Lewis C., "Shade and Ornamental Tree Evaluation," *Journal of Forestry,* 69(7):411–413, 1971.

Purcell, C., "The Realty Value of Trees," in *Proceedings of International Shade Tree Conference,* 32:128–135, 1956.

Schiff, C., "What Is Happening in Municipal Arboriculture in New York," in *Proceedings of the International Shade Tree Conference,* 45:121–217, 1969.

Spicer, O.W., *Appraising Shade and Ornamental Trees,* Bartlett Tree Experts, Stanford, Conn., 12 p., 1969.

Stone, Christopher D., *Should Trees Have Standing—Towards Legal Rights for Natural Objects,* William Kaufmann, University of California, Los Altos, California, 1974.

Tilford, P., "How Many Street Trees?" *Tree Magazine,* 17(5):24, 1957.

Weeds, Trees and Turf, "More Funds for Tree Care," *Weeds, Trees and Turf,* 9(12):16–17, 1970.

8
MUNICIPAL
FORESTRY
ADMINISTRATION

How well the urban forest is managed depends on attitudes, knowledge, and financial resources of its various owners, both public and private. The degree of management of the municipally owned forest is largely an expression of the priority given by city officials. This priority is in turn largely a manifestation of citizen concern. Successful management of the municipal forest generally requires: (1) strong administration; (2) effective legislation; (3) efficient organization; (4) sound planning; and (5) adequate funding.

Administrative Structure

Most municipal forestry programs are administered by commissions, boards, or other authorities. These generally take three forms: (1) advisory; (2) policymaking; and (3) operational.

Advisory boards or commissions have no direct authority or responsibility for policy or administration. Their duties are to study and investigate and give counsel to the city administration. They have no authority to expend funds or to conduct actual operations. Figure 8.1 shows the relationship of such boards to the city government.

Policymaking boards are semi-independent with policymaking and administrative authority for municipal forest management (Figure 8.2). Legislative authority varies, but they generally have responsibility for program planning and implementation. They are responsible for program budgets, but are answerable to higher administrative authority in program conduct and expenditure of funds. Most of the small towns involved in the Kansas Community Forestry Program operate with such boards. This program is discussed in detail in Chapter 9.

Operational commissions are independent of municipal administrative structures. They have full responsibility for policy formulation and program implementation. They are clearly distinguished from the other types by independent financing based on tax levies. Fund disbursement is the clear responsibility of such commissions and cannot be interferred with. Decision making is not passed to another body. Such commissions are similar to school boards in legislative authority and responsibility.

Operational responsibilities of commissions vary depending on organizational structures. Chadwick has listed some possible combinations (Chadwick, 1972):

1. A municipal street tree commission with jurisdiction over street, boulevard, and highway trees only.

2. A municipal shade tree commission with jurisdiction over all trees on streets, parkways, and in parks and public places.

Parks and Recreation Department

Administrative Board

Advisory Board

Parks and Recreation Department

Figure 8.1 An organizational chart of a park and recreation department having an advisory shade tree board.

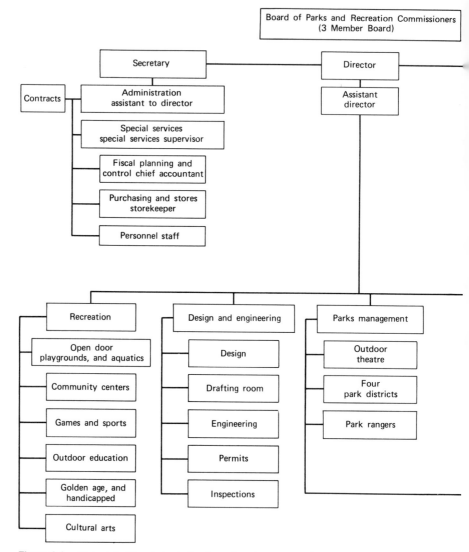

Figure 8.2 An organizational chart of a city park and recreation department having a policymaking board.

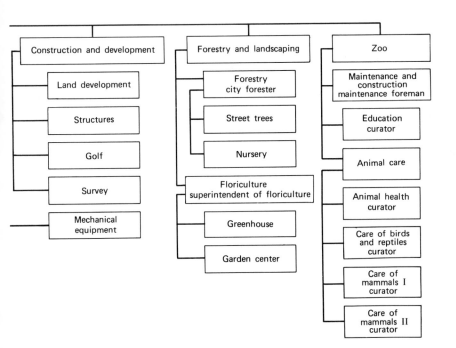

```
┌─────────────────┐
│    Planning     │
└─────────────────┘
```

Construction and development	Forestry and landscaping	Zoo
Land development	Forestry city forester	Maintenance and construction maintenance foreman
Structures	Street trees	Education curator
Golf	Nursery	Animal care
Survey	Floriculture superintendent of floriculture	Animal health curator
Mechanical equipment	Greenhouse	Care of birds and reptiles curator
	Garden center	Care of mammals I curator
		Care of mammals II curator

3. A municipal park and/or park and forestry commission that is similar to the two commissions just mentioned but encompasses other park activities beyond jurisdiction over shade or ornamental trees.

4. A municipal park and recreation commission that combines parks and forestry.

However structured and organized, municipal forestry boards or commissions should have clearly defined responsibilities and should be as free from political interference as possible. It is very important that capable people serve. They should be public-minded citizens, dynamic, and able to make and carry out decisions.

There must be ready access to technical and legal expertise, either through the qualifications of individual board members or through available outside experts. In cities with professional staffs, technical forestry input is from the city forester. In other cases, it may be from consultants or state or federal agency professionals. Legal expertise is most often from city attorneys. Often an attorney is included as an ex officio member of the board.

Ordinances

City tree ordinances form the legal base for municipal forestry programs. They authorize and require city governments to care for trees and other vegetation in specific ways in order to provide for the health, safety, and well-being of residents. City tree ordinances vary from simple statements of authority and responsibility to lengthy prescriptions for management. For the most part, ordinances deal with streetside and other public trees. However, consideration is given to trees on private property that represent hazards to public well-being. They may include some or all of the following:

1. Definitions.
2. Establishment of a tree board or commission (composition, terms of office, duties, procedures).
3. Title to and responsibility for trees on public property.
4. Designation of a city forester and other officials (duties, authority).
5. Planting requirements (permits, official species, spacing, and location).
6. Maintenance (specifications and clarifying the responsibility of adjacent property owners).
7. Removal requirements and specifications.

8. Condemnation of trees on private property.

9. Requirements of public utilities and private tree care firms (licensing and insurance).

10. Prohibition of interference with commission or its agents.

11. Violations and penalties.

12. Specifications and standards of practice (may be written into the ordinance or attached as an appendix).

Detailed ordinances that require the intensive management of streetside and other public trees by adjacent property owners are often difficult to enforce. Knowledge of this difficulty has led many people to conclude that city tree ordinances are of generally little value. There is indeed little relationship between lengthy and detailed ordinances and the quality of municipal forest management. There is, however, a strong relationship between the quality of management and the quality of program administration. There should be no doubt that ordinances are necessary as well as basic to municipal forestry administration. They legalize commissions or boards and municipal forestry departments. They set forth requirements for public safety and authorize management. How well the forest is managed depends on how well what is authorized is provided for.

Ordinances must be specific to the needs of individual cities. Needs vary by city size, location, planting history, vegetation types and organizational structure, and by the requirements of state and federal governments. The International Society of Arboriculture has prepared "A Standard Municipal Tree Ordinance" as a model that has been widely used (ISA, 1972). Appendix II contains two model ordinances—one used in the Kansas Community Forestry Program, and another developed for the Atlanta, Georgia, area. In both cases, the ISA ordinance was used as a base.

Municipal Tree Inventories

Before an effective municipal tree program can be developed, it is essential to know the situation of the public tree population. This can best be determined by a formal inventory. The information acquired is invaluable in program planning and subsequent management. Inventories may be divided by street and park trees or trees on other areas. Street tree inventories may be further divided by land use zones or other geographic or developmental areas within the city.

In city tree inventories, it is desirable to obtain the following information:

1. Total number of trees.
2. Species composition.
3. Tree location.
4. Size composition.
5. Age composition.
6. Condition class.
7. Management needs (pruning, wound treatment, insect and disease control, and removals).
8. Planting needs.
9. Total tree values.

A difficult problem in tree inventories is locating trees for future reference. One solution has been to number trees on a street individually; however, such a system is invalidated when trees are removed or planted. In another system of inventory house or lot numbers have been given to tree locations. This is made difficult by trees on lot boundary lines. Probably the surest system involves distances from street intersections. This fixes the location so that any question as to what tree to prune or remove (etc.) can be resolved by measuring the distance noted. An inventory system we have developed is given in Appendix III. This system can be used manually or by computer.

A computer inventory system lends itself well to city tree management by providing easy access to data for developing planting plans, planning for dead tree removal, implementing systematic maintenance schedules, and controlling insect and disease situations. A useful aspect of computerized inventory data is that some system of cross tabulation can provide combinations of variables and can enable specific areas of management needs to be mapped. Information such as condition class by species, management needs by species and location, planting needs by size and location, removal needs by location and difficulty class is readily available. In all cases, it can be retrieved very rapidly and with minimal effort.

Based on the information obtained from the inventory, municipal foresters can revise and update street tree management programs. For example, planting requirements can be determined by location, concentration, species, and number. This can be determined citywide by area, by street, or by block. Proper selections of species can then be made, purchase requirements determined, and planting schedules formulated.

Tree removals follow the same format. Location and concentrations are known as well as removal difficulty class. Thus projections of equipment and man-hours, along with systematic schedules, can be formulated.

Tree maintenance can also be addressed fully. From the inventory, maintenance needs (e.g., pruning, wound repair, insect and disease control) can be determined citywide. Systematic schedules can then be developed and priority areas designated for effectively assigning work crews and equipment.

In larger cities, subsample techniques may be considered to reduce inventory expense. Usually tract development areas are quite homogenous with respect to tree species. Therefore, instead of 100 percent inventories, 10 or 20 percent subsamples of tree populations might be all that are needed to provide adequate information for various projects. Although the specifics for individual trees are lost, all aspects of an overview are retained.

Inventory data can also be used to estimate shade tree values. By using shade tree valuation formulas, values can be produced for the total tree population, for each species, or for individual trees. Such values can be used to stress the importance of a city's tree resources and to support budget requests.

Formulating an annual budget requires factual information. How many trees need pruning, fertilizing, insect and disease control, or removal? What are the total planting requirements? The inventory data can answer those questions. Based on the data, purchases of supplies and materials can be accurately forecast, manpower requirements determined, and assessments made regarding contract and in-service work.

A tree inventory system provides only data. Effective use of the data is the key to budget maximization. Savings in annual operating costs alone may offset inventory costs. Those responsible for municipal forestry programs benefit from efficient operation, the urban forest benefits from proper care, and the residents have a better environment.

A sample city street tree inventory system adaptable for either manual or computer data retrieval is given in Appendix III.

Financing

Municipal forestry programs cannot be effective without adequate financing. There are many services competing for public funds. Forestry programs have often a lower priority and thus are sometimes not sufficiently funded to carry out necessary management activities. It is important that good public relations be maintained and programs actively "sold" as to their benefits. Principal funding sources for municipal forestry programs include: (1) general funds; (2) capital funds; (3) municipal front-foot assessment; (4) special block or street assessments; and (5) permit fees.

Most municipal forestry programs are financed through general funds on the basis of a budget request made by the tree commission or the department under which the program is operated. Budgets are based on program needs and requests have to be justified. Major items are wages and salaries, supplies and new equipment, plant materials, operation and repairs, and equipment. These requests are submitted to the municipal governing body where final appropriations are made.

Capital funds are outlays for improvements that require the passing and issuance of revenue bonds. They most often involve specific needs such as tree planting after widespread disasters such as Dutch elm disease, tornados, or windstorms. In these cases, a special capital outlay is needed over normal operations. This need is presented to the populace and they decide by vote whether or not to issue the revenue bonds.

Another method of funding street tree programs is by property assessments. Here real property is assessed a certain amount for each foot of frontage. Resulting funds are then earmarked for personnel and equipment to perform the necessary management operations. Usually the right to levee such an assessment is based on state statutes. This type of funding does not have to be approved by public vote but by the action of the city council. It does, however, have to be voted on by the council from year to year.

Block or street assessment funding starts when a majority of the homeowners vote to subscribe to a tree management program. Once this majority has made this decision, the assessment is levied for all property owners on the block or street involved.

A permit method is often used in tree planting programs. Here the property owner pays for a tree to be planted by the city forestry department. It should be noted that the latter three funding sources (front-foot assessment, block assessment, and permit fee) often do not generate sufficient funds for good tree programs. When coupled with a general fund appropriation, however, they can provide for excellent programs.

In recent years, federal revenue sharing and other federal programs have provided additional sources of funds for municipal forestry programs. Table 8.1 gives sources of tree care funds as reported by Kielbaso and Ottman.

In smaller municipalities there may not be a sufficient public fund to conduct all operations. In developing programs for such communities, tree boards or commissions must look at three areas: (1) What can individual property owners do? (2) What can be accomplished by community action projects? And (3) what must require a city budget?

In most small towns, property owners are responsible for the planting and maintenance of street trees. It should thus be made as easy as possible for them to do whatever is necessary for street trees. This can be done by helping them select proper species, by providing accurate information, and by sponsoring projects where they are given opportunities to participate in tree management.

Nearly every community has organizations that want to become involved in city improvement programs each year—civic groups, service clubs, garden clubs, senior citizen groups, youth organizations, and the like. Forestry projects are often welcomed by them. Their efforts can accomplish much if they are coordinated to assure that program goals and priorities are considered.

Individual or group efforts will not accomplish everything as some tasks require the commitment of public funds. Most community governments expect to spend money on a forestry program provided that they are assured that the money will be spent effectively. Thus, as mentioned earlier, the program or plan should define priorities. In most cases, top priority for public funds will have to be for the maintenance and removal of trees on public property—projects that do not lend themselves well to individual or community group efforts.

Maintenance Contracts

Many communities find that it is more economical to let contracts for tree planting, pruning, and removal rather than to invest in equipment and staff to conduct the work. In an article Plinkerton (1968) states that before bids are called for the city forester or responsible individual should check with the administrative or legal branch of municipal government to comply with the law and to determine procedures and requirements for all contracts (e.g., in regard to licenses or insurance).

Here are 12 points that should be considered in preparing bid specifications (Plinkerton, 1968):

1. *Bidders should be required to carefully examine the site of the proposed work and judge for themselves as to the nature of work to be done and the conditions under which it has to be accomplished. A proposal from each bidder should be requested so that it is assured that he has accomplished this task and understands the character, quantity and quality of the work to be done.*

2. *Bids should be submitted in a sealed envelope, opened in public and read at a prearranged time. All bids should show the proposed prices clearly, legibly and must be properly signed by the bidder.*

3. *Bidders must be competent and capable of satisfactorily performing the work covered by the proposal. They should be able to furnish references as to similar work experience, the plan or*

TABLE 8.1

Sources of Tree Care Funds

Classification	No. of Cities Reporting (A)	General Property Tax		Special Frontage Tax		Tree Mill Levy		City Income Tax		Endowment		Vehicle Tax		Emergency Employment Act		Revenue Sharing		Other[2]	
		No.	% of (A)	No.	% of (A)	No.	% of (A)	No.	% of (A)	No.	% of (A)	No.	% of (A)	No.	% of (A)	No.	% of (A)	No.	% of (A)
Total of all cities	700	596	85	12	2	63	9	79	11	9	1	53	8	49	7	132	19	124	18
Population group																			
Over 500,000	23	21	91	1	4	2	9	4	17	0	0	5	22	5	22	5	22	6	26
250,000–500,000	20	16	80	1	5	2	10	4	20	0	0	2	10	4	20	7	35	4	20
100,000–249,999	67	60	90	3	4	9	13	9	13	3	4	4	6	7	10	27	40	16	24
50,000– 99,999	148	120	81	6	4	12	8	16	11	2	1	12	8	9	4	21	14	29	20
25,000– 49,999	273	234	86	1	...	23	8	34	12	1	...	19	7	15	5	49	18	51	19
10,000– 24,999	100	84	84	0	0	8	8	6	6	2	2	9	9	5	5	14	14	12	12
5,000– 9,999	39	34	87	0	0	2	5	3	8	1	3	0	0	2	5	3	8	4	10
2,500– 4,999	30	27	90	0	0	5	17	3	10	0	0	2	7	2	7	6	20	2	7
Geographic region																			
Northeast	167	150	90	2	1	5	3	13	8	3	2	5	3	10	6	22	13	14	8
North Central	223	181	81	4	2	30	13	32	14	4	2	23	10	18	8	38	17	34	15
South	134	114	85	1	1	12	9	17	13	0	0	2	1	8	6	43	32	26	19
West	176	151	86	5	3	16	9	17	10	2	1	23	13	13	7	29	16	50	28

Metro/city type																		
Central	215	179	83	6	3	22	10	33	15	5	2	18	8	22	10	50	23	45	21
Suburban	341	300	88	6	2	24	7	35	10	0	0	29	9	17	5	54	16	55	16
Independent	144	117	81	0	0	17	12	11	8	4	3	6	4	10	7	28	19	24	17
Form of government																		
Mayor-council	219	188	86	1	. . .	16	7	27	12	4	2	15	7	19	9	41	19	30	14
Council-manager	427	370	87	11	3	36	8	46	11	5	1	37	9	29	7	79	19	83	19
Commission	31	20	65	0	0	10	32	4	13	0	0	1	3	1	3	11	35	9	29
Town meeting	12	10	83	0	0	1	8	0	0	0	0	0	0	0	0	1	8	1	8
Rep. town meeting	11	8	73	0	0	0	0	2	18	0	0	0	0	0	0	0	0	1	9

Note: Percentages, when totaled, exceed 100% because some respondents indicated more than one source.

Leaders (. . .) indicate rounds to less than 0.5%.

[1]Vehicle tax includes both state and local taxes on motor vehicles.

[2]Some of the other sources of tree care funds reported by cities were: tree sales (27), gas and weight taxes (26), state and federal categorical grants (20), and municipal water and utility charges (10). Cities also reported that some tree care funds were obtained from subdivision developer fees, city sales taxes, parking meter revenues, bond issues, and miscellaneous other sources.

Source: Kenneth A. Ottman and J. James Kielbaso, *Managing Municipal Trees*, Urban Data Service Reports, Vol. 8, No. 11 (Washington, D.C.: International City Management Association, November 1976).

procedure proposed to accomplish the work and the organization and equipment available to accomplish the task.

4. *The award of the contract should be to the lowest responsible and qualified bidder whose proposal complies with the requirements. However, the right to reject any and all bids should be reserved to best serve the interests of the city.*

5. *The contractor should understand that he is required to perform and complete the work in a thorough and workmanlike manner and to furnish and provide all the necessary labor and equipment to accomplish the task.*

6. *In the case of a cash contract, the city or agency should reserve the right to make an increase or decrease in the quantity of work to be performed and to correspondingly increase or decrease the amount to be paid to the contractor.*

7. *The contractor should be required to clean the site of rubbish or debris caused by his activity at the end of each working day and leave the site in a neat, orderly, and presentable condition.*

8. *All work to be performed should be subject to the direct supervision of the city forester or duly appointed official and should meet with his approval concerning the provisions and requirements of the bid.*

9. *The contractor should be required to carry public liability insurance as required by the city and to furnish a 10-day cancellation notice clause certificate to the city or agency in charge. In addition he should be required to secure, maintain in full force and effect, and bear the cost of complete workmen's compensation insurance for the duration of the contract. It should be understood that the city or agency will not be responsible for any claims or suits relative thereto.*

10. *The contractor should make adequate provisions to accommodate normal traffic over the public streets during the duration of the work so as to minimize public inconvenience. This includes ingress and egress of occupants of private property and the furnishing of the necessary barriers, guards, and lights to protect the public.*

11. *The contractor should be aware that he is responsible for the preservation of all public and private property in the work area and should exercise due caution in his operation to include protection of plant materials, street signs and lights. He should further understand that he will be required to bear the*

expense of correcting such damage and repair it in an accepta-
ble manner if it occurs.

12. *At the completion of his work the contractor should notify the*
responsible public official that he is ready for final inspection.
When this inspection is completed and the work passed, pay-
ment can then be made.

In addition to a written list of bid specifications, bidders should be given an idea of what a finished product is expected to look like. The contract should be awarded after weighing carefully the price, reputation, experience, and physical ability of the contractor to accomplish the work in the time specified. Prior to starting the job, it would be wise to meet with the contractor and review all of the conditions including requirements for traffic control and public safety. A sample call for bids can be found in Appendix 4, which illustrates how a bid is worded to cover the 12 points listed previously.

BIBLIOGRAPHY

Chadwick, L.C., "Some Important Aspects of a Municipal Tree Ordinance," *International Shade Tree Conference Proceedings,* 48:53–58, 1972.

Neely, D. and E.B. Himelick, eds., *A Standard Municipal Tree Ordinance,* International Shade Tree Conference, Inc., 2nd ed., 14 p., 1972.

Plinkerton, C.J., "Contracting of Tree Work and Cost Accounting," *International Shade Tree Conference Proceedings,* Western Chapter, 44:284–293, 1968.

9
INFORMATION,
EDUCATION
AND TRAINING

Information, education, and training programs are necessary for effective management of the urban forest. Property owners have the obvious need to be informed and educated concerning care of their trees. Private tree care firms benefit from an informed clientele and have special training needs for their personnel. In this chapter, we will look at information, education, and training largely from the standpoint of municipal forestry departments, as these departments have the largest responsibility and opportunity to influence management of the urban forest.

Information and Education

Information and education cannot be clearly separated. It can easily be argued that one is impossible without the other. The distinction was perhaps best made by the sage old school superintendent who said, "information is telling them what and education is them understanding why."

Information and education are necessary for three basic reasons: (1) to generate action by private property owners; (2) to gain acceptance of forestry programs; and (3) to create a favorable image of the department.

Generation of action by property owners

Municipal forestry departments have a responsibility to manage the total urban forest environment. As discussed in Chapter 6, this responsibility has limitations, as forestry departments have direct control over a limited part of the urban forest. They have direct control as prescribed by ordinance, policy, and tradition over city-owned areas such as parks and treelawns. However, areas of the urban forest in private ownership must largely be managed indirectly by the city. There is a limited opportunity for direct management as provided by ordinances that empower the city to remove hazardous trees and control epidemic insects and diseases, for example. However, most of what is done is by private owners. It is the objective of responsible city forestry departments to influence the forestry efforts of private owners in the best interests of the total forest environment. Therefore a vigorous information and education program is necessary.

The two objectives in such a program are: (1) to effect better general tree management by private owners; and (2) to make private owners more receptive to specific management needs. The former is self-explanatory, as proper selection, planting, pruning, and other maintenance are in the best interests of all the forest. In the latter, a certain practice might be desired by the city forestry department, but authority to require it is lacking. Examples are nonepidemic insect outbreaks where control measures would be desirable but not vitally necessary. In such cases, specific procedures would be recommended to property owners. A specific example is on the Great Plains where cities often have a preponderance of Siberian elms, and infestations of elm leaf beetles are common. These insects rarely cause trees to die but make them unsightly and result in annoyance to residents. Many cities instigate spray programs on public trees and request that property owners spray their trees. Cooperation is often good and felt to be proportional to information and education efforts.

Acceptance of forestry program

Acceptance of the urban forestry program by the public is absolutely necessary, both from the standpoint of existence of the department and the implementation of specific practices. Programs of city government are largely proportional to citizen interest and demand. It is a political and practical reality that interest in a forestry program must be fostered, particularly in an environment of intense competition for public funds.

Urban forestry practices cannot be carried out without some degree of inconvenience to the public. Traffic must be rerouted, parked automobiles must be moved, and noise and dust are often raised. Obviously, if citizens are to tolerate these inconveniences, they must believe that the work is worthwhile. Public acceptance comes from an understanding of what is to be done and why it is necessary plus tangible, positive results of the work. This is closely related to another reason for information and education programs: a favorable image.

Creation of a favorable image

A favorable public image makes urban forest management easier. There is more acceptance of management practices if the department is respected. A favorable image is vital also to adequate budgets. This is a practical and political reality as suggested previously.

A favorable image results from doing the job well and having the public recognize that it was done well. Thus, the public relations program of a forestry department must be its total activity. It cannot be a veneer campaign to tell everyone what good guys they are. As suggested by Cook (1974), every organization has, by its existence, PR—good, bad, or indifferent—and any management decision transferred into action says something about the organization. A PR person or campaign does not "create" the department's image, but can articulate the policies and draw attention to the activities that qualify it for its reputation.

Public relations must permeate every function of a forestry department. Any specific activity (e.g., tree removal, pruning, or insect control) should be preceded by public announcements of what is to be done, why it is necessary, what it will involve, and how long it will take. The key effort should be in explaining the "what" and "why," based on the premise that understanding leads to acceptance. The limitations should be recognized, however, as there will inevitably be people who will not hear, will not understand, and may not accept.

Information and education methods and opportunities

Few municipal forestry departments are large and complex enough to have separate information and education divisions. Thus, PR must be the job of the total department. It takes two forms: (1) PR as a part of the everyday job; and (2) special PR efforts.

As suggested, every organization has, by its existence, PR. In the case of municipal forestry departments, equipment and personnel are noticed by everyone and the results of planting, pruning, and other work are also often visible. It is important that this visibility be in the best light. The ingredients of good on-the-job PR are simple: (1) good equipment—well maintained and clean; (2) good personnel—well trained and courteous; and (3) high quality work. There can be little doubt that courteous personnel in clean work clothes or department uniforms make a better impression. Likewise, clean, well-maintained equipment with the city seal and department name clearly displayed contribute to a good impression. The overall impression of a job well done, however, must result from just that—the job being well done.

The successful completion of a job and the correct impression that it was done well requires preliminary work. The job should result in as little inconvenience to the public as possible. Thus, it should be scheduled around events or activities that concentrate people and vehicles in a particular area. Through the media the public should be given notice about what is to be done, why, and how long it will take. If traffic is to be rerouted, alternate routes should be suggested. Specific notices to residents of the neighborhood where the work is to be done may also be necessary or desirable. It is obviously poor PR to surprise a neighborhood by showing up one morning, blocking off the street and starting chainsaws, trucks, and chippers.

Public relations communications must be two-way. The public must have access to the forestry department, and response to questions and problems should be quick. The public must be able to contact the department. The telephone number should be easy to find. There is no surer way of frustrating the public than to be unreachable by telephone, or to have inquiries responded to by unqualified personnel.

In addition to utilization of local news media for announcements, special projects are also desirable. Feature articles concerning forestry programs can be arranged. There is perhaps no better method of putting the good works of the department before the public than through a well-written and illustrated feature story. Most major newspapers have lawn and garden editors responsible for daily or weekly columns. These columns can be very helpful in recommending species and practices. A good working relationship with the media is extremely important. This relationship should be cultivated and maintained and should transcend personnel changes.

There are many clubs and organizations that can be helpful in the total forestry program. Civic and service clubs often seek environmental projects. Such projects can be designated by the city forester and their existence made known to club members. Projects should, of course, be a part of the city forestry plan and consistent with the overall program.

Garden clubs can be excellent ambassadors of city forestry programs. Their meetings offer an opportunity to explain the programs. Their projects in parks and other public areas can also make a significant contribution.

Many city forestry departments conduct special projects with schools, Scouts, and other youth groups. These can be informational or active projects such as tree planting or cleanup. Their long range purpose is to foster an appreciation of the urban forest.

Arbor Day ceremonies offer excellent opportunities for focusing attention on the urban forest. Ceremonies can be as simple or elaborate as desired, and can involve young and old people. Though normally associated with tree planting, Arbor Day can also stress the management of the total urban forest environment. Mayors, other city officials, and community leaders are generally happy to participate in Arbor Day ceremonies, often from a genuine concern for trees and often because of a "photo opportunity."

PR opportunities are as varied as the urban forester's imagination. Historic or heritage tree identification, specimen tree designation, and participation in the Tree City USA program are examples.* Each must be kept in perspective, however, and careful assessment made of their potential contribution to the urban forestry mission.

Communication with consulting urban foresters, commercial arborists, landscape architects, nursery people, university extension personnel, and other professionals is extremely important. In many cities, periodic meetings are held with such professionals to discuss common problems, update knowledge, and coordinate activities. All of them have an interest in managing the urban forest, and each can have a positive (or negative) impact on the city forestry program.

Commercial arborists have a large influence on the urban forest, as they are physically responsible for much of what is done. Arborists vary from highly trained competent professionals to unskilled laborers with little knowledge of the resource with which they work. A good rapport with commercial arborists is important in that it can provide the base for better

*For a description of the Tree City USA program, see Chapter 10, pp. 215.

management of the forest. Policies, standards, and specifications can be made available for licensing and contract bid purposes. Many cities require commercial arboriculture firms to be licensed for work within the city. In some situations, work on private property can be coordinated with management activities on public areas. This is particularly applicable in cases of insect or disease outbreaks.

Information and education (public relations) are key facilitators of municipal forestry programs. They are necessary to both short-range activities and long-range goals. They involve a communications flow from the forestry department to the public, and from the public to the department.

Training

The distinction between training and formal education is not clear. It can be argued that one is not possible without the other, or that they are one and the same. However, for the purposes of this chapter, we will attempt to separate them and will consider training as continuing education, beyond the prerequisite educational requirements of the job.

The training of urban forestry personnel is necessary for the following reasons:

1. To meet basic job standards.
2. To meet requirements of federal, state, and local laws.
3. To apply new technology.
4. To meet standards for certification or licensing.

Training to meet basic job standards

The necessity for training to meet basic job standards becomes apparent when the tasks and decisions of various urban forestry field operations are considered. Before considering these, it should be noted that a complex process of decisions and tasks is also necessary at the administrative level prior to field operations. Obviously, decisions must be made about priorities, locations, designs, information and education, and a host of other factors.

In the example of field operations, shown in Table 9.1, tasks are identified and decisions necessary to each are noted. The position level (C = crew, F = foreman, P = professional) at which each task is carried out and each decision made is indicated. Such a listing of task and decision levels helps to identify the expertise necessary to each. Training needs by levels can be determined then more readily. This listing also suggests the necessity of communicating decisions to the position level where the task is carried out. For example, the decision on the methods and materials to be used in staking and guying newly planted trees is made at the professionl level. These decisions are communicated to the crew level where they become policy or standard operating procedure. The communication process is at the heart of personnel training.

Training can be formal or informal and can vary from structured courses to show and tell sessions between supervisors and employees. In-service training can be on a recurring schedule or during inclement weather. The advantage of scheduled training is that instructors and employees know when to expect it and can be better prepared. Training during inclement weather has the obvious advantage of efficient use of otherwise unproductive time. Most urban forestry organizations utilize both approaches according to need.

After training needs are clearly identified, there is the problem of finding qualified instructors. Baumgardt suggests to look first within the organization (Baumgardt, 1974). There might well be staff personnel qualified by work experience who could do a good job of training with proper reference materials and tools. Instructors can also be found through public agencies or professional or trade associations. Qualified consultants can also be engaged.

The content of the training course is extremely important. It must be relevant and presented at a level consistent with employee ability to comprehend. Most training in urban forestry work involves classroom explanation and outdoor demonstrations. Training of tree and shrub pruning perhaps illustrates this best.

Proper pruning involves not only a knowledge of tools and techniques, but an understanding of plant materials, plant growth, and response to pruning. Teaching this important job should include lectures, demonstrations, chalk-talk, the use of visual aids, and supervised practice. Employees should understand the "why" as well as the "how" of pruning. There are practical limits here, though, depending on employee ability and job needs.

Training to meet requirements of laws

Training is necessary to meet requirements of federal, state, and local laws. At the federal level, two recent laws have had a profound influence on urban forestry: (1) the Federal Environmental Pesticide Control Act of 1972; and (2) the Occupational Safety and Health Act of 1971. Both laws are based on the government's right to protect the health and safety of the public.

The Federal Environmental Pesticide Control Act requires all state laws concerning pesticide use to conform to its provisions. Under law, applicators of pesticides must be certified. Certified applicators are either "private" or "commercial." Commercial applicators, including most arborists, are certified to apply "restricted use" pesticides. A pesticide is clas-

TABLE 9.1

Tasks and Decisions in
Urban Forestry Field Operations

Task	Position Level of Task	Decisions	Decision Level
Tree Planting			
Designate spots where trees are to be planted	F P	Planting spots by species based on plan or site factors	F P
Supply trees to planting site	C F	Vehicle to be used, handling procedures, and on-site storage system	F P
Dig planting hole	C	Size of hole needed and digging equipment needed	C F
Prune roots if bareroot	C	Which roots to prune and how	C
Cut twine if balled & burlapped backfill	C	Planting depth and backfill material to be used	C F
Construct watering basin around tree	C	Width, depth, and shape of basin	C
Prune branches	C	Which branches to prune and how	C
Stake and guy tree	C	Method and materials	P
Wrap trunk	C	Method and materials	P
Mulch tree	C	Materials, method, and depth	P
Pruning and Repair			
Situation appraisal	C F	Species, treatments required, and equipment required	C F
Climb tree	C	Method and equipment	C F
Cut branches	C	Which limbs to cut, methods, and equipment	C F
Lower branches	C	Methods and equipment	C F
Paint pruning wounds	C	Method and materials	C F
Repair wounds	C	Which wounds to repair, method, and equipment	C F
Brace splits or weak crotches	C	Methods, materials, and equipment	C F

Task	Decision area		
Install cables	Locations, methods, materials, and equipment	C	C F
Dispose of debris	Method, equipment, and disposal site	C	C F
Tree Removal			
Designate trees to be removed	Dead, or otherwise in need of removal, how designate	F P	F P
Situation appraisal	Procedure—top and section, fell, etc.	F	F
Go aloft	Climb tree or use bucket truck (method and equipment)	C	F
Cut branches or portions of branches	Where to cut, method, and equipment	C	C
Lower branches	Methods and equipment	C	C F
Chip smaller branches	Material to be chipped	C	C
Load larger materials	Method and equipment	C	C F
Remove stump	Method and equipment	C	F
Dispose of debris	Disposal site	C	F
Insect and Disease Control			
Diagnose problem	Cause	P	P
Prescribe control	Control method, chemical, amount, timing, and equipment	P	P
Designate trees	Degree of potential damage and how to designate	F P	F P
Mix chemicals	Amount of chemical and carrier	F	F
Calibrate equipment	Amount of materials	F	F
Apply chemicals	Method, amount	C F	F
Clean equipment	Method, materials	C	F
Dispose of unused material	Method	C	P

E = crew.
F = foreman.
P = Professional.

Note. Tasks could be further divided. For example, cable installation requires hole drilling, holding with block and tackle, eye screw insertion, and cable attachment, each of which could be considered as tasks. A task is simply a part of an operation that is generally the responsibility of a single position level.

sified as "restricted use" if its dermal or inhalation toxicity presents a hazard, or if its use may cause unreasonable adverse environmental effects.

Standards for certification of applicators are prescribed, and provide that in order to be certified individuals must be competent in the use and handling of pesticides. Administered by appropriate state agencies, training and testing programs have been developed according to pesticide use category. The three categories that apply to most urban forestry operations are as follows:

Ornamental and Turf Pest Control: Includes commercial applicators that use or supervise the use of restricted use pesticides to control pests in the maintenance and production of ornamental trees, shrubs, flowers, and turf.

Right-of-Way Pest Control: Includes commercial applicators that use or supervise the use of restricted use pesticides in the maintenance of public roads, electric powerlines, pipelines, railway rights-of-way, or other similar areas.

Forest Pest Control: Includes commercial applicators that use or supervise the use of restricted use pesticides in forests, forest nurseries, and forest seed producing areas.

In most states, certification is given after the successful completion of written tests. Manuals and other materials for self-study are provided and training classes are scheduled. Provisions are also made for certification renewal, which require either class attendance or written testing.

The Occupational Safety and Health Act is an expression of the right of employees to a safe and healthful working environment. It requires employers to provide such an environment but protects their right to take disciplinary action against employees who violate safety and health rules.

Compliance with the Act requires that certain standards be maintained. In the area of urban forestry, the American National Standards Institute, Inc., has developed safety requirements for tree pruning, trimming, repairing, or removal (ANSI, 1972). Adherence to these requirements assures reasonable compliance. The International Shade Tree Conference (now the International Society of Arboriculture) was secretariat of the committee that developed the standards. They were developed in counsel with the Occupational Safety and Health Administration of the U.S. Department of Labor.

The six areas covered are: (1) general safety requirements; (2) electrical hazards; (3) mobile equipment safety requirements; (4) portable power hand tool safety requirements; (5) hand tool safety requirements; and (6) safe work procedures. These standards and requirements form a solid base for a safety program. Such a program begins with administrative policies, involves standards for types and condition of tools, equipment, and materials, and culminates with requirements for use. A summary of safety requirements for urban forestry work is given in Appendix V.

Compliance with state and local laws also often requires training. Licensing of persons or firms who do urban forestry work may be required by state law. An example of such requirements will be discussed later in this chapter. Licensing is often required by municipal ordinances also and may be based on oral or written tests, or acceptance of state licensing or certification in states where such programs are in effect. Training for meeting licensing requirements usually involves studying a manual or book prior to a test. In a few cities, however, practical training courses are presented. A copy of the examination required by the City of Boise, Idaho is shown as Appendix VI.

Training to apply new technology

The continuing development of equipment, materials, and procedures makes apparent the need for continued training. In recent years there has been rapid advancement in tree planting technology. New equipment and materials for digging, transporting, and transplanting trees have come on the scene. An array of new chemicals is now on the market with complex systems for their use. There are new materials and techniques for fertilizing, watering, aerating, controlling insects and diseases, and new equipment for application.

The necessity of training to apply new technology is well illustrated by the recent development of new Dutch elm disease control systems. This development also illustrates the training needs required by law. In early 1972, the Environmental Protection Agency gave label approval for the fungicide, benomyl, to be used in Dutch elm disease control. The label approved either a foliar spray or trunk injection. The spray was to be applied with a mist blower after trees reached full leaf in the spring. Trunk injections were also to be made after full leaf. Equipment systems were developed for injection. The EPA label restricted benomyl use to "trained arborists," but ironically did not define the term or say who was to train them. Training did occur, however; it was conducted largely by chemical company sales personnel and by representatives of manufacturers of injection systems.

Benomyl was successful when used under proper conditions. Its effectiveness was restricted by a frequent lack of understanding of limiting factors. Effectiveness was further restricted by benomyl's frustrating insolubility and frequent resistance to uptake in trees.

A soluable form of benomyl was developed and tested from 1973 to

1975. This material, Lignasan BLP, was given label approval in the spring of 1976. The major educational need of Lignasan BLP appears to be an understanding of the proper conditions for its use. This is a need of both applicators and consumers. There is also the continuing need to train users in the physical handling and use of the material.

Training to meet standards for certification or licensing

The certification or licensing of arborists and others concerned with the urban forest is often required by state or local laws. Although this discussion might properly be included in the previous section, it is considered separately because certification or licensing is generally professionally motivated. Certification can be required by law or can be a voluntary program that is sponsored and administered by an association or other organization. The requirements for certification or licensing usually result from a desire to be more "professional." This desire may be based on a combination of profit oriented and consumer protection reasons. It is also based on a genuine concern for the quality of work done in the urban forest.

The Kansas Certified Arborist program is an example of a voluntary approach without legislative authority. The program is sponsored by the Kansas Arborists Association, an organization of professional and lay people concerned with shade and landscape trees. As required by the Association's bylaws, certified arborists must meet the following standards:

1. Membership in the Kansas Arborists Association.
2. Successful completion of a course in arboriculture as prescribed or approved by the KAA.
3. A minimum of two years experience as a practicing arborist.
4. Practice of a code of ethics.
5. Payment of an annual certification fee.
6. Possession of insurance in the amount of $50,000 property damage and $100,000 personal liability or ample amount to meet current needs.

The Association does not certify competency. To do so would be extremely difficult. It does, however, certify that the holder meets the above standards, which should reasonably help to provide competency. The program's strength is that it requires the "successful" completion of a prescribed or approved course in arboriculture and two years' experience as a practicing arborist.

An annual arborist training course is sponsored by the Kansas Arborists Association and Kansas State University. The week-long course includes both classroom and field work. Of necessity, it deals with fundamentals and is designed to serve as a basis for further development (Figure 9.1). In addition to the training course, continuing membership in the Association is required. This provides an opportunity for further training at conferences and field days.

Kansas Arborist Training Course Outline

Monday:
9:00	Intruduction
	Welcome, course outline, requirements, crew assignments, information, questions
9:30	Definitions, history
9:45	The tree, its parts, and how it grows
11:00	Trees and the soil
1:00	Tree forms and sizes, selection and use
2:00	Field trip—soils, space and other site factors, tree identification methods
5:00	Problem and reading assignments, adjourn

Tuesday:
8:00	Quiz
9:00	Pruning (classroom)
	Why Prune?
	Pruning response
	Pruning methods and practices
	Pruning for structure
	Training young trees
	Pruning at planting time
	Pruning mature trees
	Pruning shrubs
1:00	Field work (by crews)
	Tree planting
	Pruning of newly planted trees
	Pruning of small trees
	Shrub pruning
5:00	Problems and reading assignments, adjourn

Wednesday:
8:00	Quiz and critique
9:00	Demonstrations and field work
	Pruning large trees
	Aerial equipment
	Ropes, saddles, knots
1:00	Safety
2:00	Field work (by crews)
5:00	Problem and reading assignment, adjourn

Thursday:
8:00	Quiz and critique
9:00	Cabling and bracing
	Bark tracing
	Wound repair
	Drain tubes

Kansas Arborist Training Course Outline *(continued)*

Thursday *(cont'd)*

11:00	Movies
1:00	Field work (by crews)
	Cabling and bracing
	Bark tracing
	Wound repair
4:00	Adjourn
6:00	Woodpecker barbecue

Friday:

8:00	Tree fertilization
9:00	Tree insects
10:00	Tree diseases and physiological problems
11:00	Tree fertilization and spraying demonstrations
1:00	Tree problem diagnosis
3:00	The professional arborist
	Arborist code of ethics
	Proper tree care alternatives
4:00	Quiz, critique and wrapup

Figure 9.1   Kansas Arborist Training Course Outline.

The New Jersey "Certification of Tree Experts" program is an example of a program based on state legislation. A bureau of tree experts is provided for within the state's department of environmental protection. The bureau administers the program and certifies "tree experts" who meet the following qualifications:

1. U.S. citizen (or declaration of citizenship intent, and legal resident of New Jersey).

2. Over the age of 21 years.

3. Good moral character.

4. Four years of college education, preferably forestry, agriculture or equivalent, or sufficient professional experience in tree care to waive college education, or five years continuous experience immediately pre-ceding the date at which an individual applies to be considered a tree expert.

5. Successful passing of examinations in the theory and practice of tree care, including such courses as botony, plant physiology, dendrology, entomology, plant pathology, and agronomy.

Examinations are held at least once a year and may be oral, written, or both. Applicants who fail to pass may be reexamined at the next scheduled examination period. The program does not restrict anyone from working in the field of tree care. It provides a means by which individuals may be examined by the bureau of tree experts, judged competent, and authorized to use the term, "certified."

BIBLIOGRAPHY

Baumgardt, John, "How to Train a Pruning Crew," Grounds Maintenance, Vol. 9, No. 2, February, 1974.

Cook, John, *John Cook's PR Without the BS,* John Cook and Company, Phoenix, 1974.

10
URBAN
FORESTRY PROGRAM,
SUPPORT ORGANIZATION,
AND RESEARCH

There is no single government agency, private corporation, association, or other organization directing or coordinating urban forestry in America. Interests and ownerships are far too diverse for a single umbrella. Rather, urban forestry involves a wide range of public and private programs, related organizations, and specific research efforts. In spite of a lack of central direction, or perhaps because of it, great progress is being made because of the willingness of the people involved in urban forestry to both share and seek knowledge. As suggested in the preface, there is considerable confusion and perhaps even less agreement about what urban forestry is. There is little confusion, however, as to the dedication of most interests involved.

For the purpose of this discussion, an urban forestry program is defined as the total effort of an organization, agency, or business toward urban forestry. Examples are city forestry programs, urban and community forestry programs of state forestry agencies, and urban forestry efforts of consulting forestry firms. City forestry programs are most familiar and have been discussed in varying detail in previous chapters. The role of state agency urban foresters and urban forestry consultants is less well known and will be explored further.

State Forestry Programs

An amendment to the Cooperative Forest Management Act in 1972 authorized the U.S. Forest Service to assist state forestry agencies in developing urban forestry programs. This amendment gave impetus to already developing programs in several states. The state forestry agencies of Georgia and Missouri placed urban foresters in Atlanta, St. Louis and Kansas City in 1967 and 1968. They have developed programs responsive to the requests of urban residents and serve a clientele holding potential support for their agencies' total programs. Their work is largely educational; it includes work with mass media, schools, trade associations, garden clubs, civic and service clubs, and youth groups. Assistance is provided to property owners, tree service companies, land developers and local units of government including park, cemetery, and planning boards. Demonstrations and training schools are sponsored for city forestry department personnel and others responsible for the maintenance of the urban forest. Similar programs have since been developed in other large metropolitan areas of the nation.

The Kansas community forestry program

Kansas has developed a forestry program for small towns that has become a model for other states. The Kansas Community Forestry Program began in 1971 in response to numerous appeals from small towns hit hard with Dutch elm disease in the late 1960s. With technical assistance provided by the Department of Forestry at Kansas State University, the program provides for the creation of local tree boards or commissions that develop and administer forestry programs for their towns.

To be effective on a continuing basis, tree boards must be legally constituted with the authority to develop and implement programs (Appendix IIa, page 228). Ideally, board members should be dynamic community leaders who are able to make and carry out decisions. A knowledge of trees is important, but perhaps secondary to leadership ability and interest.

Before programs can be developed, tree boards must know the public tree situation in their towns. With assistance from state forestry department personnel, an inventory of street and park trees is taken. Trees are inventoried by species, size, age, and condition class, and from these data species and condition class percentages are computed.* The inventory serves as a planning base from which planting, tree removal, and maintenance needs can be determined. Priorities are then determined and program goals set. It then becomes necessary to identify what is needed to reach the goals. For example, if a tree board gives priority to a street tree planting project, the following questions must be answered: (1) What species will be made available? (2) How will orders be taken? (3) How will the program be publicized? (4) How will payment be arranged? (5) How will planting spots be located? (6) How will trees be planted and maintained? And (7) what ordinances are desirable to regulate street plantings? Similar questions must be asked for tree removal and maintenance projects. The answers to these questions constitute annual or project work plans.

Ideally, tree boards should serve in a planning and advisory capacity, with qualified city employees to physically implement work plans. Realistically, however, most small towns do not have employees with either the responsibility or qualifications for such work. Hence, in most towns tree boards actually administer and implement the program. Board members purchase and distribute trees, arrange publicity, mark trees for removal, stake planting sites, and the like. This approach has the obvious weakness of being dependent on the board members' interest. However, in small towns with limited resources, it is perhaps the most practical approach.

Provision of technical service is vital to the Kansas community forestry program. At the outset, few towns have the capability or available funds for the development of landscape plans, dead and diseased tree marking, planting site location, or insect and disease diagnosis. If work plans are to be carried out, these services must be made available. Urban foresters and a landscape architect from the state forestry department provide such services. Private landscape firms also play a role.

*A sample inventory summary is shown in Chapter 3, page 32.

The staff landscape architect makes a strong contribution to the program. Many towns give high priority to the development of park and recreation area plans or the landscaping of other public areas such as city squares, highway entrances, and central business districts. The first determination is whether or not funds are available to contract with a private landscape firm. If not or if the project is too small to be economically feasible for a private firm, the service is provided by the state forestry department. If funds are available, a list of private contractors is furnished to town officials.

Many plans are developed on site by simply staking planting locations. This is a direct, positive way of getting plantings in the ground. It provides for efficient use of the urban forester or landscape architects' time and is applicable in cases where planting funds are available. In other cases where implementation funds must be budgeted, drafted plans are necessary.

In addition to assisting the tree board organization, program development, and implementation, Kansas urban foresters provide training for tree board members, city employees, and private arborists. All are involved in the Kansas Arborists Association—tree board members, private arborists, and foresters.

As of this writing, there are 130 towns in Kansas that have developed comprehensive community forestry programs. They range in populations from 151 to 28,000—the average is 4756. Some are extremely successful. Some flounder, and some have failed. Those that are successful have common ingredients: (1) a supportive and positive attitude of city officials and residents; (2) legal sanction and authority—a part of city government; (3) a readily available source of accurate technical information and assistance; (4) projects that are practical and consistent with community abilities; and (5) consideration of the rights and wishes of individual property owners. It is our conviction that these same ingredients are necessary in any city in the nation regardless of size.

Virtually every state forestry agency offers some form of urban forestry assistance. Programs vary greatly, depending on interest and budgets. Involvement may be comprehensive or limited to responding to requests by individuals or groups. Urban forestry programs take many forms and may involve any combination of the following:

Audience	Involvement
Local government (city) commission, council, etc.)	Counsel on program organization and development—for example, ordinances and sample costs
Tree boards, commissions (action or advisory)	Forestry program development, project planning, information, and training

Planning boards, commissions, and authorities	Tree protection and environmental assessments, for example
City forestry departments	Information, training, and project planning
Private developers	Tree protection, planting information, and environmental protection
Private arborists	Information, education, and training, (e.g., schools and workshops)
Clubs and organizations	Information and project assistance
Property owners	Information and education (media, direct contact, demonstrations, and workshops)

Urban forestry programs of state forestry agencies are well summarized in a 15-minute movie, *The Urban Forest,* produced at Kansas State University in cooperation with the U.S. Forest Service. The movie shows program examples in various states and appeals to city officials for action. Development and production of the film were part of an urban forestry program that obtained technical input from state forestry agencies, the Urban Forestry Committee of the National Association of State Foresters, and personnel of the U.S. Forest Service.

Consulting Urban Foresters

A limited number of private consultants offer urban forestry services. A directory of urban foresters compiled by the Society of American Foresters indicates that there were 15 consultants in the United States in 1974 (SAF, 1974). This directory lists professional foresters only, and does not include other tree care personnel from firms offering arboriculture services. Our observations suggest that this number has increased substantially since the directory was compiled. It can be concluded that this is a result of an increasing awareness of urban forestry and the role of urban foresters.

Services of consultants vary according to the localized demand and expertise available. Services are offered to municipalities, other governmental units, corporations, and individuals; they include the following:

• Information on tree care
• Street and park tree surveys and inventories

211

- Program development counsel
- Insect and disease inspections and diagnosis
- Tree care contract service including specifications and inspections
- Land development tree surveys
- Vegetative management plans
- Studies for environmental impact assessments and statements
- Advice on selecting, planting, and moving trees
- Evaluation reports on losses from fire, storms, accidents, and other causes
- Tree problem diagnosis
- Expert testimony in court cases

Support Organizations

Various organizations, by virtue of their dedication to trees, give support to urban forestry. Notable among them are the International Society of Arboriculture, the Urban Forestry Working Group of the Society of American Foresters, the National Arbor Day Foundation, and various state arborists associations.

International Society of Arboriculture

Formerly the International Shade Tree Conference, the International Society of Arboriculture has the following purposes:*

> *To promote and improve the practice of professional arboriculture.*
>
> *To stimulate greater public interest in the planting and preservation of shade and ornamental trees.*
>
> *To promote public education to develop a greater appreciation for trees of shade and ornamental value, and to promote cooperation in the conservation of trees and in the beautification of the countryside.*
>
> *To recommend and uphold a* Code of Ethics *established to maintain a high level of practice by those engaged in the profession.*
>
> *To initiate and support the scientific investigation of problems concerned with arboriculture and to publish the results of such investigations.*
>
> *To sponsor an annual meeting devoted to the exchange and presentation of information of interest and value to professional*

*International Society of Arboriculture, *An Invitation to Join the International Society of Arboriculture,* 3 Lincoln Square, Urbana, Illinois.

arborists and others interested in improving tree planting and maintenance practices.

To afford the producers of materials, services, and equipment of value to arboriculture an opportunity to advertise, exhibit, and demonstrate their value to arborists.

A wide range of tree interests is represented by the nearly 3000 members—commercial arborists, municipal arborists, urban foresters, research scientists, park and grounds superintendents, consultants, city tree commission and board members, landscape contractors, landscape architects, nursery people, educators, and others.

The ISA has 10 chapters organized on a regional basis. At the national level, much of the work is done in subject matter committees such as those concerned with safety, pesticides, shade tree evaluations, and urban forestry. Other committees involve administration and affiliated associations. These associations include the Municipal Arborists Association, Utility Arborists Association, and Arboricultural Research and Education Academy. Other related or affiliated organizations are the American Society of Consulting Arborists, various state arborists associations, and associations of shade tree commissions.

The ISA publishes a monthly *Journal of Arboriculture* containing articles by researchers and practitioners. Educational materials such as slides and films are made available. In addition, a "Standard Municipal Tree Ordinance" has been published, and a shade tree evaluation formula developed.

Society of American Foresters

The Society of American Foresters is the primary organization of professional foresters in the nation. The objectives of the Society are to "advance the science, technology, education, and practice of professional forestry in America and to use the knowledge and skill of the profession to benefit society" (SAF, 1975). Professional foresters have long been involved with the urban forest environment. The major emphasis of Society members, however, has naturally been on matters relating to forest resources beyond urban environs. In 1972, working groups were formed within the Society. The Urban Forestry Working Group provides a focal point for foresters interested or involved in this area. Its objectives are (SAF, 1972):

1. *Establish liason with such associations as the International Society of Arboriculture and the Society of Municipal Arborists to:*

   a. *Exchange information on purposes and objectives of the respective organizations.*

213

  b. *Avoid duplication of effort in setting up training meetings and/or conferences or other educational projects where interests and purposes are common to the respective organizations.*

  c. *Exchange results of research and field testing.*

2. *Represent the interests and needs of urban-oriented foresters as a means of holding their interest in the society.*

3. *Serve as the advisory branch of the Society of American Foresters in the field of urban forestry.*

4. *Determine educational needs and career opportunities in urban forestry and encourage educational institutions to develop a curriculum in urban forestry or to improve existing courses.*

5. *Communicate with public and private planning agencies to encourage their employment of professional foresters.*

6. *Coordinate programs and plans with other appropriate Society working groups.*

7. *Serve as consultants to sections of the Society of American Foresters when assistance is needed to set up regional technical conferences.*

8. *Identify areas of needed research in urban forestry.*

In addition to the setting of these objectives, these projects of immediate priority were identified:

1. *Prepare a directory (listing by states) giving the names of professional foresters (public or private) working in the field of urban forestry* [completed (SAF, 1974)].

2. *Prepare a compendium of state laws and municipal codes on urban/community forestry.*

3. *Prepare a bibliography of major publications in the field* [completed (Andresen, 1973)].

4. *Collect and distribute job descriptions and salary schedules currently in use for urban forestry positions.*

5. *Prepare a policy statement for the Society on the importance of urban forestry including a definition of urban forestry in the statement (see Chapter 1, page 8).*

National arbor day foundation

The Arbor Day Foundation is a nonprofit corporation directed by a board of trustees made up of conservation and business leaders in the nation. The purposes of the Foundation are to:*

> *Properly and officially promote the observance of Arbor Day each year.*
>
> *Create an awareness and appreciation among all peoples through all forms of communication of the fundamental role that trees play in man's day-to-day existence.*
>
> *Endorse, support, or otherwise implement education programs that will stimulate and inspire youth to better understand the bounty and joy of trees.*
>
> *Recognize achievement among all elements of society through an annual Awards Program for contributions made to the understanding, appreciation, conservation and wise use of trees.*
>
> *Initiate programs that encourage the planting of trees and create an awareness of those resource programs that will assure the perpetuation and growing abundance of this basic resource.*
>
> *Establish and maintain a National Arbor Day Center at Nebraska City, Nebraska, the birthplace of Arbor Day. The basic purpose of the Center will be to educate Americans on Arbor Day, the resource of trees, and tree planting . . . past, present and future.*

A specific urban forestry activity of the Arbor Day Foundation is the "Tree City USA" program. Tree City USA is designed to recognize cities and towns that are effectively managing their urban forests. It is also designed to encourage the implementation of local forestry programs by meeting the following standards:

1. *A legally constituted tree body (a department, board, commission, or other authority) with statutory responsibility for developing and administering a comprehensive city forestry program.*

2. *City ordinances or statutes providing for tree planting, maintenance, and removal according to proper urban forestry principles.*

3. *An active comprehensive forestry program, supported by a minimum one dollar per capita public funds.*

*National Arbor Day Foundation, *Your Opportunity to Improve Your Town,* Arbor Lodge 100, Nebraska City, Nebraska.

215

4. *A formal Arbor Day proclamation by the mayor and a com-
memorative tree planting each year.*

The program was begun in 1975 and is administered locally by
cooperating state forestry agencies. Its impact as an incentive for development of local city forestry programs is yet to be determined.

Research

Research in urban forestry is a dynamic need, because the changing face of
the urban environment presents a challenge requiring new trees and new
technology. Seven broad classes of research needs were suggested by Doolittle in order to meet this challenge and improve living in the northeast
(Doolittle, 1969). With the inclusion of two additional needs, these represent
a summary of the major thrust of relevant urban forestry research in the
nation in recent years:

1. Evaluate and develop tree species. *Evaluate the adaptability of
species to the extremes of urban growing conditions, soil, and
air pollutants. Trees and groups of trees will also be evaluated
for effectiveness in sound abatement, light attenuation, deposition of suspended matter, and the reflectance of radiant energy.*

2. Determine methods for improving sites for planting trees. *We
must find better answers to these questions: What exactly are
the factors of soil, nutrition, air, and water that affect or control
tree survival and growth? What are the optimum levels or requirements, such as fertilization or soil amelioration, for the
various species over the wide range of growing conditions found
in urban areas?*

3. Develop more effective and efficient ways to establish trees.
*We must find out what morphological and physiological attri-
butes of young trees account for high survival and more rapid
growth in high-density population areas; and also what cultural measures, weed control, and protection will be necessary
on the various planting sites.*

4. Determine the nature and extent of the effect of trees on the
amenities or human environment. *We must answer these relevant questions: How much solar energy is transformed into
latent energy of evapotranspiration by a tree, by groups of trees,*

or by various species? How effective is a tree in changing pol-luted air to a more favorable mixture? How much change in climate can be effected by trees in a city park or by tree plantings in a suburb? How can trees affect pollution through the soil–water–plant interrelationship?

5. Provide ways to improve water yield and quality on municipal and private watersheds. *We must determine how several uses of forested watersheds can be coordinated to provide for higher yield and quality. We need to evaluate current, preliminary watershed results, and correlated information. And we must undertake more intensive cooperative research on a network of municipal watersheds to provide better future management methods for forested watersheds in the Northeast.*

6. Develop methods of protecting trees from insects, diseases, and adverse environment of air pollutants. *We need to know which insects, diseases, and pollutants are most critical, and how to manage trees and forests to protect them. Critical air pollutants include ozone, chlorine, fluorine, photochemical smog, and oxides of sulfur and nitrogen. A change in tree species, stand composition, or breeding for resistance may be necessary.*

7. Develop effective methods of culturing and maintaining trees and forests. *The critical questions in this research are: What are the owner's objectives in maintaining or improving existing trees and stands? Is he interested in aesthetics, recreation, amenities, water, wildlife, wood products, or some combination of these uses? What methods of culture are best adapted to the various objectives?*

The two additional needs appear to be as follows.

1. Develop systems for harvesting, marketing, utilization, and disposal of products and debris from the urban forest.

2. Develop structure and systems by which urban forestry programs can be more effectively administered.

Research relating to urban forestry is conducted primarily by industries, federal agencies, state and local government agencies, colleges and universities, private research corporations, institutes, and academies. Research is funded largely by these organizations, but may also be supported or endowed by private contributions, trusts, foundations, or other sources.

Research by private industries is primarily product oriented and involves the development and testing of plant materials, equipment, and supplies. Systems for the use of equipment and supplies are also researched. Selection, breeding, and testing of "new" trees by nursery people is a prominent example of private industry research. From this work has come an array of new plant varieties displaying special form, color, and other qualities in recent years. There is continuing research by chemical companies in insect and disease control, tree fertilization, and growth control. The recent development of injection capsules for insecticides, fungicides, fertilizers, and other chemicals is a result of research of application systems. Large equipment such as mechanical tree transplanters, aerial buckets, and sprayers are obvious products of research and development.

A great amount of research is done for private industry by university scientists working under grants and contracts. Such arrangements can be particularly important in situations requiring the testing of materials or the methods for application in different areas of the nation.

The Elm Research Institute is a unique program of research and promotion involving private industry and public institutions. The Institute is a nonprofit organization dedicated to the perpetuation of American elms. It serves as a mechanism through which research, development, and promotional projects can be coordinated. Research funds are made available through the Institute to university scientists and others for work on the Dutch elm disease fungus and insect vector control, elm tree improvement, and other areas. The Institute also conducts an enthusiastic elm promotional campaign involving a "Specialized Elm Care" program, film distribution, and other projects (Elm Research Institute, 1975).

Research related to urban forestry by federal agencies is conducted primarily by the Agricultural Research Service and the U.S. Forest Service. Research by the Agricultural Research Service is generally in the area of shade and windbreak tree improvement. The U.S. Forest Service is involved in research specific to urban forestry and also conducts research in other areas that have application to urban forestry.

Authority for U.S. Forest Service research is granted by the following acts:

- McSweeney-McNary Forest Research Act of 1928
- Agricultural Experiment Stations Act of 1955
- Cooperative Forestry Research Act of 1962
- Whitten Act of 1956
- Public Laws 85-934 and 89-106 (Research Grant Acts)

These laws authorize in-service research and also provide for cooperative programs with universities and other institutions. The Pinchot Institute of Environmental Forestry is an excellent example of both and constitutes the Forest Service's main effort in urban forestry research.

The Pinchot Institute was organized in 1970 and addresses itself to the urban forestry situation of the northeastern states (Riddle, Moeller and Smith, 1976). The Institute is coordinated at the Northeastern Forest Experiment Station headquarters of the U.S. Forest Service at Upper Darby, Pennsylvania. Research is conducted by Forest Service and university scientists. The university researchers are organized as the Consortium for Environmental Forestry Studies. Research is divided among eight working groups, each considering a specific aspect of urban forestry:

Air: Investigation on the ways trees remove air pollutants and the ways that pollution damages trees.

Water: Attempts at determining the effect of human activities on water quality; the use of forests as a medium for the disposal of municipal waste water; and the use of soil and vegetation to remove effluent for groundwater recharge.

Land Use: Study of ways to preserve and maintain forests and green spaces in and around cities. Evaluation of economic, social, and environmental effects of new land-use control systems, and present state and local government ordinances designed to maintain urban vegetation.

Wildlife: Study of urban wildlife habitat requirements and urban stress on wildlife, and development of management practices to increase the benefits of wildlife to urban residents.

Physical Amenities: Research on the role of trees in influencing the physical environment of urban areas—how trees affect metropolitan climate and energy consumption. Study of ways to use trees to reduce noise in urban settings.

Social Amenities: Development of methods to assess forest qualities such as beauty and suitability for recreation, and the impact of urbanization on forest land resources.

Soils: Investigation of the effect of urbanization on soil properties and its subsequent impact on trees.

Forest Genetics: Selection and breeding of trees to better withstand the rigors of the urban environment.

The National Forest Management Act of 1976 has implications for urban forestry research. Section 20 of this act requires the following (USDA/Forest Service, 1976):

The Secretary of Agriculture, in consultation with officials of both the States and political subdivisions thereof, shall conduct a study of the incidence of Dutch elm disease and evaluate methods for controlling the spread of such disease. The Secretary shall prepare and submit to the President and both Houses of the Congress on or before March 1, 1977, a report which includes—

    (1) *the results of such a study;*

    (2) *plans for further research into the control of Dutch elm disease; and*

    (3) *an action plan which includes a program of outreach and public information about the disease, and recommendations for controlling the spread of the disease.*

As of this writing, the study is underway. When completed, it can give a comprehensive picture of the disease in the nation, and serve to indicate the direction of future research.

BIBLIOGRAPHY

Andresen, John W., *Community and Urban Forestry, A Selected and Annotated Bibliography,* USDA Forest Service, Southeastern Area, Atlanta, Georgia, 1974.

Doolittle, Warren F., "Research in Urban Forestry," *Journal of Forestry,* Vol. 67, No. 9, p. 650, 1969.

Elm Research Institute, *Progress Report–Spring, 1975,* ERI, Waldwick, New Jersey, 1975.

Riddle, Jane R., George H. Moeller, and William H. Smith, "Breaking New Ground in Urban America," *American Forests,* Vol. 83, No. 11, p. 26, 1976.

Society of American Foresters, *Directory of Urban Foresters,* SAF Urban Forestry Working Group Publication, 1974.

Society of American Foresters, Objectives, SAF Urban Forestry Working Group, unpublished, 1972.

Society of American Foresters, *SAF Constitution and Bylaws,* 1976.

USDA Forest Service, *The National Forest Management Act of 1976,* Current Information Report No. 16, December 1976.

USDA Forest Service, *The Principal Laws Relating to Forest Service Activities,* Agricultural Handbook No. 453, U.S. Government Printing Office, Washington, D.C., p. 83, 1974.

11
URBAN
FORESTRY ISSUES

Of the issues facing urban forestry perhaps none is more important than energy. Scarcity and high costs of fossil fuels have focused attention on the utilization of wood from the urban forest for heating. There is little doubt that this trend will continue. Manufacturers of wood-burning stoves, furnaces, and fireplaces are currently hard-pressed to keep up with demand, and retail stores for heating equipment have opened in many cities. In addition to accelerating utilization of "waste" wood from the urban forest, there is increasing interest in the establishment of energy forests. Many of these are plantings on vacant lots or small acreages in urban vicinities to be managed and harvested for fuelwood.

There is increasing emphasis on the use of trees and other plants to conserve energy. Trees for wind barriers and shrubs for insulation are becoming more important in the landscape. More consideration is being given to precise locations of deciduous trees to provide summer shade yet allow incoming solar radiation in winter. An interesting application of this concept is the use of deciduous vines on passive solar collector walls to prevent excessive heat generation in summer.

Changing energy sources have long-term implications for the urban forest. There are certain to be changes in our automobile-oriented society. It is conceivable that we will experience a vast reduction in automobile numbers as gasoline prices continue to increase. What is more likely, however, is a general conversion to smaller, more energy-efficient autos. In either situation, the design of urban areas will be influenced—perhaps the results will be narrower streets, more neighborhood shopping centers, parks, and other facilities. And this will certainly influence the composition and distribution of the urban forest.

Recent state and local legislation providing for solar easements also has implications for the urban forest. An example of this legislation is House Bill 2096 introduced in the 1977 Kansas legislature. A brief of this bill is as follows:

> *HB 2096 would provide that any easement obtained for the purpose of exposure of a solar energy device could be in writing and subject to the same conveyance and recording requirements as other easements. Written instruments creating the solar easement would contain a description of the vertical and horizontal angles of the easement, any terms or conditions under which the easement is granted or terminated, and any compensation the property owner would be allowed if the easement is violated or the compensation of the owner of the property subject to the solar easement for maintaining the easement.*

The right presently exists in the common law for a landowner to secure an easement for sun light from an adjacent landowner. HB 2096 provides that such easements may be in writing, and it sets forth certain specific information such written easements shall contain.

As of this writing, various federal public works programs are being proposed. Designed primarily to ease unemployment, these programs will focus on public service jobs in cities. It is reasonable to expect that a substantial part of these jobs will involve the urban forest. At issue will be local program administration, conflict with the private sector, and project priorities.

The general area of public vs. private involvement in urban forestry is an ongoing issue. Appropriations have been made for federal funding through the USDA Forest Service of urban forestry programs by state forestry agencies. Proponents assert that such funding will provide technical urban forestry assistance to cities and small towns that cannot reasonably be provided by private urban forestry firms. Pilot programs indicate that this is so. Opponents argue that public urban forestry programs compete unfairly with private enterprise, and tend to make the private sector subservient to public foresters. That this will continue to be an issue is as certain as the fact that it will not soon be resolved.

Concerns for environmental protection will continue to influence urban forestry. Of direct concern are materials and equipment such as pesticides and noisy machinery that may adversely affect the environment. Also of direct concern are governmental regulations on the use of these items. Of less direct concern are the environmental factors that will influence the future of urban areas. Many of these are related to changing energy sources for heating, cooling, and transportation. Others are related to society's desires for a "green" environment of grass, trees, and open spaces.

These issues and others will influence urban forestry in the future. What is perhaps more important is the influence that urban forestry itself will have. The well-being and the better life for urban society are at issue. By properly manipulating the components of the urban forest—vegetation, water, soil, and animals (including people)—the urban forester can enhance its contributions to a better quality of life.

APPENDICES

APPENDIX 1

Schools for Urban Forestry in North America

On the following page are schools in North America that offer urban forestry and related instruction at the university baccalaureate or graduate student level (from Andresen and Williams, 1975).

APPENDIX 2a

Sample City Tree Ordinance for a Small Midwest Community

Be it ordained by the City Commission of the City of _____ , Kansas:

Section 1: Definitions

Street trees: "Street trees" are herein defined as trees, shrubs, bushes, and all other woody vegetation on land lying between property lines on either side of all streets, avenues, or ways within the City.

Park Trees: "Park trees" are herein defined as trees, shrubs, bushes and all other woody vegetation in public parks having individual names, and all areas owned by the City, or to which the public has free access as a park.

Section 2: Creation and Establishment of a City Tree Board

There is hereby created and established a City Tree Board for the City of _____ , Kansas, which shall consist of five members, citizens and residents of this city, who shall be appointed by the mayor with the approval of the Commission.

Section 3: Term of Office

The term of the five persons to be appointed by the mayor shall be three years except that the term of two of the members appointed to the first board shall be for only one year and the term of two members of the first board shall be for two years. In the event that a vacancy shall occur during the term of any member, his or her successor shall be appointed for the unexpired portion of that term.

Section 4: Compensation

Members of the Board shall serve without compensation.

University	Current Courses[a] U.G.	G.	Current Curriculum U.G.	G.	Planned Courses U.G.	G.	Planned Curriculum U.G.	G.	Instructional Materials Available
Colorado State	+	+	−	+	−	−	−	−	+
Duke	+	+	+	+	−	+	−	−	+
Florida	−	−	−	−	+	−	+	−	−
Georgia	+	−	−	−	−	−	−	−	+
Humbolt State	+	−	+	−	+	−	−	−	+
Illinois	−	−	+	−	−	−	−	−	+
Kansas State	+	+	+	−	−	−	−	+	+
Maine	−	−	+	−	+	−	−	−	+
Massachusetts	−	+	−	−	−	−	−	−	+
Michigan	+	−	+	−	−	−	−	−	+
Michigan State	+	−	+	−	+	−	−	−	+
Michigan Tech.	+	−	−	−	−	−	−	−	+
Minnesota	−	−	+	−	+	−	−	−	+
Missouri	+	−	+	−	+	−	−	−	+
Nebraska	+	−	+	−	+	−	+	−	+
Nevada	−	−	−	−	+	−	+	−	−
New York State (Syracuse)	+	−	+	−	−	−	−	−	+
North Carolina State	+	−	−	−	−	−	−	−	+
Oklahoma State	−	−	+	−	−	−	−	−	+
Pennsylvania State	+	−	+	−	−	−	−	−	+
Purdue	+	−	+	−	−	−	−	−	+
Rutgers	−	−	−	−	+	−	−	−	−
Southern Illinois	+	−	+	−	−	−	−	−	+
Stephen F. Austin	+	−	+	−	−	−	−	−	+
Texas A & M	+	−	+	−	−	−	−	−	+
Toronto	+	+	+	+	−	−	−	−	+
Vermont	+	−	−	−	−	−	−	−	+
Virginia Polytech.	−	−	−	+	−	−	−	−	−
Washington	−	−	−	−	+	−	+	−	−
West Virginia	+	−	−	−	−	−	−	−	+
Wisconsin (Madison)	+	−	−	+	−	−	−	−	+
Wisconsin (Stevens Point)	+	−	−	−	−	−	+	−	+
Yale	−	+	−	+	−	−	−	−	+
Total 33	22	6	18	6	10	1	5	1	28

[a] U.G. = undergraduate. G. = graduate.

Section 5:   Duties and Responsibilities

It shall be the responsibility of the Board to study, investigate, council, and develop and/or update annually, and administer a written plan for the care, preservation, pruning, planting, replanting, removal, or disposition of trees and shrubs in parks, along streets and in other public areas. Such plan will be presented annually to the City Commission and upon their acceptance and approval shall constitute the official comprehensive city tree plan for the City of _____, Kansas.

The Board, when requested by the City Commission, shall consider, investigate, make finding, report, and recommend upon any special matter of question coming within the scope of its work.

Section 6:   Operation

The Board shall choose its own officers, make its own rules and regulations, and keep a journal of its proceedings. A majority of the members shall be a quorum for the transaction of business.

Section 7:   Street Tree Species to be Planted

The list on the following page constitutes the official Street Tree species for _____, Kansas. No species other than those included in this list may be planted as Street Trees without written permission of the City Tree Board.

Section 8:   Spacing

The spacing of Street Trees will be in accordance with the three species size classes listed in Section 7 of this ordinance, and no trees may be planted closer together than the following: Small Trees, 30 ft (9.1 m); Medium Trees, 40 ft (12.2 m); and Large Trees, 50 ft (15.2 m); except in special plantings designed or approved by a landscape architect.

Section 9:   Distance from Curb and Sidewalk

The distance trees may be planted from curbs or curblines and sidewalks will be in accordance with the three species size classes listed in Section 7 of this ordinance, and no trees may be planted closer to any curb or sidewalk than the following: Small Trees, 2 ft (0.61 m); Medium Trees, 3 ft (0.91 m); and Large Trees, 4 ft (1.22 m).

Small Trees	Medium Trees	Large Trees
Apricot	Ash, green	Coffeetree, Kentucky
Crabapple,	Hackberry	Maple, silver
flowering (sp.)	Honeylocust	Maple, sugar
Goldenraintree	(thornless)	Oak, bur
Hawthorn (sp.)	Linden or basswood	Sycamore
Pear, Bradford	(sp.)	Sycamore, London
Redbud	Mulberry, red	planetree
Soapberry	(fruitless, male)	Cottonwood (cottonless,
Lilac, Japanese	Oak, English	male)
tree	Oak, red	
Peach, flowering	Pagodatree, Japanese	
Plum, purpleleaf	Pecan	
Serviceberry	Birch, river	
	Osageorange (male,	
	thornless)	
	Persimmon	
	Poplar, white	
	Sassafras	

Section 10: Distance from Street Corners and Fireplugs

No Street Tree shall be planted closer than 35 ft (10.67 m) to any street corner, measured from the point of nearest interesecting curbs or curblines. No Street Tree shall be planted closer than 10 ft (3.05 m) to any fireplug.

Section 11: Utilities

No Street Trees other than those species listed as Small Trees in Section 7 of this ordinance may be planted under or within 10 lateral ft (3.05 m) of any overhead utility wire, or over or within 5 lateral ft (1.52 m) of any underground water line, sewer line, transmission line, or other utility.

Section 12: Public Tree Care

The City shall have the right to plant, prune, maintain, and remove trees, plants, and shrubs within the lines of all streets, alleys, avenues, lanes, squares, and public grounds, as may be necessary to insure public safety or to preserve or enhance the symmetry and beauty of such public grounds. The City Tree Board may remove or cause or order to be removed, any tree or part thereof which is in an unsafe condition or which by reason of its nature is injurious to sewers, electric power lines, gas lines, water lines, or other public improvements, or is affected with any injurious fungus, insect, or other pest. This Section does not prohibit the planting of Street Trees by adjacent property owners provided that the selection and location of said trees is in accordance with Sections 7 through 11 of this ordinance.

Section 13: Tree Topping

It shall be unlawful as a normal practice for any person, firm, or city department to top any Street Tree, Park Tree, or other tree on public property. Topping is defined as the severe cutting back of limbs to stubs larger than three inches in diameter within the tree's crown to such a degree so as to remove the normal canopy and disfigure the tree. Trees severely damaged by storms or other causes, or certain trees under utility wires or other obstructions where other pruning practices are impractical may be exempted from this ordinance at the determination of the City Tree Board.

Section 14: Pruning, Corner Clearance

Every owner of any tree overhanging any street or right-of-way within the City shall prune the branches so that such branches shall not obstruct the light from any street lamp or obstruct the view of any street intersection and so that there shall be a clear space of 8 ft (2.43 m) above the surface of the street or sidewalk. Said owners shall remove all dead, diseased, or dangerous trees, or broken or decayed limbs that constitute a menace to the safety of the public. The City shall have the right to prune any tree or shrub on private property when it interferes with the proper spread of light along the street from a street light, or interferes with the visibility of any traffic control device or sign.

Section 15: Dead or Diseased Tree Removal on Private Property

The City shall have the right to cause the removal of any dead or diseased trees on private property within the city, when such trees constitute a hazard to life and property, or harbor insects or disease that constitute a potential threat to other trees within the city. The City Tree Board will notify in writing the owners of such trees. Removal shall be done by said owners at their own expense within sixty days after the date of service of notice. In the event of failure of owners to comply with such provisions, the City shall have the authority to remove such trees and charge the cost of removal on the owners property tax notice.

Section 16: Removal of Stumps

All stumps of street and park trees shall be removed below the surface of the ground so that the top of the stump shall not project above the surface of the ground.

Section 17: Interference with City Tree Board

It shall be unlawful for any person to prevent, delay, or interfere with the City Tree Board, or any of its agents, while engaging in and about the planting, cultivating, mulching, pruning, spraying, or removing of any Street Trees, Park Trees, or trees on private grounds, as authorized in this ordinance.

Section 18: Aborists License and Bond

It shall be unlawful for any person or firm to engage in the business or occupation of pruning, treating, or removing street or park trees within the City without first applying for and procuring a license. The license fee shall be $___annually in advance; provided, however, that no license shall be required of any public service company or City employee doing such work in the pursuit of their public service endeavors. Before any license shall be issued, each applicant shall first file evidence of possession of liability in-surance in the minimum amounts of $_____ for bodily injury and $_____ property damage, indemnifying the City or any person injured or damaged resulting from the pursuit of such endeavors as herein described.

Section 19: Review by City Commission

The City Commission shall have the right to review the conduct, acts, and decisions of the City Tree Board. Any person may appeal from any ruling or order of the City Tree Board to the City Commission who may hear the matter and make a final decision.

Section 20: Penalty

Any person violating any provision of this ordinance shall be, upon conviction or a plea of guilty, subject to a fine not to exceed $_____.

APPENDIX 2b

Model Municipal Tree Ordinance for the Atlanta, Georgia Area

Regulating the Protection, Maintenance, Removal, and
Planting of Trees on Certain Areas in the

City of _____

county of _____

state of _____ Georgia _____

ordinance No. _____

An ordinance regulating the protection, maintenance, removal, and planting of trees in the public streets, parks, other public places, and tree protection zones on designated private property under development; establishing a tree commission and establishing the office of a municipal arborist, as the agencies prescribing regulations relating to the protection, maintenance, removal, and planting of trees in the above-mentioned places; providing for the maintenance or removal of trees on private property when the public safety is endangered; and prescribing penalties for violations of its provisions.

Except for sections 12 and 13, this ordinance in no way regulates protection, maintenance, removal, or planting of trees on the property of a one or two-family dwelling, where the owner of the property resides thereon.

Be it ordained by the Council of the Municipality of _____, County of _____, State of Georgia.

Section 1: Value of Urban Trees

_____, Georgia, is situated in an area covered with a wide variety of trees and shrubs that are a vital part of the heritage passed to us by nature and our forefathers. This vegetation creates such an impression on visitors that the Atlanta area is nationally recognized for the beauty of its plant life. However, there is much concern over the recent, indiscriminate destruction of trees in both public and private places.

Trees are recognized as a valued asset, providing a healthier and more beautiful environment in which to live. They provide oxygen, shade, esthetics, and a priceless psychological counterpoint to the manmade, urban setting. Trees aid in preventing erosion, siltation of streams and reservoirs, flash flooding, and air, noise, and visual pollution.

Trees are economically beneficial in attracting new industry, residents, and visitors. Healthy trees of the right size and species, growing in the right places enhance the value and marketability of property, and promote the stability of desirable neighborhoods, thus helping to prevent the emergence of blighted areas and slum conditions.

Section 2: Short Title

This Ordinance shall be known and may be cited as the Municipal Tree Ordinance of the Municipality of _____, County of _____, State of Georgia.

Section 3: Definitions

For the purpose of this Ordinance the following terms, phrases, words, and their derivations shall have the meaning given herein. When not inconsistent with the context, words used in the present tense include the future, words in the plural include the singular, and words in the singular include the plural. The word *SHALL* is mandatory and not merely directory.

A. *Municipality* is the municipality, city, town, village, subdivision, or otherwise designated political jurisdiction of _____, County of _____, State of Georgia.

B *Council* is the council, board, commission, or otherwise designated governing body of the municipality.

C. *Park and Street Tree Department* is the department of "Parks and Street Trees," "Parks and Forestry," "Forestry," "Street Trees," or other designated department of the Municipality under whose jurisdiction park and/or street trees fall.

D. *Municipal Arborist* is the Municipal Arborist, Forester, Horticulturist, Landscape Architect, or other qualified designated official of the Municipality assigned to carry out the enforcement of this Ordinance.

E. *Person* is any person, firm, partnership, association, corporation, company, or organization of any kind, including public utility and municipal department.

F. *Street or Highway* is the entire width of every public way or right-of-way when any part thereof is open to the use of the public, as a matter of right, for purposes of vehicular and pedestrian traffic.

G. *Park* shall include any public parks having an individual name.

H. *Public Place* shall include any other ground owned by the Municipality.

I. *Property Line* shall mean the outer edge of a street or highway.

J. *Treelawn* is that part of a street or highway, not covered by sidewalk or other paving, lying between the property line and that portion of the street or highway usually used for vehicular traffic.

K. *Tree:*

(1) Any living pine that has a well-defined stem with a caliper of at least 6 in. (15.24 cm), at 4.5 ft (1.4 m) from the ground level.

(2) Any living, self-supporting nonpine (except in 3 below) that has a well-defined stem with a caliper of at least 3 in. (7.62 cm), at 4.5 ft (1.4 m) from the ground level.

(3) Any dogwood, redbud, or other conspicuously flowing tree, as listed by the Municipal Arborist, which has a well-defined stem of at least 2 in. (5.1 cm), at 4.5 ft (1.4 m) from the ground level.

L. *Public Trees* shall include all trees now or hereafter growing on any street, park, or any other public place.

M. *Property Owner* shall mean the person owning such property as shown by the County Plat of _____ County, State of Georgia.

N. *Tree Removal* includes any act that will cause a tree to die within a three (3) year period.

Section 4: Establishment of a Tree Commission

A. There shall be created a commission to be known and designated as the "Tree Commission" composed of nine (9) citizens of the Municipality of _____, a majority of whom shall be residents of the Municipality of _____, or of _____ County. Six (6) of said members shall be appointed by the Mayor with approval of the Council and three (3) of these shall be persons professionally trained in fields such as forestry, botany, horticulture, and landscape architecture. The seventh (7th) member shall be the Director of Public Service who shall be an ex-officio member, the eighth (8th) member shall be the Superintendent of the Department of Parks and Street Trees who shall be an ex-officio member, and the ninth (9th) member shall be the Municipal Arborist who shall be an ex-officio member. All members of the Commission shall serve without pay. The six (6) members appointed by the Mayor shall be appointed as follows: two (2) for two (2) years; two (2) for three (3) years; and two (2) for four (4) years, and serve until their successors are duly appointed and approved by the Council. Successors to those members appointed by the Mayor shall, thereafter be appointed for terms of four (4) years. Vacancies caused by death, resignation, or otherwise, shall be filled for the unexpired term in the same manner as original appointments are made.

B. The duties of said "Tree Commission" shall be as follows:

To study the problems and determine the needs of the Municipality in connection with its tree planting program.

To recommend to the Municipal Arborist, the type and kind of trees to be planted upon such municipal streets or parts of municipal streets, parks, public places, and other tree protection zones.

To assist the properly constituted officials of the Municipality, as well as the Council and citizens of the Municipality, in the dissemination of news and information regarding the protection, maintenance, removal, and planting of trees on public or private property, and to make such recommendations from time to time to the Municipal Council as to desirable legislation concerning the tree program and activities for the Municipality.

To provide monthly and special meetings at which the subject of trees may be discussed by at least three members of the Commission, officers, and personnel of the Municipality, and all other persons interested in the tree program.

To hear appeals as set forth in Section 19.

C. That within a reasonable time after the appointment of said Commission and the approval of the members thereof, upon call of the Mayor, said Commission shall meet and organize by the election of a chairman and the appointment of the Municipal Arborist as secretary. The said Commission shall then provide for the adoption of rules and procedures and for the holding of regular and special meetings as said Commission shall deem advisable and necessary in order to perform the duties set forth.

Section 5: Appointment and Qualifications of the Municipal Arborist

The Municipal Arborist shall, where possible, be appointed from a Merit System roster established by competitive examination after a personal interview, or where a Merit System does not exist, by a competitive examination and interview given by the Tree Commission of the Municipality. Upon satisfactory completion of a six (6) months probationary period he or she shall hold office as long as he satisfactorily performs the duties of his office. He shall be a person skilled and trained in the arts and sciences of municipal arboriculture, and shall hold a college degree or its equivalent in arboriculture, ornamental, or landscape horticulture, forestry, or other closely related field. If and when there is a State (Forester, Arborist, Horticulturist, etc.) Examining Board, he shall have passed the state examination. He shall have had at least three (3) years experience in municipal shade tree work or its equivalent.

The position of Municipal Arborist shall be funded and filled within one year of the adoption of this Ordinance.

Section 6: Salary of the Municipal Arborist

The Municipal Arborist shall receive a salary commensurate with his training and experience, as full compensation for all services rendered and in lieu of all fees.

237

Section 7: Duties of the Municipal Arborist

The Municipal Arborist shall affirm the rules and regulations of the *Arboricultural Specifications and Standards of Practice* (appended to this Ordinance) governing the protection, maintenance, removal, and planting of trees on the streets, parks, public places, and other Tree Protection Zones in the Municipality. He shall direct, regulate, and control the protection, maintenance, removal, and planting of all trees growing now or hereafter in the streets, parks, public places, and other tree protection zones of the Municipality. He is also charged with planning, constructing, and maintaining a plant nursery/tree bank for the purpose of supplying trees and shrubs for planting on public land. He is further charged with keeping informed of environmental and technical changes that could affect the trees of the Municipality. He shall cause the provision of this Ordinance to be enforced. In his absence these duties shall be the responsibility of a qualified alternate designated by the Municipal Arborist.

Section 8: Authority of the Municipal Arborist

A. Jurisdiction: The Municipal Arborist shall have the authority and jurisdiction of regulating the proteciton, maintenance, removal, and planting of trees on streets, parks, public places, and other tree protection zones.

B. Enforcement: The Municipal Arborist shall be vested with police power for the purpose of enforcing this Ordinance and to insure that provisions of this Ordinance are not violated including, but not limited to, the issuance of citations for the violation of any provisions of this Ordinance.

C. Supervision: The Municipal Arborist shall have the authority and it shall be his duty to supervise or inspect all work done under a permit issued in accordance with the terms of this Ordinance.

D. Condition of Permit: The Municipal Arborist shall have the authority to affix reasonable conditions to the granting of a permit in accordance with the terms of this Ordinance.

E. Inventory of Existing Trees: The Municipal Arborist shall have the responsibility of inventorying (and classifying as to location, species, size, condition, and evaluation) the existing trees on streets, parks, and other public places, as an integral part of the Master Street Tree Plan. This Inventory shall be periodically updated.

F. Master Street Tree Plan: The Municipal Arborist shall also have the authority to formulate a Master Street Tree Plan with the advice and approval of the Tree Commission. The Master Street Tree Plan shall include the Inventory of Existing Trees, and shall specify the species of trees to be protected, maintained, removed, and/or planted on each of the streets, parks, and other public places of the Municipality. From and after the effective date of the Master Street Tree Plan, or any amendment thereof, all tree work shall conform thereto.

(1) The Municipal Arborist shall consider all existing and future utility and environmental factors when recommending the planting of a tree species or other tree work for each of the streets, parks, and other public places of the Municipality.

(2) The Municipal Arborist, with the approval of the Tree Commission, shall have the authority to amend or add to the Master Street Tree Plan at any time that circumstances make it advisable.

Section 9: Tree Protection Zone

The Tree Protection Zone shall:

A. Include all streets, parks, and other public places such as the grounds of public buildings, schools, libraries, etc.

B. Include all property planned for, or under development, redevelopment, razing, or renovating ... unless the property is judged (based on current zoning) by the Municipal Arborist to be commercial forest land and the trees to be removed are to be utilized for some wood product.

C. Include that land fifteen (15) feet (4.57 m) beyond the roof line of any building.

D. Include all land within a horizontal distance of fifty (50) feet (15.24 m) from the right-of-way of any street or highway.

E. Include that portion of designated private property identified as the front, side, and rear yard, set-back requirements as established by the Municipal Zoning Code.

This section shall not be interpreted to prohibit the removal, as determined by the Municipal Arborist, of:

1. Dead, dying, diseased, insect infested, or hazardous trees.
2. Unwanted weed species.
3. The necessary minimal amount of trees and limbs by survey parties.

Nor shall this Section be interpreted to prohibit the protection, maintenance, removal, or planting of trees on the property of one- or two-family dwellings where the property owner resides thereon.

Section 10: Protection of Trees

Within each Tree Protection Zone:

A. During development, redevelopment, razing, or renovating no more

239

than 50 percent of the trees shall be cut, damaged, destroyed, or removed except by specified permit.

B. All trees within 30 ft (9.1 m) of any excavation or construction of any building, structure, or street work shall be guarded through the length of the project with a good substantial fence, frame, or box not less than 4 feet (1.2 m) high and 8 ft (2.4 m) square, or at a distance in feet from the tree equal to the diameter of the trunk in inches at 4.5 ft (1.4 m) from the ground, whichever is greater. All equipment, building materials, chemicals, dirt, or other debris shall be kept outside the barrier at all times.

C. No person shall excavate any ditches, tunnels, trenches, or lay any drive within a radius of 10 ft (3.05 m) from any tree without first obtaining a written permit from the Municipal Arborist.

D. No person shall intentionally damage, cut, carve, transplant, any tree; attach any rope, wire, nails, advertising posters, or other contrivance to any tree; allow any gaseous, liquid, chemical, or solid substance that is harmful to such trees to come in contact with them; or set fire or permit any fire to burn when such fire or the heat thereof will injure any portion of any tree without first obtaining a written permit from the Municipal Arborist.

E. No person shall deposit, place, store, or maintain any stone, brick, sand, fill dirt, concrete, or other materials that may impede the free passage of water, air, and fertilizer to the roots of any tree growing therein, except by written permit of the Municipal Arborist.

Section 11: Site Plan

The Site Plan for development or improvement of any tract or parcel of land shall be evaluated and approved by the Municipal Arborist before a building permit can be issued. The Municipal Arborist may inspect the site before approving or disapproving the site plan and at any time during the development, redevelopment, renovating, or razing thereafter.

The Site Plan, in addition to the usual requirements of the Zoning Code, shall show the following:

A. Approximate location, size, and species of all existing:

1. Trees to be maintained.
2. Trees to be removed.

B. Specifications for:

1. Protection of existing trees during the development, redevelopment, renovating, or razing.

2. Grade changes or other work within a tree's drip line.

3. Disposal of trees to be removed.

C. Any intended replanting, specifying the location, species, size, and a completion date for the seasonable planting of trees.

Section 12: Obstruction: Trees Pruned

It shall be the duty of any person or persons owning or occupying real property bordering on any street upon which property there may be trees, to prune such trees in such manner that they will not obstruct or shade the street lights, obstruct the passage of pedestrians on sidewalks, obstruct vision of traffic signs, or obstruct the view of any street or alley intersection. The minimum clearance of any overhanging portion thereof shall be 10 ft (3.05 m) over sidewalks, and 12 ft (3.66 m) over all streets except truck thoroughfares, which shall have a clearance of 16 ft (4.88 m).

A. Notice to Prune. Should any person or persons owning real property bordering on any street fail to prune trees as herein above provided, the Municipal Arborist shall order such person or persons, within three (3) days after receipt of written notice, to so prune such trees.

B. Order Required. The order required herein shall be served by certified mail to the last known address of the property owner.

C. Failure to Comply. When a person to whom an order is directed shall fail to comply within the specified time, it shall be lawful for the Municipality to prune such trees.

Section 13: Insects and Diseases

The Municipal Arborist shall have the authority to direct private property owners to treat or remove a tree suffering from a transmittable disease or insect infestation when such tree is on private property but may affect the health of trees on public property. The owner of said tree shall be notified of the condition and recommended treatment in writing and shall be given a period of one (1) week to instigate the treatment or removal. If not treated or removed within a period of one (1) additional week, the Municipal Arborist shall cause the treatment or removal to be carried out and the cost may be assessed to the tree owner.

Section 14: Emergencies

In the case of officially declared emergencies, such as windstorms, ice storms, or other disasters, the requirements of Sections 10 and 16 shall be waived so that the requirements of this Ordinance would in no way hinder private or public work to restore order in the Municipality. This work shall follow maintenance standards as outlined by the Municipal Arborist.

Section 15: Moving Large Objects

No person shall move any building or other large objects that may injure public trees, or parts thereof, without first having obtained the approval of the Municipal Arborist.

Section 16: Permits Required

A. Planting, Maintenance, or Removal

(1) Within any tree protection zone, during development, redevelopment, razing, or renovating, no person shall spray, prune, cut above ground, remove or otherwise disturb more than 50 percent of the tree without first filling an application and procuring a permit from the Municipal Arborist.

(2) No person shall plant, spray, fertilize, prune, cut above ground, remove, or otherwise disturb any tree on any street, park, other public place, or other tree protection zone without first filling an application and procuring a permit from the Municipal Arborist.

(3) The person receiving the permit shall abide by the *Arboricultural Specifications and Standards of Practice.*

(4) Application for permits must be made at the office of the Municipal Arborist not less than seventy-two (72) hours in advance of the time the work is to be done.

(5) The Municipal Arborist shall issue the permit provided for herein if, in his judgment, the proposed work is desirable and the proposed method and workmanship to be used are of a satisfactory nature. Any permit granted shall contain a definite date of expiration and the work shall be completed in the time allowed on the permit and in the manner as therein described. Any permit shall be void if its terms are violated.

(6) Notice of completion shall be given to the Municipal Arborist for his inspection within five (5) days.

B. Planting

(1) The application required herein shall state the number of trees to be set out or planted in public places, the location, grade, species, cultivar or variety of each tree, the method of planting, and such other information as the Municipal Arborist shall find reasonably necessary to a fair determination of whether a permit should be issued.

(2) Whenever any tree shall be planted or set out in conflict with the

provisions of this section, it shall be lawful for the Municipal Arborist to remove or cause removal of the same.

C. Maintenance

The application required herein shall state the number and kinds of trees to be sprayed, fertilized, pruned, or otherwise preserved; the kind of treatment to be administered; the composition of the spray material to be applied; and such other information as the Municipal Arborist shall find reasonably necessary to a fair determination of whether a permit should be issued.

D. Removal, Replanting, and Replacement

1. Wherever it is necessary to remove a tree from a treelawn in connection with the paving of a sidewalk, or the paving or widening of the portion of a street or highway, the Municipality shall replant the tree or replace it. Provided that conditions prevent planting on treelawns, this requirement will be satisfied if any equivalent number of trees of the same size and species as provided in the *Arboricultural Specifications and Standards of Practice* are planted in an attractive manner on the adjoining property.

2. No person shall remove a tree from any tree protection zone for the purpose of construction, or for any other reason, without first filing an application and procuring a permit from the Municipal Arborist, and without replacing the removed tree in accordance with the adopted *Arboricultural Specifications and Standards of Practice*. Such replacement shall meet the standards of size, species, and placement as provided for in a permit issued by the Municipal Arborist. The person or property owner shall bear the cost of removal and replacement of all trees removed.

E. Permit Fees

A fee of _____ dollars ($ _____) shall be assessed for each permit and shall be applicable to the particular job as specified by the permit. The Municipality and public utilities companies shall be exempt from acquiring individual job permits to perform necessary tree maintenance on public rights-of-way or public lands.

All permits issued for the installation or maintenance of public utilities or public works that affect trees shall be certified annually (semiannually) by the Municipal Arborist. The work of trimming or other operations affecting public trees shall be limited to the actual necessities of the service of the public utility or Municipal Department and shall be performed according to the *Arboricultural Specifications and Standards of Practice*. Permits shall expire one (1) year (6 months) from date of issuance.

Section 17: Registration of Tree Experts

To protect the public, the Municipality shall require any person who removes or maintains trees as a business on public or private lands to be:

A. Examined by the Tree Commission on his or her ability to carry out such work before he is granted a specific license (in addition to the normal business license) to practice as a tree expert. The examination shall consist of a standardized field test and written test. Supervisors of field crews shall be examined in the field on their ability to properly treat and remove trees. When a statewide licensing law for tree experts exists, the above examination and specific license might not be required.

B. Bonded.

C. Insured (medical and liability).

A nonrefundable _____ dollar ($ _____ fee shall accompany each application for examination.

Employees of the Municipality responsible for maintaining public trees shall be examined in the field but shall not be subject to registration as a tree expert. They shall, however, be required to attend at least one day of training per year. Such training shall be sponsored by the Municipal Arborist and shall consist of up-to-date information and techniques on the planting, care, removal, and insects and diseases of trees.

Section 18: Nurseries and Botanical Gardens

All state-approved and governmental plant and tree nurseries and botanical gardens shall be exempt from the terms and provisions of this Ordinance only in relation to those trees that are so planted and growing for the sale or intended sale to the general public in the ordinary course of business or for some public purpose.

Section 19: Interference with Municipal Arborist

No person shall hinder, prevent, delay, or interfere with the Municipal Arborist or any of his assistants while engaged in carrying out the execution or enforcement of this Ordinance; provided, however, that nothing herein shall be construed as an attempt to prohibit the pursuit of any remedy, legal or equitable, in any court of competent jurisdiction for the protection of property rights by the owner of any property within the Municipality.

Section 20: Appeals

Any adjustment of the standards required by this Ordinance or an appeal of a decision of the Municipal Arborist shall be taken to the Tree

Commission. The Tree Commission, upon receipt of such request, on forms provided by the Municipal Arborist, shall have the authority and duty to consider and act upon the request. This application shall clearly and in detail state what adjustments or requirements are being requested, reasons such adjustments are warranted, and shall be accompanied with such supplementary data as is deemed necessary to substantiate the adjustment. The Tree Commission may approve, modify, or deny the requested adjustment, based upon protection of public interest, preservation of the intent of this Ordinance, and possible unreasonable and unnecessary hardships involved in the case.

The Tree Commission shall act on the application as expeditiously as possible and shall notify the applicant in writing within five (5) days of the action taken.

Within fourteen (14) days after notification of the decision, but not thereafter, any decision of the Tree Commission may be appealed by the applicant to the Council. This appeal shall be on a form provided by and filed with the Municipal Arborist and the applicant shall be notified of the time and place this appeal will be heard.

The Council shall act on the application as expeditiously as possible and shall notify the applicant in writing within five (5) days of the action taken.

Section 21: Violation and Penalty

Any person violating or failing to comply with any of the provisions of this Ordinance shall be subject to court action and may be found guilty of a misdemeanor, and upon conviction thereof, shall be fined a sum not exceeding $250.00 or may be imprisoned for a term not exceeding ninety (90) days, or both.

In addition, the person shall replace the tree with a size and species recommended by the Municipal Arborist.

Each tree affected by noncompliance with this resolution shall constitute a separate violation.

Violation of this Ordinance shall be the basis of withholding a final inspection permit until such violation is corrected to the satisfaction of the Municipal Arborist, Tree Commission, Council or courts.

Section 22: Legality of Ordinance and Parts Thereof

Should any section, clause, or provisions of this Ordinance be declared by the Courts to be invalid, the same shall not affect the validity of the Ordinance as a whole, or parts thereof, other than the part so declared to be invalid.

All other Ordinances pertaining to shade trees are hereby repealed.

Section 23:   Effective Date

This Ordinance is hereby declared to be of immediate necessity for the preservation of public peace, health, and safety, and shall be in full force and effective from and after its passage and publication as provided by law.

Passed this _____

day of _____

19 _____

Signed this _____

day of _____

19 _____

_____

Mayor

Attest _____

Municipal Clerk

APPENDIX 2c

Arboricultural Specifications and Standards of Practice

The Municipal Arborist shall have the authority to affirm the rules and regulations of the *Arboricultural Specifications and Standards of Practice* governing the planting, maintenance, removal, fertilization, pruning, bracing, and spraying of trees in the streets, parks, other public places, and tree protection zones in the Municipality.

A. Policy

(1) All work on protected trees shall comply with the "Municipal Tree Ordinance" of the Municipality of _____, County of _____, State of Georgia.

(2) The *Arboricultural Specifications and Standards of Practice* shall be adhered to at all times, but may be amended whenever experience, new research, or laws indicate improved methods, or whenever circumstances make it advisable, with the approval of the Tree Commission.

(3) The policy of the Department of Parks and Street Trees shall be to cooperate with the public, property owners, other Municipal departments, and appropriate not-for-profit organizations at all times.

(4) No trees shall be removed from any tree protection zone unless they constitute a hazard to life or property, a public nuisance, or because a revision of planting plans necessitates.

B. Species, Cultivars, or Varieties

(1) The Municipal Arborist shall prepare lists of trees acceptable for planting in tree protection zones of the Municipality. Undesirable trees shall not be recommended for general planting and their use, if any, shall be restricted to special locations where, because of certain characteristics of adaptability or landscape effect, they can be used to advantage.

(2) Only desirable, long-lived trees of good appearance, beauty, and adaptability that are generally free from injurious insects or disease shall be planted in tree protection zones. The Tree Commission, in conjunction with the Municipal Arborist, shall review at least once every two (2) years the species, cultivars, and varieties included on the approved list to determine if any should be removed for any reason or if certain new species, cultivars, or varieties of proven dependability and value should be added.

(3) Where street blocks have been assigned a particular species or variety on the Master Street Tree Plan, only these shall be planted subject to revision by the Municipal Arborist and approved by the Tree Commission.

C. Planting

(1) Size

a. Unless otherwise specified by the Municipal Arborist, all medium to large deciduous tree species and their cultivars and varieties shall conform to American Association of Nurserymen Standards and be at least 1¼ to 1½ in. (3.17 to 3.81 cm) in diameter, 6 in. (15.24 cm) above ground level, and at least 8 to 10 ft (2.44 to 3.05 m) in height when planted. The crown shall be in good balance with the trunk.

b. All small deciduous tree species and their cultivars or varieties, shall be at least 5 to 6 ft (1.52 to 1.83 m) or more in height and have six (6) or more branches.

(2) Grade

Unless otherwise allowed for specific reasons, all trees shall have comparatively straight trunks, well-developed leaders and tops, and roots characteristic of the species, cultivar, or variety and shall show evidence of proper nursery pruning. All trees must be free of insects, diseases, mechanical injuries, and other objectionable features at the time of planting.

(3) Location and Spacing

a. Based on a 40-year cycle, no tree that will attain a trunk diameter greater than 12 to 15 in. (30.48 to 38.1 cm) shall be planted in a treelawn less than 3 to 5 ft (0.91 to 1.52 m) in width. In treelawns less than 3 ft (0.91 m) in width, or where overhead lines or building setback presents a special problem, the selection of site and species shall be determined by the Municipal Arborist.

b. Where there is a treelawn less than 3 ft (0.91 m) in width, legal steps should be taken to obtain easement rights to plant beyond the sidewalk on private property. Such easements should contain provisions that grant the Municipality permission to select, plant, maintain, and remove such trees under the direction of the Municipal Arborist.

c. Trees shall be planted at least 30 ft (9.14 m) from street intersections and at least 15 ft (4.54 m) from driveways and alleys.

d. No tree shall be planted closer than 10 ft (3.05 m) to a utility pole.

e. Spacing of trees should be determined by the Municipal Arborist according to local conditions, the species, cultivars, or varieties used and their mature height, spread, and form. Generally, all large trees shall be planted 40 to 60 ft (12.19 to 18.29 m) on center; all medium-sized trees shall be planted a minimum of 35 ft (10.64 m) on center; and all small trees shall be planted a minimum of 25 ft (7.62 m) on center.

f. All planting on unpaved streets without curbs must have the special permission of the Municipal Arborist who shall determine the tree's location so it will not be injured or destroyed when the street is curbed and paved.

(4) Methods of Planting and Support

a. Most small deciduous trees may be moved bare-rooted unless otherwise indicated. Roots of bare-rooted trees should be protected against drying out.

b. All coniferous trees shall be moved balled and burlapped. Balled roots should be prevented from drying out at the surface of the ball and protected against injurious freezing.

c. Pits dug for planting of bare-root plants shall be a minimum of 12 in. (30.48 cm) larger in diameter than the root system so as to be of sufficient size to accommodate the roots without crowding. For balled trees, the pits shall be a minimum of 12 in. (30.48 cm) larger in diameter than the diameter of the ball of soil to allow proper backfill.

d. Plants shall be planted no deeper than previously grown, with due allowance for settling.

e. In poorly drained soil, artificial drainage shall be provided to properly drain the soil about the plant roots or tolerant species selected.

f. Acceptable top soil, compost, peat moss, or other acceptable soil mixtures shall be placed about the roots, or in the backfill around the ball. When the planting is completed, the entire root area shall be thoroughly saturated with water.

g. Excessive pruning at the time of transplanting should be avoided. The extent of top pruning should be based on the ability of the plant roots to function.

h. Trees shall be suitably wrapped and guyed, or supported in an upright position, according to accepted arboricultural practices. The guys or supports shall be fastened so that they will not girdle or cause serious injury to the tree or endanger public safety.

D. Early Maintenance

(1) General

Newly planted trees require special attention to maintenance practices during one or two growing seasons following planting. All maintenance practices shall follow approved arboricultural standards.

(2) Watering

Ample soil moisture shall be maintained following planting. A thorough watering each five (5) to ten (10) days, depending on soil type and drainage provisions, is usually adequate during the growing season. A soil auger or sampling tube is used to check the adequacy of moisture in the soil ball and/or backfill.

(3) Fertilization

Provision of good drainage and adequate moisture of the prepared backfill, and the soil ball of balled plants, is more important than fertilization immediately following planting. However, adequate quantities of the essential nutrient elements should be available after new growth starts.

(4) Insect and Disease Control

Measures for the control of insects and diseases shall be taken as shown necessary by frequent and thorough inspections. Plants in a weakened condition following transplanting are often more susceptible to insects, especially borers, and some diseases than are vigorously growing trees. Where it is necessary to spray, insecticides or fungicides shall be used that are recommended for safe and effective control.

(5) Pruning

a. Pruning practices to be followed in the first few years after planting shall consist of removing dead, broken, or injured branches, the suppression of rank, uneven growth, and usually the removal of water sprouts. Feather growth shall be removed when it reaches pencil size in diameter.

b. Pruning shall be practiced subsequent to transplanting and as necessary thereafter to assure sturdy crotch development.

c. Tree heads shall be raised as growth characteristics and location dictates. Newly planted trees need not have lower branches removed until they are well established. Eventually, trees should have the lower branches removed to a height of at least seven (7) feet, unless they are located in areas where the lower branches do not impede traffic.

E. General Maintenance

(1) Pruning and Removal

a. No topping or dehorning of trees shall be permitted except by written permission of the Municipal Arborist. Proper cabling and bracing shall be substituted for this practice wherever possible.

b. All large, established trees shall be pruned to sufficient height to allow free passage of pedestrians and vehicular traffic; 10 ft (3.05 m) over sidewalks and 12 ft (3.66 m) over all streets except those that are subject to truck traffic, which shall have a clearance of 16 ft (4.88 m).

c. It shall be the policy of the Municipal Arborist to cooperate with the Municipal or Utility Lighting Engineer, and vice-versa, in the placement and height of lighting standards and in the development of a system of tree pruning to give effective street illumination.

d. All cuts shall be made with a saw or pruner and only at the nodes or crotches. No stubs shall be left. No spurs or climbing irons shall be used in the trees, except when trees are to be removed.

e. All dead, crossed, and rubbing branches shall be removed.

f. All wounds over 2 in. (5.08 cm) in diameter shall be treated with a suitable tree wound dressing.

g. All tools being used on a tree suspected to be infected with a contagious disease shall be disinfected before being used on another tree.

h. Whenever streets are to be blocked off to public service, police and fire departments shall be notified of the location and length of time that the street will be blocked. Notification shall be given to these departments upon the removal of such barriers or if such barriers are to remain longer than originally expected.

i. To protect the public from danger, suitable street and sidewalk barriers, highway cones, or signs shall be placed on all barriers or obstructions remaining in the street after dark.

j. The stumps of all removed trees shall be cut to at least 3 in. (7.62 cm) below the ground, and soil shall be replaced and the area leveled. If the area where the tree is removed is to be paved, the tree should be cut or stump removed at least 6 in. (15.24 cm) below the ground.

(2) Spraying

a. Suitable precautions shall be taken to protect and warn the public that spraying is being done.

b. Spraying shall be done only for the control of specific diseases or insects, with the proper materials in the necessary strength, and applied at the proper time to obtain the desired control. All spraying practices shall conform to federal and state regulations.

c. Dormant oil sprays shall not be applied to sugar maple, Japanese maple, beech, flowering dogwood, hickory, walnut, and most crabapple trees. Dormant oil sprays shall be applied to other trees only when the air temperature is 40°F (5°C) or above and when it is not likely to drop below this temperature for a period of twenty-four (24) hours.

(3) Fertilization

a. Fertilization of public trees shall follow the National Arborist Association or other accepted arboricultural standards.

b. Formulations, rates, and methods of application of fertilizers shall be specified by the Municipal Arborist.

(4) Cavities

Extensive cavity work should be performed on trees only if they are sufficiently high in value to justify the cost. All cavity work shall conform to the National Arborists Association or other accepted arboricultural standards.

(5) Cabling and Bracing

a. As a general rule, cables should be placed approximately two-thirds (2/3) of the distance between the crotch and top branch ends. Rust-resistant cables, thimbles, and lags should be used. The ends of a cable should be attached to hooks or eyes of lags or bolts, and thimbles must be used in the eye splice in each end of the cable. Under no circumstance shall cable be wrapped around a branch.

b. All cabling and bracing practices with screw rods shall follow National Arborists Association or other accepted arboricultural standards.

F. Amend

The Municipal Arborist shall have the authority to modify, amend, or extend, with the approval of the Tree Commission, the *Arboricultural Specifications and Standards of Practice* at any time that experience indicates improved methods or whenever circumstances make it advisable.

APPENDIX 3

A City Street Tree Inventory System

	Instructions
City and Date:	Fill in on first tally sheet of the day.
Street:	Use a street name
Block	Use map code or block number. Blocks are always inventoried from south to north and west to east.
Side:	Street side—east, west, north, or south.
Species:	Use species codes on card. Record vacant spots as "Blank."
Diameter:	DBH—to nearest even numbered inch.
Condition:	Use codes 1 through 4.

Code	
1 (good)	Healthy vigorous tree. No apparent signs of insect, disease, or mechanical injury. Little or no corrective work required. Form representative of species.
2 (fair)	Average condition and vigor for area. May need corrective pruning or repair. May lack desirable form characteristic of species. May show minor insect injury, disease, or physiological problem.
3 (poor)	General state of decline. May show severe mechanical, insect, or disease damage, but death not imminent. May require major repair or renovation.
4 (dead or dying)	Dead or death imminent from Dutch elm disease or other causes.

Management Needs:	**Use codes 1 through 8.**

Code	
1	Minor pruning
2	Major pruning
3	Wound repair
4	Feeding (fertilizer, iron, or other elements)
5	Insect control
6	Disease control
7	Removal
8	None

Removal Difficulty:

Code*

1	Easy
2	Medium
3	Difficult

Planting Needs:

Base on vacant spots, and use 30 to 50 ft (9.14 to 15.24 m) spacing. Consider all restricting factors.

Code§

1	Small (mature height, 25 ft) (7.62 m)
2	Medium (mature height, 60 ft) (18.28 m)
3	Large (mature height, 90 ft) (27.43 m)

*Related to time and cost. §Species codes could be used directly.

Species Codes: City Street Tree Inventory

001 Ash, green	024 Kentucky coffeetree	047 Pine, white
002 Ash, white	025 Locust, black	048 Poplar, Lombardy
003 Baldcypress	026 Magnolia	049 Poplar, white
004 Basswood	027 Maple, Norway	050 Purpleleaf plum
005 Birch (sp.)	028 Maple, red	051 Redbud
006 Boxelder	029 Maple, silver	052 Redcedar
007 Bradford pear	030 Maple, sugar	053 Smoke tree
008 Buckeye	031 Mountain ash	054 Soapberry
009 Catalpa	032 Mulberry, red	055 Spruce (sp.)
010 Cottonwood	033 Oak, bur	056 Sweetgum
011 Elm, American	034 Oak, chinquapin	057 Sycamore or planetree
012 Elm, hybrid	035 Oak, English	058 Tree of heaven
013 Elm, Siberian	036 Oak, pin	059 Tulip poplar
014 Fir (sp.)	037 Oak, red	060 Walnut, black
015 Flowering crab (var.)	038 Oak, shingle	061 Willow
016 Fruit (sp.)	039 Oak, white	062
017 Ginkgo	040 Osage orange	063
018 Goldenraintree	041 Pawpaw	064
019 Hackberry	042 Pecan	065
020 Hawthorn (sp.)	043 Persimmon	066
021 Hickory (sp.)	044 Pine, Austrian	067
022 Honeylocust	045 Pine, ponderosa	068
023 Japanese pagodatree	046 Pine, Scotch	069

Tally Sheet
City Street Tree Inventory

City _Anytown_   Date _12/1/76_

Street _Pine_ Block _1_ Side _W_   Street _Pine_ Block _1_ Side _E_

Sp.	DBH	Cond.	Mgt. Needs		Sp.	DBH	Cond.	Mgt. Needs
037	14	1	0		019	22	2	1
022	16	2	1					
001	36	3	2, 3			ETC.		
011	32	4	7 (3)					
Blank								
	ETC.							

Planting needs ___2___   Planting needs _____

    In this example, we worked north on Pine Street. The west side of the street is on the left of the tally sheet and the east on the right. The first tree on the left side is a red oak, 14 inches in diameter, in good condition with no present management needs. The second is a honeylocust, 16 inches, in fair condition in need of minor pruning. The third is a green ash, 36 inches, in poor condition in need of major pruning and wound repair. The fourth is an American elm, 32 inches, dead or dying, in need of removal. Removal is difficult because of wires and other obstructions. There is no need for replanting after removal. The fifth tree space is blank and should be planted with a potentially medium-sized tree, for example.

    With this system the computer can locate a particular tree only as being in a particular block and street side. For a more precise location, one would have to go to the tally sheets and count down. Distances from intersecting curb lines at the end of the block could be recorded, but practical use of such precise data might not justify the cost.

APPENDIX 4

Sample Format for a Call for Bids in City Tree Maintenance Contracts*

Organization
City of _____   **Date** _____
                                Call For Bids

Bidders will be required to carefully examine the site of the proposed work and to judge for themselves as to the nature of the work to be done and the general conditions relative thereto; and the submission of a proposal hereunder shall be considered prima-facie evidence that the bidder has made the necessary investigation and is satisfied with respect to the conditions to be encountered, the character, quantity, and quality of the work to be performed.

Each bid shall be in a sealed envelope submitted to the _____, and will be publicly opened and read by the Park Superintendent of his duly appointed officer at 2:00 P.M., on _____. All proposals presented shall show the proposed prices clearly and legibly and must be properly signed by the bidder, giving address and telephone number.

Bidders must be thoroughly competent and capable of satisfactorily performing the work covered by the proposal and, when requested, shall furnish such statements relative to previous experience on similar work, the plan or procedure proposed and the organization and equipment available for the contemplated work, and any other as may be deemed necessary by the Park Superintendent in determining such competence and capability.

The award of the contract will be to the lowest responsible and qualified bidder whose proposal complies with all the prescribed requirements; but until an award is made, the right will be reserved to reject any or all bids, if to do so is deemed to best serve the interests of the City. In no event will an award be made until all necessary investigations are made as to the responsibility and qualifications of the bidder to whom it is proposed to make such award.

It shall be understood that the contractor will be required to perform and complete the proposed work in a thorough and workmanlike manner, and to furnish and provide in connection therewith all necessary labor, tools, implements, equipment, materials, and supplies except such thereof as may otherwise be specified will be furnished by the City. The City re-

*This appendix from C. J. Plinkerton, "Contracting of Tree Work and Cost Accounting." *International Shade Tree Conference Proceedings,* Western Chapter, 44:284–293, 1968.

serves the right in the case of a cash contract to make such increase or decrease in the quantity of any item of work to be performed or furnished under such contract; and in the event that any such increase or decrease in the quantity of work to be performed or furnished is so ordered, the amount to be paid the contractor under his or her contract shall be correspondingly increased or decreased, as the case may be, in proportion to the increased or decreased quantities of work.

At the end of each working day the contractor shall clean the site thereof, and all grounds that he has occupied in connection therewith, of all rubbish and debris caused by him; and all parts of the work shall be left in a neat, orderly, and presentable condition. All rubbish and debris as a result of this contract may be disposed of, free of charge, at the Municipal Dump.

All work to be performed shall be subject to the direct supervision of the Park Superintendent and his duly appointed officer, and in all respects shall meet with his approval as conforming with the provisions and requirements prescribed therefor.

Public liability insurance in the amount of not less than $100,000.00 for injuries to or death of any one person, and in the amount of not less than $300,000.00 for injuries to or death of any two or more persons in any one accident and property damage insurance in an amount of not less than $25,000.00 shall be taken out and maintained by the contractor for the duration of the contract. The contractor shall furnish the Park Superintendent with a certificate containing a ten (10) day cancellation notice clause.

The contractor shall secure, maintain in full force and effect, and bear the cost of, complete Workman's Compensation Insurance for the entire duration of the contract, and the City will not be responsible for any claims, or suits in law or equity, occasioned by the failure of the contractor so to do.

When the work is completed and ready for final inspection, the contractor shall so notify the Park Superintendent. As soon as possible thereafter the Park Superintendent or his duly appointed officer will make the necessary inspection and if he finds that the work has been properly performed and completed in accordance with all terms of the specifications and contract, he will accept it and notify the finance officer to that effect.

During the progress of the work adequate provisions shall be made by the contractor to so accommodate the normal traffic over the public streets as to cause a minimum of inconvenience to the general public. Means of ingress and egress for occupants of property adjacent to the work, with convenient access to driveway, housing, or building shall be provided as far as possible.

The contractor will be required to provide and maintain barriers, guards and lights when and where it may be necessary so to do in order to effectively guard the public from danger as a result of the work being done.

He will also be required to post proper notices and signals to the public regarding detours and the condition of the work under construction, all in accordance with applicable provisions of the Vehicle Code.

The contractor will be held responsible for the preservation of all public and private property along and adjacent to the work being done, and will be required to exercise due precaution to avoid and prevent any damage or injury thereto as a consequence of his operation. All trees, shrubs, ground covers, fences, warning signals, and street signs shall be adequately protected and should not be removed or disturbed without permission from the Park Superintendent.

Should any direct or indirect damage or injury result to any public or private property by or on account of any act, omission, neglect or misconduct in the execution of the work, or as a consequence of the nonexecution thereof, on the part of the contractor or any of his employees or agents, such property shall be restored, by and at the expense of the contractor, to a condition equivalent to that existing before the damage or injury occurred, by repairing or rebuilding the same, or by otherwise making good such damage or injury, in an acceptable manner.

APPENDIX 5

Safety Requirements for Urban Forestry*

Many of us have recently become aware of a new federal act that has an important effect on the conditions of our workplace. This new law is from the Williams-Steiger Occupational Safety and Health Act of December 29, 1970. The act became an official part of the national labor law on April 28, 1971.

The mission of OSHA is ". . . to assure so far as possible every working man and woman in the Nation safe and healthful working conditions and to preserve our human resources. . . ." OSHA is to reach its objective by implementing the following:

a. Encouraging employers and employees to reduce hazards in the workplace, and start or improve existing safety and health programs.
b. Establishing employer and employee responsibilities.
c. Authorizing OSHA to set mandatory job safety and health standards.
d. Providing an effective enforcement program.
e. Encouraging states to assume the fullest responsibility for administering and enforcing their own occupational safety and health programs that are to be at least as effective as the federal program.
f. Providing for reporting procedures on job injuries, illnesses, and fatalities.

OSHA applies to every employer in a business affecting commerce who has one or more employees. The Act does not affect workplaces covered under other federal laws. Federal, state, and local government employees are covered under separate provisions in the Act for public employment. Whether a city has public employees for urban forestry work or a city tree board contracts with private tree care companies, all are concerned with OSHA and the rights and responsibilities of employers and employees under the new law.

General Safety

The act requires each employer to provide a workplace free from safety and health hazards and to comply with its standards. Employees similarly shall comply with safety and health standards and those rules, regulations, and orders that affect their own actions and conduct.

Employers should be familiar with mandatory occupational safety and health standards and examine conditions of the workplace to make sure they conform to these standards. It is also the responsibility of the employer

*From a term paper presented by Tim Martz, student in a 1976 Urban Forestry class at Kansas State University.

259

to make sure the employees have and use safe tools and equipment, including required personal protective gear, and that they are properly maintained. Always use color codes, posters, labels, or signs to warn employees of potential hazards and to make sure they too are familiar with OSHA. Employers must keep required OSHA records of work-related injuries and illnesses and post the annual summary during the entire month of February each year. Each injury or health hazard that results in a fatality or the hospitalization of five or more employees should be reported to the nearest OSHA area office. The OSHA poster informing employees of their rights and responsibilities must be displayed in the workplace or in a prominent place in the main building.

Every employee has the responsibility to read the OSHA poster at the workplace and comply with any applicable OSHA standards. All of the employer's safety and health standards and rules must be followed. Employees must wear or use prescribed protective equipment and should report hazardous conditions to the immediate supervisor. It is the employee's responsibility to report any job-related injuries or illnesses to the employer and seek treatment promptly.

Personal protective equipment must be worn by all employees if there is a reasonable probability of injury or illness. Head protection must be worn by workers engaged in tree operations and should conform to Industrial Head Protection, Z89.1–1969. Respiratory, eye, and face protection shall be provided as required and should conform to Respiratory Protection Z88.2–1969 and Eye and Face Protection Z87.1–1968. The employee should wear clothing and footwear that is appropriate for the work location and condition. Safety belts or saddles must be worn by workers at all times when they are in a tree. Saddles should have forged support rings and be designed so that the snaps will not roll off accidentally. Safety and climbing ropes must also be used when working in trees. The ropes should have a minimum diameter of 0.5 inch and a nominal breaking strength of 2650 pounds. If snaps are used with the ropes, they must be of the self-closing safety type.

A first-aid kit that is adequately stocked and maintained must be provided by the employer wherever operations are being carried on. Probably each truck will need to have a kit available. Every employee should be instructed in first-aid and rescue techniques. All employees should also be taught to identify poison ivy, poison oak, and poison sumac and be instructed to avoid such poisonous plants. In addition, it should be stressed that an injury of any kind, irrespective of severity, should be reported promptly to the employer.

An adequate supply of potable water must be provided for employees. Portable drinking water dispensers shall be designed and serviced so that sanitary conditions are maintained; dispensers must be designed so that they can be closed and must come equipped with a top. Where single service cups are supplied, both a sanitary container for the unused cups and a receptacle for disposing of the used cups shall be provided. A common drinking cup is prohibited.

To avoid injury or property damage to vehicles, an effective means for the control of pedestrian and vehicular traffic shall be instituted on every job site where necessary. Traffic control devices used in tree operations must conform to the applicable federal and state regulations or to Uniform Traffic Control Devices for Streets and Highways, D6.1–1971.

Fire protection for tree operations in urban forestry programs must comply with federal, state, and local regulations. The engines of trucks and all other gasoline-powered equipment must be shut off before refueling, and any spilled fuel shall be removed from the equipment before restarting. Gasoline equipment should not be operated within 10 ft of any refueling operation. Only approved metal containers and safety cans should be used to store, handle, and dispense flammable liquids. All smoking by employees is prohibited when they are handling or working in the vicinity of any flammable liquid. Local regulation or codes should be followed in the handling of slash, chips, or other refuse.

Protection against the effects of noise exposure for employees shall be provided when the sound levels exceed those shown in Table 1 when measured on the A scale of a standard sound level meter at slow response. When employees are subjected to sound levels that exceed those listed in Table 1, the employer shall take appropriate measures to suppress the noise to safe levels. If noise levels cannot be reduced adequately, personal protective equipment shall be provided and used to reduce sound levels within the

TABLE 1

Permissible Noise Exposure

Duration per Day, Hours	Sound Level dBA Slow Response
8	90
6	92
4	95
3	97
2	100
1½	102
1	105
½	110
¼ or less	115

levels of the table. In no case should impulsive or impact noise exceed a peak sound pressure level of 140dB. In every case where sound levels exceed safe levels, a continuing, effective hearing conservation program shall be administered.

Many injuries in tree operations are caused by the improper lifting of brush and logs. If a weight is to be carried from one area to another, there should be clear ground between the two points. One should decide exactly how the object should be grasped to avoid the sharp edges, slivers, or other objects that might cause injury. Usually it is best to make a preliminary lift to be sure the load can be safely handled. When lifting, you should keep your back as straight as possible and not arched. Try to lift with the legs, not the back.

Working Near Electrical Hazards

Before work is started near electrical hazards, each employee should be informed that all overhead and underground electrical conductors and all communications wires and cables shall be considered to be energized with potentially fatal voltages and shall never be touched either directly or indirectly. Every tree worker should be instructed that direct contact is made when any part of his or her body touches any energized electrical fixture or apparatus. Indirect contact is made by a worker when he touches an energized tool, tree branch, truck, equipment, cable, fence, or guy wire. The organization that operates or controls the electrical conductors involved (the system operator or the owner) must be advised before any work is performed in proximity to energized conductors. This is not necessary if one is working on behalf of system operator or owner.

The supervisor or person in charge must make a close inspection of the tree prior to working in it to determine whether an electrical conductor passes through the tree or passes within reaching distance of the tree worker. If any of these conditions are found, it is considered that an electrical hazard exists, unless the system operator or owner has caused the hazard to be removed. Only a qualified line-clearance trimmer or qualified line-clearance trimmer trainee should be assigned to the work if it is found that an electrical hazard exists. Line-clearance trimmers and trainees must maintain clearances from energized conductors as given in Table 2. If safe clearances cannot be maintained, the system operator or owner shall be contacted to provide protective measures or devices before any work is begun in or near the tree. Branches that are hanging on a conductor may be removed using appropriately insulated equipment. Employees should not place their trust in the dielectrical capabilities of rubber footwear, helmets, ladders, platforms, and aerial devices. If an aerial lift device contacts an

TABLE 2

Minimum Working Distances from Energized Conductors from Line-Clearance Tree Trimmers and Line-Clearance Tree-Trimmer Trainees

Voltage Range (Phase to Phase) (KV)	Minimum Working Distance
2.1 to 15.0	2 ft 0 in. (0.61 m)
15.1 to 35.0	2 ft 4 in. (0.71 m)
35.1 to 46.0	2 ft 6 in. (0.76 m)
46.1 to 72.5	3 ft 0 in. (0.91 m)
72.6 to 121.0	3 ft 4 in. (1.01 m)
138.0 to 145.0	3 ft 6 in. (1.07 m)
161.0 to 169.0	3 ft 8 in. (1.12 m)
230.0 to 242.0	5 ft 0 in. (1.52 m)
345.0 to 362.0	7 ft 0 in. (2.13 m)
500.0 to 552.0	11 ft 0 in. (3.35 m)
700.0 to 765.0	15 ft 0 in. (4.57 m)

electrical conductor, the truck supporting the aerial lift device is considered as energized, and contact with the truck should be avoided.

Safety Requirements for Mobile Equipment

All the equipment should be operated by qualified personnel only and must be equipped and operated in compliance with applicable federal, state, and local laws and regulations, and with manufacturers specifications. Any exposed drive belts, gears, mufflers, or exhaust pipes must be guarded to prevent contact during normal operations. If there are any defects or malfunctions in the equipment, they must be corrected before the equipment is put into use. All material and equipment carried on vehicles must be stored or fastened to prevent them from falling off the truck while moving. This includes such things as shovels, rakes, axes, brooms, pitch forks, tar poles, and traffic control signs. No worker shall be permitted to ride outside of, or on top of, the vehicle or its load unless it is an operation like roadside spraying. This means that no employee should be allowed to hang their legs from the back of the truck, no matter how hot the back of the truck is. If there are any step surfaces on the equipment, they should be skid-resistant.

When aerial lift equipment is used it must be operated in accordance with Vehicle-Mounted Elevating and Rotating Work Platforms. A92.2–1969. A visual inspection in accordance with manufacturer's instructions should be conducted prior to the daily use of an aerial lift device. The controls should be guarded to prevent accidental operation. Buckets or platforms shall be provided with some means of anchorage to which a safety belt or lanyard can be secured. The rated lift capacity must be conspicuously and permanently posted on the lift and the combined load, including workers, material, and tools, should not exceed this figure. If the lift is being operated on an incline wheel, chocks are used, provided that they can be installed safely. The booms should not be operated unless outrigger feet are down, where necessary. Pads for the outrigger feet must be provided on soft surface and traction shall be insured when ice or snow is present. When hydraulic and pneumatic tools are not in use or are being serviced, they must be disconnected except where manufacturer's procedures require otherwise. Whenever booms are operated over roads, safe clearances from passing vehicles should be maintained or traffic control must be provided. Operators must be alert and look in the direction of travel of the bucket, but should also be aware of the boom elbow action. If a hydraulic leak should occur, no part of the body should be used to locate or attempt to stop the leak. Wounds permitting hydraulic fluid to get into the circulatory system have caused death. Workers should never ride in the bucket while the truck is being moved.

In almost every urban forestry operation brush chippers are used and are a likely hazard. All such equipment should have a locking device to prevent unauthorized starting. If the equipment is unattended, the key should be removed. The chipper should be equipped with an infeed hopper of sufficient length so as to prevent workers from contacting the blades or knives of the machine during normal operation. Throwing rocks and metal objects through chipper should be avoided. Workers in the immediate area shall wear eye and noise protectors where necessary.

Log and brush trucks should have a steel bulkhead or equivalent protection must be provided to protect the occupants of vehicles from load shifts. Logs and brush should never obscure the taillights, brakelights, and vision, or should never overhang the side. Red flags must be used at the ends of brush or logs when they extend beyond the confines of the truck. The logs and brush should be secured with rope or cable or prevent it from falling off during transit. Wood chips shouldn't be left in trucks for extended periods because of spontaneous combustion hazard.

Tool Safety Requirements

The gasoline powered chain saw is probably the most common and most used tool in urban forestry operations. It can be the most dangerous if improperly used. The manufacturer's operating and safety instructions are the best safety requirements to follow when operating a chain saw. In all cases, the operator should have secure footing when starting and operating the saw, and extra precautions should be taken in slippery areas. When the worker is bucking up a log on the ground or pruning in the tree, he or she should be aware of which way the limb will fall or move, after it is cut and make sure he will not be in its path. The engine should be stopped when carrying the saw on the ground or in the tree. The saw should be clean of sawdust, oil, and gas, but should be stopped before cleaning and refueling operations are started. The saw muffler must be maintained in good condition. The chain should have the proper tension before it is operated. All co-workers should be clear of the saw before it is started.

There are many hand tools used in tree operations, and the worker should always select the correct tool for the job. If there are tools that have been made unsafe by damage or defect, they should not be used. Tree trimmers should not carry any tools in their hands while climbing, other than pole pruners or pole saws. Other tools should be raised and lowered by means of a handline. Workers should be alert and keep a safe distance from other workers when using hand tools. When tools are not in use they should be properly stored out of the immediate work area. Tools should never be thrown or dropped from a tree unless a warning has been given and the area is clear below. When using the tools the workers should have a secure grip and firm footing. All tools must be properly maintained and inspected before use.

Safety and climbing ropes must always be used when working aloft in trees. Again it should be stressed that they must be at least 0.5 in. (1.27 cm) thick and have a breaking strength not less than 2650 pounds (1192.5 kg). If the rope is made unsafe by damage or defect, it shall not be used. When the rope is not being used it should be coiled and stored so that air can circulate through the coils. It should be stored away from all cutting edges, sharp tools, corrosive chemicals, gas, and oil. Both ends of the rope should be secured to prevent unraveling. Ropes should never be spliced to effect repair. If safety snaps are used they should be rotated from one end of the rope to the other, as needed, and the worn end cut off.

Safe Work Procedures

When a worker is climbing he or she must use an approved safety rope and saddle even if working from a ladder or scaffold. A safety strap can be used for additional protection but is not required. The tree should be examined before starting work and its overall health and vigor noted. Worker should also examine limbs while climbing and prior to applying weight to them. It is recommended that workers never trust solely in one limb but have their feet or hand on separate limbs. Generally workers should not shin a tree that is taller than 15 ft (4.57 m) or beyond their

265

physical capabilities. Workers should note the location of all electrical conductors prior to climbing and work away from these areas if possible. It is usually best to crotch as high as possible in the tree and pass the rope around the main leader or an upright branch, using the limb as a stop. If possible, use wide crotches and avoid tight V-shaped crotches. If the worker is in a tall tree or has a short rope, a figure-eight knot should be tied in the end. This prevents pulling the rope accidentally through the taut line-hitch. The worker should break off all small dead limbs as he or she climbs up. The worker should be crotched-in as soon as possible in the tree and remain tied-in until the work is completed and has returned to the ground.

Before any pruning is started, the worker should inspect the rope for cuts or abrasions. If any defects are found the rope should be discarded, used for other purposes, or the defective section cut off. The climbing rope should be used for no other purpose than climbing. During pruning, pole pruners and pole saws should be hung securely to prevent dislodging. They should never be hung on utility wires or cables, or left in the tree overnight. Likewise ropes should never be left in a tree overnight but removed at the end of the working day. Each worker should have a scabbard or sheath hooked on to their saddle to carry the handsaw when not in use. Whenever necessary warning should be given by the worker to others in the tree and to people on the ground before a limb is dropped. "Timber," "heads up," or "headache" are common terms used for this purpose. If the limbs are too heavy to control by hand, they should be roped off and lowered with a separate line held by workers on the ground. Never use the same crotch for both safety rope and work rope. Whenever there is a person in the tree there should be a second worker in the vicinity.

Before a tree is to be felled the worker should consider the surrounding area, shape of the tree, lean of the tree, wind force and direction, and decay or weak spots in the tree. The work area should be cleared to permit safe working conditions and a speedy exit in the direction of a planned escape route. All workers involved should know exactly what they are to do and others should stay clear. The felling should be planned thoroughly, because once the tree is falling, you have little control. A notch should be used in trees over 5 in. (12.7 cm) DBH. The backcut shall be made higher than the point or apex of the notch to prevent kickback. Just before the tree is ready to fall an audible warning should be given. If there is any danger that the tree may fall the wrong way, wedges or ropes should be used. The worker should stand to the side of the tree before it starts falling, not directly in line with the direction of fall, in case it should "jump the stump."

During pruning operations brush and logs should be removed from beneath the tree. Workers feeding brush into chippers must wear eye protection. The chipper should be fed from the side of the center line and should be operated from the curbside whenever possible. Hands, arms, feet, legs, or any other part of the body should be kept out of the feed table when the chipper is running. Sweepings and foreign material should not be thrown into the chipper. Workers should not wear loose clothing, chains, necklaces, watches, rings, or anything else that could be caught by the brush when feeding the chipper.

If your forestry operation does have a visit by a compliance officer, you as an employer have the right to request and receive proper identification prior to the inspection of your workplace. You also have the right to be advised as to the reason for the inspection. The employer can also participate in the walkaround inspection of the workplace and have an opening and closing conference with the compliance officer. If a violation is found it must be corrected within a specified time or a notice of contest filed within 15 working days after receiving citation and notice of penalty. A temporary variance can be applied for if you are unable to comply because of unavailability of materials, equipment, or personnel to make changes within the required time. A permanent variance is also possible if you can prove that your facilities or method of operation provide protection for your employees that is at least as effective as that required by the standard. If found in noncompliance, an employer could be fined $1000 a day and given six months to a year in prison for willful violation resulting in a fatality. Employers must remember that the purpose of the law is not to fine people but to save lives and prevent injuries.

If employers comply with the law and prepare in advance for the OSHA visit that may or may not come, they are improving their position from a safety standpoint. In the long run, they will save money. The cost of insurance will decrease as employee safety increases. Granted, initially they might incur some expenses in acquiring the necessary safety devices, but over a long term this can be recovered in reduced cost to workman's compensation insurance, reduced lost time due to injuries, and increased efficiency.

BIBLIOGRAPHY

1. American National Standard; safety requirements for tree pruning, trimming, repairing, or removal; ANSI Z133.1–1972.
2. *Federal Register;* Occupational Safety and Health Standards, Part II, Volume 39, Number 125.
3. *All About OSHA*, U.S. Department of Labor, OSHA 2056.
4. Felix, Robert, "OSHA and the Tree Man," *Weeds, Trees and Turf*, June 1974.

APPENDIX 6

Examination for Commercial Tree Firms, City of Boise, Idaho

The answers to the 50 questions in this section are either true or false. Each question has the value of one point.

TRUE   FALSE

1. A healthy tree is able to overcome many insect and disease attacks. _____ _____
2. Violators of the Tree Ordinance shall be deemed guilty of a felony. _____ _____
3. Since the streets, sidewalks, and parking strips now belong to the Ada County Highway District, the City Forester no longer has any legal jurisdiction over the trees that lie therein. _____ _____
4. A nail driven into a tree 10 years ago at 4 ft (1.22 m) above the ground would be about 6 ft (1.83 m) above the ground now. _____ _____
5. Slime flux can be controlled with methoxychlor. _____ _____
6. Anthracnose in sycamores is usually immediately fatal to the tree. _____ _____
7. Property and liability insurance is required *before* a tree license is issued. _____ _____
8. A sanitation program is very important in the control of Dutch elm disease. _____ _____
9. A City Tree License expires on December 31 of each year. _____ _____
10. A secondary function of leaves is to prevent sunscald. _____ _____
11. Dutch elm disease fungus enters the tree through the leaves. _____ _____
12. The elm leaf beetle is a carrier of Dutch elm disease. _____ _____
13. Stumps may be left on right-of-way if they have been treated with ammonate. _____ _____
14. The most important time to water large trees is during the summer drought period. _____ _____
15. There are certain cases where the City may do tree removal or hazard-reduction work on private property. _____ _____
16. Brown streaking in elm twig samples is a good indication that the tree has Dutch elm disease. _____ _____
17. The City Forester may examine your equipment. _____ _____
18. When it is necessary to block off a street or portion of a street you should notify the fire departments. _____ _____

19. When working on elm trees, tools should be sterilized
    once a week. ⎯⎯⎯ ⎯⎯⎯
20. Rough and irregular tree wounds usually heal faster
    than smooth, regular wounds. ⎯⎯⎯ ⎯⎯⎯
21. Sunscald of trees occurs only in the summer. ⎯⎯⎯ ⎯⎯⎯
22. The license for which you are now being tested will
    enable you to do limited commercial spraying on
    private property as well as general tree work
    throughout the City. ⎯⎯⎯ ⎯⎯⎯
23. Sap flow is usually most active in the spring. ⎯⎯⎯ ⎯⎯⎯
24. Mushroomlike growth on live tree trunks often
    indicates the presence of a root rot. ⎯⎯⎯ ⎯⎯⎯
25. Elmwood may be left with the property owner for
    fireplace wood. ⎯⎯⎯ ⎯⎯⎯
26. Elm bark beetles lay their eggs in dead elm wood that
    still has tight bark on it. ⎯⎯⎯ ⎯⎯⎯
27. Aphids are the main cause of the "honeydew" that
    falls from most trees during the summer. ⎯⎯⎯ ⎯⎯⎯
28. According to Boise City Code any plant, tree or shrub
    that grows 3 ft or higher is considered a tree. ⎯⎯⎯ ⎯⎯⎯
29. The City will supply and plant a tree, on the
    right-of-way, for a charge of $10.00 + tax to the
    property owner. ⎯⎯⎯ ⎯⎯⎯
30. The property owner may not furnish his own tree. ⎯⎯⎯ ⎯⎯⎯
31. A permit is necessary before trees may be removed
    from the parking. ⎯⎯⎯ ⎯⎯⎯
32. Trees under 3 in (7.62 cm) diameter may be removed
    from a right-of-way without a permit. ⎯⎯⎯ ⎯⎯⎯
33. Diseased *street* trees will be removed by the City at
    City expense. ⎯⎯⎯ ⎯⎯⎯
34. Large limbs should be pruned off using at least three
    cuts. ⎯⎯⎯ ⎯⎯⎯
35. Painting cuts and wounds helps discourage the
    entrance of insects. ⎯⎯⎯ ⎯⎯⎯
36. Narrow crotches are stronger than those with a wider
    angle. ⎯⎯⎯ ⎯⎯⎯
37. Clorox is a satisfactory disinfectant for sterilizing
    pruning tools. ⎯⎯⎯ ⎯⎯⎯
38. Spurs may be used while pruning. ⎯⎯⎯ ⎯⎯⎯
39. It is okay to leave elm stumps with bark intact as long
    as they are on private property. ⎯⎯⎯ ⎯⎯⎯
40. Drop-crotching is a pruning technique used to lower

the height of a tree, while allowing it to maintain its
natural shape.   _____ _____

41. For safety reasons, two men are a minimum crew for
    pruning and removal.   _____ _____

42. All stumps must be removed from the right-of-way
    when trees are removed.   _____ _____

43. The City Forester may condemn a tree on private
    property only if it interferes with public travel.   _____ _____

44. Sunscald may result in oaks if the crown is thinned
    too severely.   _____ _____

45. "Sucker" or "volunteer" growth on elms may be
    removed from a tree without a permit.   _____ _____

46. Asphalt base paints are not good for painting cuts
    because they are toxic to the tree.   _____ _____

47. A first-aid kid is required as part of the equipment of
    a tree crew.   _____ _____

48. Limbs should be cleared from the right-of-way at the
    end of each working day.   _____ _____

49. A tree proven to have Dutch elm disease must be
    removed within five days after proper notice is given
    by the City Forester.   _____ _____

50. "Potted" trees, like those in the downtown area may
    be set out by the/a property owner without a permit
    since they are not planted in the ground.   _____ _____

The following 15 questions are multiple choice. Each question may
have more than one right answer. Circle all the answers for each question
that you believe to be correct. This section is worth 30 points. *If one part of a
question is wrong, the entire question is wrong.*

51. According to the approved street tree list, which of the following are
    acceptable for planting under power lines?

    a. Class I trees

    b. Class II trees

    c. Class III trees

    d. All of the above.

52. The time(s) to prune a tree and cause the least amount of damage due to
    shock is/are:

    a. Just after the leaves have started to grow in the spring.

270

b. When the tree is in full summer foliage.

c. Just before the leaves drop in the fall.

d. When the tree is leafless during winter.

53. Dutch elm disease may be transmitted from tree to tree.

a. On pruning tools

b. By root grafts

c. By the elm bark beetle

d. By the wind

54. The growing parts of a tree are

a. Buds

b. Heartwood

c. Cambium

d. Root tips

55. Pruning cuts that should be painted are

a. 0.5 in. (1.27 cm) in diameter or greater

b. The size of a silver dollar or greater

c. 3 in. (7.62 cm) in diameter or greater

d. 5 in. (12.70 cm) in diameter or greater

56. Street trees should be pruned for the following reason or reasons

a. To promote their health

b. To provide adequate clearance for traffic and pedestrians

c. To remove dead, dying, diseased or broken branches

d. To provide firewood for the property owner

57. Clearance pruning means removal of all limbs that are:

a. Above utility wires

b. Below 8 in. (2.44 m) over the sidewalk and 14 in. (4.27 m) over the road

    c. Below 6 in. (1.83 m) over the sidewalk

    d. Below 10 in. (3.05 m) over the road

58. Drop-crotching is:

    a. A method of lowering the height of a tree

    b. A special method of lowering limbs to the ground by use of a crotch

    c. An alternative to flat-topping a tree

    d. Not permissible under Boise City Code

59. If you should notice any serious defect while pruning a tree on public right-of-way you should:

    a. Notify the City Forester's office so that they may take any necessary action.

    b. Notify the property owner so that he or she does not pay for pruning of a tree that may have to be removed.

    c. Repair the defect to the best of your ability.

    d. Recommend to the property owner that the tree be removed and then remove it.

60. Brown streaks in the wood of elm branches are:

    a. A sure sign of Dutch elm disease

    b. An indication that Dutch elm disease could be present

    c. Has no bearing on Dutch elm disease

    d. Could be the result of an old wound

61. Who may prune or remove trees on the parking:

    a. The property owner

    b. A licensed tree firm

    c. City tree crews

    d. Anyone as long as they get permission from the property owner first

62. Chlorosis is:

a. A solution used for sterilizing tools

b. Yellowing of leaves resulting from mineral deficiency

c. The result of improper pruning

d. Yellowing of leaves due to chlorine in the water

63. Which of the following are control measures for Dutch elm disease:

a. Fertilizing the tree with a high nitrogen fertilizer

b. Pruning out dead elm wood

c. Dormant spray using methoxychlor

d. Cutting off all "sucker" growth

64. The City's charge for removing a nonhazardous and nondiseased tree on the right-of-way is set by the City Council. These charges are currently set at:

a. Fifty dollars for all removals

b. Thirty-five dollars minimum

c. One hundred dollars maximum

d. One hundred and twenty-five dollars maximum

65. A deciduous tree is one that

a. Is more commonly known as an evergreen

b. Loses its leaves each year

c. Has been defoliated by scale

d. Has cones

The 10 questions in this section are worth two points each. There are 20 possible points in this section.

66. Name the three major parts of a tree and briefly explain their function.

67. What are the types and amount of insurance required to obtain a tree license?

68. List three ways that Dutch elm disease can be carried from tree to tree.

69. Name 10 species of trees approved for use on rights-of-way in Boise.

70. Name four species of trees that may not be planted on the parking.

71. If a property owner asked you to prescribe treatment for a private property tree that had Dutch elm disease according to the City Forester, what would you say?

72. How does anyone go about getting a street tree removed?

73. Under what tree circumstances will the City Forestry crews remove trees at no charge to the property owner.

74. What does safety pruning consist of?

75. What is a girdling root?

APPENDIX 7

Conversion Factors

English to Metric

To convert from	to	Multiply by
Inches	centimeters	2.540
Sixteenths of an inch	millimeters	1.587
Eighths of an inch	millimeters	3.175
Fifths of an inch	millimeters	5.080
Fourths of an inch	millmeters	6.350
Thirds of an inch	millimeters	8.467
Halves of an inch	millimeters	12.70
Feet	meters	0.3048
Number per bushel	number per hectoliter	2.838
Pounds per bushel	kilograms per hectoliter	1.287
Ounce per bushel	grams per hectoliter	80.44
number per pound	number per kilogram	2.205
Number per pound	number per gram	0.002205
Number per ounce	number per gram	0.3527
Number per square foot	number square meter	10.76
Number per linear foot	number per linear meter	3.281
Degrees, Fahrenheit (F)	degrees, Centigrade (C)	0.55 (F − 32)

Metric to English

To convert from	to	Multiply by
Millimeters	1/16 of an inch	0.6301
Millimeters	1/8 of an inch	0.3150
Millimeters	1/5 of an inch	0.1968
Millimeters	1/4 of an inch	0.1574
Millimeters	1/3 of an inch	0.1181
Millimeters	1/2 of an inch	0.07874
Millimeters	Inch	0.03937
Centimeters	Inch	0.3937
Meters	Feet	3.281
Number per hectoliter	number per bushel	0.3524
Kilograms per hectoliter	pounds per bushel	0.777
Grams per hectoliter	ounces per bushel	0.0124
Number per kilogram	number per pound	0.4536
Number per gram	number per pound	453.6
Number per gram	number per ounce	28.35
Number per square meter	number per square foot	0.0929
Number per linear meter	number per linear foot	0.8048
Degree Centigrade (C)	degrees, Fahrenheit (F)	(1.8 × C) + 32

INDEX